The
HIDDEN PLACES

WELSH BORDERS

Front Cover:
Ross on Wye
by PAUL BENNETT

D0381436

Acknowledgements

*The Publishers would like to thank the following for their assistance in the
production of this book: ;*
*Deborah , and Jean for Administration. Joanna, Gerald , Shane, and Sarah
f or Writing. Peter and Bob for research, Simon at Graphix for the maps.
Typesetting by Gerald Bolton. Paul Bennet for Artwork.*

ALL MAPS COPYRIGHT MAPS IN MINUTES
RH Publications 1996

TITLES IN THE HIDDEN PLACES SERIES
Ireland
Wales
Scotland
The Channel Islands
Thames & Chilterns
The Lake District
Northumberland & Durham
Lancashire, Cheshire and the Isle of Man
Yorkshire
Devon and Cornwall
Dorset, Hampshire, I.O.W
Somerset, Avon, Glos, Wilts.
East Anglia
The Heart of England
The South East
(ORDER FORM AT BACK OF BOOK)

© M &M PUBLISHING LTD.. 118 Ashley Rd .Cheshire. U.K. WA14 2UN

Foreword

The Hidden Places Series

This is an established collection of travel guides which covers the U.K and Ireland in 16 titles.

The aim of the books is to introduce readers to some of the less well known attractions of each area whilst not ignoring the more established ones.

We have included in this book a number of hotels, inns, restaurants, various types of accommodation, historic houses, museums, and general attractions which are to be found in this part of the country, together with historical background information.

There is a map at the beginning of each chapter with line drawings of the places featured, along with a description of the services offered.

We hope that the book prompts you to discover some of the fascinating "Hidden Places " which we found on our journey , and we are sure the places featured would be pleased if you mentioned that our book prompted your visit.

We wish you an enjoyable and safe journey.

THE HIDDEN PLACES
OF
The Welsh Borders

1. North Shropshire   1

2. Much Wenlock, Ironbridge
   and Shrewsbury   47

3. South Shropshire   97

4. Worcester and the Malverns   145

5. The Vale of Evesham   173

6. Droitwich to Kidderminster   195

7. Bewdley to Leominster   219

8. Eardisland and the Marshes   235

9. Hay-on-Wye to Hereford via
   the Golden Valley   265

10. Ross-on-Wye and the Wye Valley   289

Tourist information Centres   319

Index   321

CHAPTER ONE

North Shropshire

Hodnet Hall

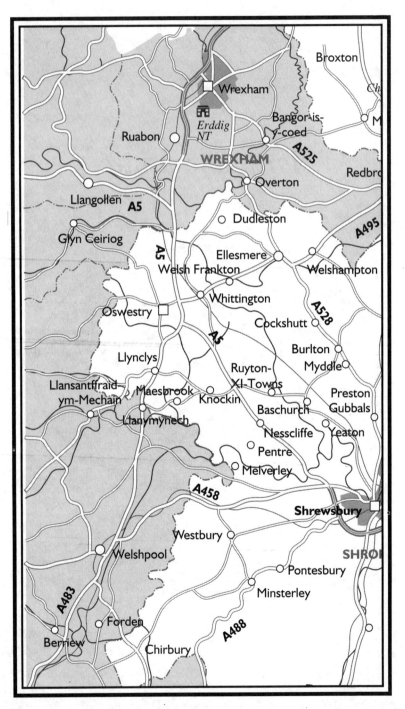

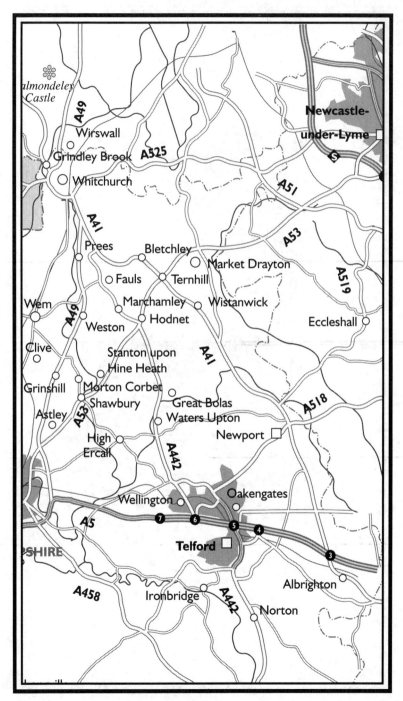

Morton Corbet Castle

CHAPTER ONE

North Shropshire

MARKET DRAYTON.

In 1651 almost all of the town of Market Drayton was sadly burnt down, with the result that there is quite a diversity of architectural styles. It is, nevertheless, a pleasant place to wander and discover for yourself. The Buttercross, for example, was built in 1842 to enable farmers wives to display their wares under cover. It bears the crest of the Corbet family, Lords of the Manor since the 1560s. The bell was used to summon the fire engine in times of need.

Clive of India can probably be called Market Drayton's most famous son, although he was actually born at nearby Styche. He was a dare-devil even as a youngster. At eleven he went to The Old Free Grammar School and was nearly always up to no good.

On one occasion he climbed the church tower and sat astride one of the gargoyles, making faces at the people down below. He is also reputed to have offered protection to shopkeepers, taking payment in fruit, cakes and sweets.

If they refused to pay, he threatened to flood their shops, which in Great Hales Street was not difficult, because there were no pavements and all he had to do was block the gutters on the sides of the road and so flood all the cellars of the shops and houses.

He actually got as far as building a sort of dam and then at the last moment diverted the water.

You could say we've come to Market Drayton for the gingerbread! Strange to think that this unique and potent blend of rich spices and rum should be so important, but it is one of the towns claims to fame. Apparently there were once four warring dynasties, all competing for Gingerbread fame. Now there are two, one of whom concentrates purely on novelty gingerbread figures. You will find it at No 72 Shropshire Street. Their recipes are a closely guarded secret.

Gingerbread-men date back to the time of Queen Elizabeth I, who liked to portray her favourite in gingerbread. Since then they have been made for religious and civil festivals and frequently given as a love token.

Naturally there is much more to Market Drayton than just gingerbread. It was twice mentioned in the Domesday book as Magna Draitune, and became Market Drayton when Abbot Simon Combermere obtained a Royal Market Charter in 1245. The towns growth in the ensuing six hundred years has been closely linked to its market, which is still held in Cheshire Street on Wednesdays.

Damsons have always been important here too. On the seventh, eighth and ninth of September every year, Drayton Damson Fair was held. The principal buyers were the mill owners from the Lancashire cotton trade, who used them to make dye. Damsons were set out in the High Street in buckets and sold in 90lb lots. Nowadays their use has become far more domestic and they also feature in the wonderful, local, Damson Cheese.

The Corbet Arms is one of the important watering holes and has been a major gathering point in the town for the last two hundred years. Anything of importance was dealt with here; political meetings, bankruptcy proceedings, inquests into lunacy, tax collecting etc. It was at one of these assemblies that two of Wellingtons Generals, Rowland Hill and Stapleton Cotton came to celebrate Wellingtons victories against Napoleon. Another famous resident was Thomas Telford who stayed here in 1832, when he came to inspect the canal he was building to the east of the town.

It has not always been peaceful here though. In 1865 there was a violent eruption at a meeting called to discuss the installation of proper drainage. It developed into a riot and troops were brought in from Manchester to calm things down.

There is a ghost story attached to Room 7 so bachelors beware, you may be at risk! The ghost, a young girl, only appears to single men. The girl was employed as a chambermaid at The Corbet Arms and happened to fall in love with a handsome stranger staying in Room 7. He made the most of his stay and then jilted her. She, broken-hearted, hung herself in the room. Nowadays, she still seeks revenge and is quite likely to kiss the occupant, providing he is single of course. She is not averse to pinching bottoms and snatching the duvet away either.

The Railway Hotel, another local landmark, was built in 1860 with the intended purpose of being in a key position for the Market Drayton Terminus, but the railway was re-routed and completely missed the new hotel. Michael and Jan are the very welcoming hosts of The Railway offering first class en-suite accommodation, really excellent food and top quality ales, wines and spirits. The restaurant seats 75 and bookings are preferred at weekends. Weddings and special events are catered for. Open all day, everyday.

The parish church of St. Mary has stood in Market Drayton for over a thousand years and has seen turbulent times. Abbot Combermere took exception to the Archbishop of Canterbury back in 1280, and refused to let him into the church - he armed his monks and they defended it like a castle.

The Railway Hotel, 79 Cheshire Street, Market Drayton, Shropshire.
Tel: 01630 652083.

AROUND MARKET DRAYTON.

Situated on the A51 at Pipegate on the Shropshire border, **The Chetwode Arms** is another interesting find. It dates back in part to the 18th century with a history as a former farmhouse with its own slaughterhouse, probably selling ale from the house at that time. Barrie and Pam arrived at The Chetwode Arms in November 1995 and through their joint efforts have produced a very popular venue for delicious food and fine ale in a lovely atmosphere. Credit also goes to Paul Jackaman, the Chef, who has been part of the team for over six years producing quality dishes which customers return for again and again. Meals are available every lunchtime and evening chosen from the blackboard selection or the very popular Carvery. The Chetwode is attractively Olde Worlde in appearance with beamed ceilings, exposed brick walls and feature fireplace and bar area. Booking advisable.

The Chetwode Arms, Pipegate, Nr. Market Drayton. Tel: 01630 647563.

"Know that we have granted and by this our present charter confirmed to Brother Simon Abbot of Combermere and the monks serving God there that they and their successors forever shall have a weekly market in their manor of Drayton on Wednesday"

8th November 1245, Henry 111

If you like spending time looking around Garden Centres look out for The Little Nursery. A wonderful family run business situated on the A41 owned and personally run by Barrie and Sheila Fisher for the past four years, though it has been in the family since 1969. Set in two and a half acres of beautiful landscaped gardens it has much to offer both amateur and professional gardeners. The emphasis here is on the personal touch and nothing seems too much trouble for Barrie and Sheila. The Nursery is beautifully laid out and features rare and unusual plants, you are even allowed to wander around their own private garden to gain ideas on how to lay things out. Clearly the Nursery is more than just a job to Barrie, it is his hobby and his dedication can be easily observed in The Little Nursery. Open seven days a week 9am to 6pm.

The Little Nursery, Tern Hill, Market Drayton, Shropshire Tel: 01630 638275 Fax: 01630 638376.

Another, more formal place to visit for people who like gardening is **Hodnet Hall Gardens,** quite easy to reach on the A53 Market Drayton to Shrewsbury road, only five miles from Market Drayton itself. The gardens here, were developed by the late Brigadier A.G.W. Heber-Percy over a period of thirty years during which time he transformed a shrub-entangled marshy valley into the beautiful landscaped gardens, that you see today. The gardens extend to over sixty acres with magnificent forest trees, sweeping lawns and ornamental lakes, which provide a perfect background for the masses of daffodils and blossoms in the early spring. A little later come the glorious colours of the azaleas, rhododendrons, laburnums and lilacs and then the peonies, roses, astilbes and primulas. If you cannot get there during this time summer produces even more beauty when the borders blossom and the hydrangeas are in full bloom. The late summer brings on the shrubs and in the autumn there's brilliant coloured foliage and berries. The gardens are a superb example of what can be done to produce a wonderful show of colour throughout the seasons. It is almost as if Brigadier Heber-Percy were an artist painting a wonderful picture.

There is an excellent Tea Room, which is decorated with an amazing collection of Big Game Trophies. This doesn't detract from the fact that you get an excellent cup of tea and some very good home-baked food. The House itself - Hodnet Hall - is built in the late Elizabethan style, high on the valley side overlooking the main lake, and has recently been modernised for the family but is not shown to the public. The Gardens are open from Good Friday until the 30th of September. Tuesdays to Saturdays (closed Mondays) from 2pm - 5pm. (gardens cleared 6.30pm) Sundays and Bank Holiday Mondays from 12 noon until 5.30pm. (gardens cleared 7.00pm).

Hodnet Hall Gardens, Hodnet, Market Drayton. Tel: 01630 685202.

HODNET.

The village of **Hodnet** is a pretty place with some attractive half-timbered houses and a splendid looking pub called The Squirrel. The parish church of St. Luke looks down on the village from a lovely hilltop position. It is of Norman origin and has, unusually, a christening gate and wedding steps and a rare 14th century octagonal tower. Here you'll find fabulous carvings of foliage, rosettes and a peacock accompanied by an eagle, a cock and a lion, set around a 17th century font. A Chapel is dedicated to the Heber-Percy family and has a fine head sculpture of

Bishop Heber-Percy who wrote so many stirring hymns. The church usually opens daily during daylight hours.

The Bear Hotel at Hodnet is particularly well placed opposite the magnificent 60 acre Hodnet Hall and close to four fine golf courses. The Bear has an interesting history originating from an old 16th century coaching inn and which today provides all the facilities of a country hotel. Old features such as the open fireplaces and oak beams help maintain the cosy ambience whilst the floodlit cellar viewed through the glass floor and Jasper the friendly ghost are always a talking point.

Norman and Irene Adams have been hosts at The Bear for seven years, their chefs catering is appreciated by many regular visitors.; food is served in both the restaurant and the bar. The Hotel has six comfortable en-suite bedrooms and during your extended stay, Jasper may put in a friendly appearance! E.T.B.- 3 Crowns Commended. A.A. ** R.A.C.

The Bear Hotel, Hodnet, Shropshire. Tel: 01630 685214 Fax: 01630 685787.

MARCHAMLEY

In the nearby village of **Marchamley** you'll find the imposing entrance drive to **Hawkstone Hall**. Between 1556 and 1906 the hall was the seat of the Hill family but is now home to the Redemptorists religious order, who conduct courses in spiritual renewal for priests and nuns from all over the world. The wonderful Georgian mansion is set in gardens and parklands that are a masterpiece of naturalistic landscaping. The gardens feature formal terraces and lawns, lily and stew ponds. There are informal pathways through the extensive woodlands, which feature a magnificent and varied collection of trees.

Because the very nature of Hawkstone is one of peace, quiet and contemplation the hall and gardens are only open to the public on Spring Bank Holiday Monday and during August from the 5th to 31st.

WESTON-UNDER-REDCASTLE

In the peaceful village of **Weston-under-Redcastle** is perhaps the most outstanding attraction of its kind in Europe, **Hawkstone Park.** An extraordinary landscape of concealed pathways, secret tunnels, hidden grottoes and spectacular follies which was created in the 18th-century by Sir Rowland Hill.

A fascinating place to spend a day, it covers almost 100 acres of beautiful Shropshire countryside between the A49 and A442 near Weston-under-Redcastle and is one of the greatest historic parklands in the UK. An acknowledged masterpiece of the romantic School of Naturalistic Landscape, this unique fantasy of caves, cliffs, towers and monuments is designated Grade I by English Heritage.

Now restored to its former glory after having been neglected for almost a century, the park is full of surprises: paths twist and turn, rise and fall to reveal something out of the ordinary around every corner. Throughout its history, Hawkstone has been visited by succession of illustrious people, including Dr Johnston and the Duke of Wellington, and in recent years it has also been linked with Arthurian legend. The park forms part of the Hawkstone Estate, 400 acres of idyllic grounds which incorporate two 18-hole championship golf courses and the renowned **Hawkstone Park Hotel.** Originally built in 1790 as an inn to accommodate visitors to the park, this superb facility has been fully updated to the standard of an English Tourist Board 41-crown country house hotel.

Its 65 fully-refurbished guest bedrooms are beautifully appointed and equipped with en suite bathrooms and a full range of extras, and there are also two first-class restaurants and a choice of licensed bars which are open to non-residents. Hawkstone Park Hotel is open all year round, and the park daily between 1 April and 31 October.

Hawkstone Park, Weston-under-Redcastle, Nr. Shrewsbury, Shropshire
Tel: 01939 200611 Fax: 01939 20031

There are some great places in the area to visit too. **Bridgemere Garden Centre**, which is Europe's largest, is approximately two miles from **Larksfield**. It is a gardeners paradise and well worth a visit. For a wealth of tourist sights take a look at **Stoke-on-Trent**, where you will find the famous potteries such as Wedgwood, Royal Doulton and Coalport.

WISTANWICK.

Driving around its very easy to inadvertently find yourself, in Shropshire one minute, then Cheshire and then Wales; very confusing! Close to each of these three borders is the rural and picturesque village of Wistanswick, which is just outside Market Drayton. A Shropshire Giant called Tom Dutton once lived in the village, who is said to have built the local church by carrying the sandstone blocks across the river on his back. Oliver Cromwell was once quite active in this area too.

NEWPORT

Back on the A41 and on to **Newport**. There is plenty to do around here, with nature trails, indoor sports at the Lilleshall National Sports Centre about two and a half miles away, a cycle hire centre, golf and horse riding and many interesting walks.

One of the most rewarding experiences must surely come from a visit to **Mischas Restaurant and Accommodation.** This elegant Georgian and Elizabethan property was all but derelict when partners Mischa and Georgina rescued it four years ago. Between them they have a wealth of talent and experience which they have put to good use in the total refurbishment of the house, adding a lovely conservatory along the way. From the moment you walk in, you are aware of the care and quality applied to the presentation, from elegant furnishings and decoration to gleaming cutlery and carefully selected china and glassware. The restaurant has an intimate atmosphere and the a'la carte menu is an achievement in balance and variety of classical cuisine carefully and imaginatively presented to satisfy the highest expectations. Three guest bedrooms are available with en-suite bathrooms allowing one the full pleasure of a complete dining experience and comfortable rest.

Mischa's Restaurant, 128 High Street, Newport, Shropshire.
Tel: 01952 820636.

It is sad that so much of the old town of Newport was destroyed by fire in the 17th century, but there are still some very nice places to see here. Both High Street and St. Mary's Street have some fine half-timbered buildings and the parish church, which sits between them, is well worth a visit.

In 1832, after partaking of luncheon, Their Royal Highnesses The Duchess of Kent and the young Princess Victoria, gave their assent to the Hotel being renamed **The Royal Victoria Hotel**. Today, this handsome listed building, now privately owned, offers excellent accommodation in twenty four en-suite bedrooms equipped to exacting standards with all luxuries and with room service provided. The Bars and Restaurant of the Royal Victoria with their strong Victorian decor are one of the Hotels most popular features. The Buttercross Restaurant has a most comprehensive a'la carte menu featuring a great variety of freshly prepared dishes using seasonally available produce from local suppliers, complimented with a well balanced wine list. Maintaining the quality and service of The Royal Victoria Hotel, the manager will gladly arrange any connecting transport and a special collection and delivery service is available.

The Royal Victoria Hotel, St. Mary's Street, Newport, Shropshire. Tel: 01952 820331.

Its nice to occasionally find cafes and eating places with a more unusual setting; **The Conservatory** is just such a place. You will find it by passing through the bakery shop on the High Street in Newport. A few paces through and there you are! Built to resemble the style of the grand old conservatory, the whole of roof area is glass with a show of greenery in troughs around its base and plants in tubs, ironwork tables and chairs, tiled floor and latticework divisions continue the theme. Air conditioning keeps the temperature very pleasant. The Conservatory is open from 8am until 5pm Monday to Saturday and is a popular venue for breakfast and morning coffee. During the day, a menu offering a wide range of truly excellent food is available supplemented by daily specials. Light snacks and afternoon teas are of course available too. Its a lively place and the service is very good. Parties can be catered for by pre-booking.

The Conservatory, 28 High Street, Newport. Tel: 01952 825053.

With a history dating from the mid 19th century as an inn, the **Shakespeare Inn** has had a total of only eight licensees. Present owners Robbie and Brenda Holme came here in 1989 as tenants and bought the inn four years ago. They have put in quite an investment of time and money in turning the Shakespeare into a really excellent pub.

Shakespeare Inn
They have received many awards for outdoor floral displays and the

whole place is very nicely presented. The neat interior with its Stone laid floors and exposed brick walls and fireplaces, also features a collection of teapots and mugs as well as other memorabilia. Appreciative regulars enjoy the well kept ales and the pub is well known for its selection of five different bitters. Sandwiches are available at lunch times. Open everyday 11am to 11pm and 12 noon until 10.30pm on Sundays. Call in and sample the friendly atmosphere and welcome.

Shakespeare Inn, 66 Upper Bar, Newport, Shropshire. Tel: 01952 811924.

AROUND NEWPORT.
SAMBROOK.
The ancient village of Sambrook can be found signposted off the A41 Newport to Whitchurch road .

Charles Dickens used to stay in this area, not very far from Chetwynd House, in which lived a jilted bride who reputedly kept her wedding cake locked up in a cupboard and only lived in the top part of the house. It is said that this is where Dickens got the idea for the character of Miss Haversham in Great Expectations.

Situated in this tiny and picturesque village just a mile from the A41, the **Three Horseshoes Inn** offers a traditionally warm welcome to visitors from many parts. Although the records show this inn as licensed premises only since the late 19th century, it was formerly an alehouse, a butchers with its own slaughterhouse and, over 250 years ago, a farmhouse.

Don't forget. ! ·
To mention Hidden Places
when you call.

When Christine and Trevor decided to take on the tenancy some two and a half years ago, the inn was just about to be closed. Fearing the loss of their village pub and obviously not wanting to see it fall into disrepair, the village and the Parish Council offered Trevor their support. Walk into the Three Horseshoes today and you'll see a successful inn with plenty of atmosphere. Both Trevor and Christine are still hard at work making sure the food is the best it can be and the ales in top condition. Make a point of calling in and enjoy some great hospitality.

Three Horseshoes Inn, Sambrook, Newport, Shropshire. Tel: 01952 550234

GREAT BOLAS.

Driving out from Newport slightly to the west, its worth seeking out the small village of Great Bolas. It was here that Tennyson found his heroine Sarah Hoggins, about whom he wrote a poem. This pretty young lady was the daughter of the village miller. One day she met and fell in love with a young man called John Jones who came to stay at her fathers farm. They married but she was later to find out that the marriage was bigamous. John Jones was not her husbands real name at all. He was really Henry Cecil, and already married to a lady named Emma Vernon who had in turn deserted him and departed with the curate. For some time the lovers were separated but Sarah remained true to her John and one day he came back for her, having confirmed that his first wife was dead. They were properly married this time, using the bridegrooms real name. This was not the end of this extraordinary story though, because Sarah had yet another discovery to make. Henry Cecil was descended from the great Lord Burghley and because the then Lord Burghley was childless, Henry succeeded to his title and estates. So the millers daughter soon found herself a countess and mistress of one of the finest stately homes in England.

SHAWBURY

Shawbury may be a disappointing if you don't like aircraft (and exciting if you do), because it is close to an RAF base and potentially noisy. The splendid ruins of Moreton Corbet Castle, which was the seat of the local Corbet family, are worth exploring regardless. It is an entrancing and romantic sight with its stark grey stone walls forming a silhouette against the sky. Hopefully neither it, nor the delightful church nearby which has a remarkable 14th century chancel, suffer from the constant shaking given to them by the jet aircraft roaring overhead.

The Elephant and Castle is an impressive pub and eating place which is situated in the heart of the village of Shawbury, seven miles Northeast of Shrewsbury on the A53 Market Drayton road. Since taking over in 1995, Robin and Clare Long have transformed this handsome 18th-century former coaching inn into a lively meeting place which offers a warm welcome to visitors and locals alike. As well as a good range of traditional ales, there is an excellent-value food menu which offers a wide choice of steaks, chicken, fish and vegetarian dishes. Clare and Robin also organise a popular programme of events, and have three recently-refurbished en suite guest rooms available for those wanting accommodation.

Elephant and Castle, Shawbury, Near Shrewsbury, Shropshire
Tel: 01939 250205

EDGEBOLTON.

A short distance north of Shawbury on the A53 at Edgebolton you'll arrive at an impressive Garden Centre. Set within 5.5 acres and with an adjacent further 9.5 acres planted to pick-your-own and ready picked fruit and vegetables, **Shawbury Garden Centre** created by Brian and Angela Humphreys has become really popular. Brilliantly set out, there's lots of room to ponder and decide on the magnificent array of shrubs, plants and trees. If you need help or advice on what to buy or how to care for your plants - just ask! There is plenty of help available. The pick-your-own section is very popular and produce can be picked from early June right up until first frost. We called in October and found strawberries still available to pick! Open seven days - 9am to 5pm in winter and until 6pm in summer. There's a good Coffee Shop on site providing anything from refreshing hot drinks to full lunch.

Shawbury Garden Centre & Fruit Farm, Edgebolton, Shawbury,
Shrewsbury. Tel: 01939 251173 Fax: 01939 251311

UPPER ASTLEY.

The Dog In The Lane was at one time a typical country house with an inn combined, which also brewed its own ale. Built in 1600, it stands on the old turnpike road, the A53, a few miles from Shrewsbury on the Market Drayton road. The inn was also known as the Talbot, which was the name of a breed of large, white hunting-hound which became extinct several centuries ago. The Talbots were also, of course, the Earls of

Shrewsbury, and presumably the inn belonged to the family estate at one time. The inn, run by Stan and Maureen Hall, is well known for its excellent food, served in normal opening hours. You can choose from a variety of light snacks and freshly prepared sandwiches to a full 3-course meal which can include several vegetarian dishes. There's a good choice of ales and bottled beers. A very suitable resting place.

The Dog In The Lane, Upper Astley, Shrewsbury, Shropshire.
Tel: 01939 210244.

Wandering to the west along lanes brings you to **Grinshill**, a mellow village running along a valley, and then on to **Clive**. The two villages are separated by a hill where building stone has been quarried since Roman times. Grinshill stone is known throughout Shropshire.

WEM

The perfect holiday base for exploring this beautiful part of the country can be found in Foxleigh Drive in the heart of Wem. **Foxleigh House** is a handsome part-17th-century residence which was extended in the 1840s and which stands in a large attractive garden containing its own croquet lawn. Now the spacious family home of Barbara Barnes, it offers comfortable centrally-heated guest accommodation in a large twin-bedded room with private bathroom, and a family suite of three rooms sleeping 4-6 with its own private bathroom; each is equipped with colour television and tea/coffee making facilities. Mrs Barnes offers the warmest of welcomes and the choice of a traditional English or continental breakfast; she also provides delicious evening meals by prior arrangement. English Tourist Board 2-crown commended, Foxleigh House is full of traditional character and ideally located for touring the many visitor attractions which lie within easy driving distance. These include the World Heritage Site at Ironbridge, the famous china factories of the Potteries, the Roman city walls and medieval remains at Chester, the castles of the Welsh borderland, and the many National Trust-owned houses and gardens which are dotted throughout the area.

Foxleigh House, Foxleigh Drive, Wem, Shrewsbury, Shropshire
Tel: 01939 233528

Well known to everyone in the locality and to many throughout the country is **T.O. Williams of Wem,** famous for its incredible selection of 100/150 cheeses and looked after as a labour of love by Alex Williams. A top judge in national competitions, he has the qualified experience to guide and help his customers. The shop is an absolute picture packed full of additional items including many different types of savouries, home made bread and cakes, home-cooked meats, and Shropshire stuffings made on the premises and sold in famous shops throughout the country.

T.O. Williams, 17 High Street, Wem. Tel: 01939 232552 Fax: 01939 235151

If you enjoy carnivals then the first Saturday in September should be marked down in your diary, because that is Wem's big day. The Carnival has the reputation for being the finest in Shropshire, which is no mean title to live up to. It is a great day out with activity from early morning until late at night. In the middle of all this activity is **The Castle Hotel** with its roots back in the 17th century, having been built after the Great Fire of Wem destroyed the majority of buildings in the town. For the past two and a half years it has been personally run by Chris and Claire Richmond, their first venture into the Licensing Trade and judging by the popularity of The Castle, it has proved to be a success. Open all day, every day from 9.30 am for morning coffee and 10.30am for alcoholic drinks. Food is available every lunchtime and can be served in various rooms or in the bar. The is plenty of the old character remaining with oak panelling,

19

The Mere. Ellesmere

wooden floors, old beams and interesting fireplaces and memorabilia. On Sunday evenings live entertainment features soloists and duets with across the board music, everything from Country and Western to the popular current sounds.

The Castle Hotel, Wem, Shropshire. Tel: 01939 232430

AROUND WEM

In 1974 Hugh and Olive Shingler purchased 31 acres of land and set about creating a caravan park. Now, 22 year later, with the help of their Son and Daughter they welcome many visitors and families to their enlarged 48 acre **Lower Lacon Caravan Park.** It is one of the best in the county offering first class facilities to those hiring a holiday home or visiting touring vans. The holiday homes are separate from the Touring Park, all connected to mains services and individually landscaped.

Lower Lacon Caravan Park

The Holiday Home season is from 1st March to 2nd January. No subletting is allowed. The general facilities are extensive and include outdoor heated swimming pool, toddlers paddling pool, play area, children's cycle hire, crazy golf, pony rides; the list is endless. A lounge bar is available for Adults with family marquee nearby. There is a cafe and shop, breakfasts and lunches are served in the Cafe and the Barn has family discos at weekends in the high season. The Touring Park is open all year and provides 200 mains hook-up points, a camping area and disabled facilities. Ask for a comprehensive brochure. Beautifully laid out and carefully run. Numerous awards including AA -3 Pennants, British Graded Holiday Parks - √√√

Lower Lacon Caravan Park, Wem, Shropshire. Tel: 01939 232376

HARMER HILL.

Heading south again along the A528, just after Harmer Hill you will discover **Pimhill Organic Farm**, the oldest established organic farm in Shropshire. Organic since 1949, this delightful place provides a vast range of mouthwatering, organically produced food including wholewheat and fine brown flour which is stone ground on the premises.

While parents browse in the beautifully laid out farm shop, children can make friends with the likes of tame pygmy goats, rabbits and chickens which wander freely around the farmyard. Above the shop you can enjoy a rest in the small cafe and choose from a wide selection of mouthwatering homemade snacks, and during the summer months you can make free use of the barbecue equipment set out by picnic tables on the lawn.

Pimhill Organic Farm Shop, Lea Hall, Harmer Hill, Nr. Shrewsbury. Tel: 01939 290342 Fax: 01939 291156

Also situated on the A528 at Harmer Hill is **The Red Castle** public house. Run personally by Tim Smith for the last twelve months, The Red Castle is a good meeting place for both locals and visitors who together create a great atmosphere. The pub is well decorated and furnished with comfortable seating for 30 dining patrons. Excellent meals are available at lunchtime and in the evenings and the pub is open all day on Saturdays. The well kept ales feature Tetley and Bass as regulars with a good selection of lagers and ciders on tap. To the rear is a beer garden where, when weather permits, barbecues are held. Suitable for children and disabled visitors with a large car park.

The Red Castle, Harmer Hill, Shrewsbury. Tel: 01939 291071

Soulton Hall is an Elizabethan Country Manor House with a long and interesting history; the present Ashton family can trace their ancestors to the 11th century when the *Manor of Suleton* features in the Domesday Book of 1086. John and Ann Ashton are very welcoming and share their lovely old house with appreciative guests who are invited to enjoy the tranquillity of the walled garden, its pillared courtyard and mature trees. Accommodation in the main house is in four well-appointed double rooms, three of which have en-suite bathrooms. All have colour television, radio and tea making facilities. Each room has its own character with many architectural features dating back to the 16th century.

Across the lawn the coach house has been transformed and offers ground-floor accommodation with two spacious bedrooms with en-suite spa bathrooms. Keepers Cottage and Shooters Lodge offer further independent accommodation within or close by the 550 acre estate. At the end of the day guests are welcome to join the residents of Soulton Hall for dinner and a relaxing evening. The leisurely five-course dinner is imaginatively prepared with the emphasis on home cooking and the use of home-grown produce, complimented by a choice of wines. Ponies are available for riding and other pursuits such as pony and trap rides, clay target shooting, musket shooting, archery and coarse fishing can be arranged. Beautifully presented with a very personal touch. E.T.B. - 4 Crowns Commended. AA Selected QQQQ

Soulton Hall Near Wem, Shrewsbury, Shropshire. Tel: 01939 232786
Fax: 01939 234097

BASCHURCH & YEATON.
Coming just a little way south and west again you'll reach **Yeaton**, a small black and white hamlet living a quiet, rural life of its own. This is in spite of the fact that the nearest village, **Baschurch**, is a busy place having become a commuter base for Shrewsbury and a retirement area for many as well.

If it wasn't for the sign on the lawn, you could easily miss The attractive **Boreatton Arms** which looks more like a large private home than a public house. On this spot once stood a coaching inn which later became an hotel and public house before finally being raised to the ground in the sixties. The replacement fared little better and eventually was closed and boarded up for nearly three years.

Then along came Jenny and Dave in January 1996. It was by then in a terrible state explained Jenny. But in just six months they have transformed the old place and it now looks a picture with it smart clean appearance and cottage style bow windows. Soon it is to have a conservatory added for the convenience of diners. Jenny and Dave have created a really atmospheric inn with delicious food and outstanding ale to match. The decorations and furnishings are tasteful and even the facilities are a picture!

They open seven days a week offering a menu from snacks and sandwiches to main meals such as The Boreatton Mixed Grill, Mushroom and Nut Fettucini and Seafood stuffed Pancakes. There's lots more on offer and with the daily specials its hard to choose. Children have their special selections too. With good access for disabled callers and a children's play area (ready in Summer 97), the owners are really providing good facilities for everyone. We mustn't forget to mention the wide selection of Ales, bottled beers, Lagers, wines and spirits. Then there's the Pool night, Bowling Club, Football team and .... Convinced? Situated in the village of Baschurch on the B4397.

Boreatton Arms, Station Road, Baschurch, Shropshire. Tel: 01939 261412

MAESBROOK.

Following the sign to Knockin, off the A5 Shrewsbury/Oswestry Road, leads to the peaceful hamlet of **Maesbrook**, which is mentioned in the Domesday Book as Meresbroc, and it's here you will meet Mina and Steve who recently became tenants of **The Blackhorse Inn**.

The Black Horse Inn

The inn has a history from the 18th century and is certainly interesting and characterful with many old beams. Mina takes care of the catering and her delicious food is served in either the restaurant or dining area. Steve looks after front of house and the bar where the ale is varied and well kept. Letting rooms are available for bed and breakfast accommodation whilst to the rear of the inn there are three self-catering cottages available all year round. Telephone for further details.

The Black Horse Inn, Maesbrook, Oswestry. Tel: 01691 682472

Be careful you don't go speeding along the A5 and miss **The Queens Head**, a really well presented country pub and restaurant. It is situated two miles south east of Oswestry on the way to Shrewsbury and sits adjacent to the recently re-opened Montgomery Canal in picturesque countryside. Mick and Di are the resident owners and together with their efficient staff will ensure you are made welcome and enjoy your visit. The decor and furnishings are outstanding and fifty percent of the area is designated non-smoking. The blackboard menus list a huge variety of dishes and making your choice takes time. Mick is the chef and his culinary abilities must require considerable dexterity to support such a selection. His seafood specialities are fresh and just that little bit different. Children have their own special menu. Theakstons ales head the wide range of beers, wine, spirits and soft drinks which may be enjoyed in the beer garden on warm days. Book at peak times.

The Queens Head, Nr. Oswestry, Shropshire. Tel: 01691 610255

OSWESTRY.

Oswestry Borderland is how Shropshire describes both the enchanting medieval town and then all the lovely places around it. Most of the surrounding area has been both Welsh and English at different stages of history, and this has left a rich heritage within the landscape.

This is an area of unspoilt, uncrowded beauty and frequently very dramatic landscapes. It is not the place for people who need to live in the fast lane. If you enjoy the peace and pace of rural Britain, appreciate quality in your surroundings and like to stray from the main tourist track, then you will be totally happy here.

Oswestry is an ancient market town which has grown up around King Oswalds Well, although it traces its origins further back in time to the huge and impressive Iron Hillfort of Old Oswestry, on the outskirts of the town.

It was in the year 642 AD that a furious battle raged between rival Saxon Kings, Oswald of Northumbria and the pagan King Penda of Mercia in which Oswald was defeated. His body was cruelly dismembered and hung on the branches of a tree. A hungry eagle swooped and carried off one of his severed arms. Where it subsequently fell to the ground, a spring bubbled up to mark the spot. And so King Oswalds Well came into being and very soon it became a place of pilgrimage renowned for its healing powers.

There are also those who would have you believe that Oswestry acquired its name because the dead kings body was hung from a tree, and that the name is a corruption of Oswalds Tree. Make your own decision!

In the 8th century Wats Dyke and later Offas Dyke were built along the Wales border to keep out the Welsh, and you can see some of the remains to the west of the town. The Normans later built a motte and bailey castle soon after the Conquest, with the intention of quelling the increasing Welsh raids. As if all this fighting was not enough, the town also had other troubles.

1559 brought the Great Plague and it killed nearly one third of the inhabitants of the town. The Croeswylan Stone is a reminder of this, marking the spot to which the market was removed at the time of all this anguish. It is sometimes referred to as the Cross of Weeping.

Ravages of fire and war also did much to destroy parts of the town. There were three horrific fires between the 13th and 18th centuries. Oswestry didn't fare well during the Civil War either - the town was Royalist, but was captured by the Parliamentarians, who wasted no time in destroying the castle. All that is left today is ruins, but the land has been turned into a small park and arboretum and is well worth visiting to get good views of the town.

Even more buildings were demolished when Oswestry became the headquarters for the railway in 1860. One that managed to escape was the 17th century Llwyd Mansion, which is by far the best example of the towns half-timbered buildings. On its side is a double headed eagle crest, granted to the Llwyd family by the Holy Roman Emperor for distinguished service during the crusades.

In Upper Brook Street is Oswestry School, founded in 1407 and believed to be the oldest secular school in the country. There are many delightful buildings to enjoy, but to get the best out of the town take a walk starting from Castle Bank. From here, wander down to Bailey Head, which once was the outer square of the castle and held the stocks and whipping post where punishments were meted out every Wednesday. There is still a market held here every Wednesday though the stocks and whipping post have now gone. The Guildhall, built in 1893 in the French style, is an imposing local landmark.

Situated in the market square of Oswestry is **The Red Lion,** attractively presented with its recessed outdoor sitting area with tables and sun shades. As with many pubs and hotels in the area, In its early days, The Red Lion was an old coaching inn. Although George and Jaki have been here only a short time, they have already established themselves and have created a nice atmosphere and a relaxing venue in which to enjoy a drink and bar snacks. A good selection of food is available in the restaurant which is open to non-residents . There are four comfortable guest bedrooms available and children are welcome. Call in and sample the welcome.

The Red Lion, Bailey Head, Oswestry. Tel: 01691 652781

From here walk down Albion Hill and into Beatrice Street, which houses the 14th century, gabled Fighting Cocks, once a coaching inn and thought to be one of the oldest buildings in the town. Further down is the site where Beatrice Gate used to stand. The road widens here, as it does at all the old gate sites, allowing traffic to pass out from the restricted space of the town.

If you turn right into King Street you come to Oswald Road with the old railway station on the left. The station yard is now the home of the Cambrian Railway Society. The Great War poet Wilfred Owen, born in 1893, was the son of the stationmaster here.

Jane and Sean are a young couple deserving of their success having recently taken up the tenancy of **The Golden Lion** and injected it with a new lease of life. This 250 year old building started life as a school before becoming a public house, though the only learning applied there today is from the experience of this hardworking couple. Jane's organisational skills are from her past duties in hotel reception whilst Sean is an experienced qualified chef, previously with the well known Bells of Peover in Cheshire. As you might therefore expect, the food served at The Golden Lion is freshly prepared and really delicious. The bar has an infinite variety of ales, wines and spirits and you are cordially invited to join in the Tuesday evening quiz nights. Call in and sample the great atmosphere.

The Golden Lion, Upper Church Street, Oswestry, Shropshire.
Tel: 01691 653747

Church Street is where you will find the Fox Inn, an old timber building which once had a gable projecting over the street. Apparently a passer-by had his silk top hat ruined when it caught on the gable, a row ensued and finally the gable was removed. At the end of the street a pillar marks the location of what was once New Gate and you will see that the road widens just in the same way as it did at Beatrice Gate.

There are a number of other attractive buildings on Church Street, some timber-framed, with a good selection of Georgian and Victorian shops and houses as well. On the left side of the street is The **Wynstay Hotel**, once a coaching inn. In fact, there are still some stables and coach houses at the rear. It is a busy place today but must have been even busier when it was the starting point for coaches leaving for Chester and Shrewsbury.

Before entering the parish church, which is dedicated to St. Oswald, take a look at Holbache House. It is a fine brick and timber building dating from the 1400s and once housed the **Holbache Grammar School,** founded by David Holbache. In the Old School Room there is even an old bench on which many pupils have carved their names.

The Church of St. Oswald has a long history and varied. It played an important part in the Civil War when it was used as an observation point and strategic position during the siege of the town by the Parliamentarians. Much damage was done and the medieval fabric has been largely remodelled and extended by restoration work over the years, especially in the 19th century. The oldest section of the building is the tower which dates from around 1200. The church is quite lovely inside, and includes a font presented by Colonel Lloyd of Llanforda in the 17th century as a thanksgiving for the restoration of the monarchy. There is also a war memorial designed by Sir Giles Gilbert Scott, and a memorial to Hugh Yale whose family founded Yale University in America.

At the gates of the church is **The Coach and Dogs Restaurant.** Built in the mid-17th century, this is a place of sheer delight. The walls and ceilings are all timbered and the atmosphere is superb. It was originally the home of one Edward Lloyd, son of Colonel Edward Lloyd of Llanforda, leader of the Royalist forces in the town in 1643. Edward was the last of the Lloyds of Llanforda and was a man of strong character. He kept a light carriage of four wheels and, as was the custom in those days, it was drawn by four dogs. It is believed that he turned the house into an inn. It was a very different kind of house then, with two projecting gables and a large entrance porch in the middle. The long mullioned window which stretched from gable to gable is still there today but, with that exception, the building has been renovated considerably, but thankfully without losing its charm.

On the opposite corner of Church Street is another timber-framed house which still has the original leaded windows, made by apprentices when the building was the dwelling of Roberts the Gas, a local plumber and glazier, between 1810-1861. The house, which is now a private dwelling, spent some time as a pub called the Raven and Bellman.

This part of the town was once known as Pentrepoeth which translated into English means the burnt end and refers, no doubt, to the fire of 1567 which did so much damage.

Passing through the War Memorial gates at the end of Church Street you enter **Cae Glas Park.** The roll of honour for the dead of two world wars is a long and proud one. In such a small town there would have been few families who did not suffer loss. There is also a memorial for railway workers who were killed in the form of a bronze angel. It used to stand in the station but was transferred to the park when the station closed in the mid-sixties.

It is a beautifully laid out park with some wonderful flower beds which in summer are riotous in colour. The bandstand, something rarely seen today, is almost surrounded by magnificent beech trees - there are tennis courts, a bowling green, children's play area, crazy golf and vast areas of open parkland.

Leaving the park through the gates brings you to Welsh Walls and then a right turn leads you to Willow Street. Here there is a plaque marking the site of the old Willow Gate, one of the four gates into the town through the old walls. The town walls were once a mile long, back in 1220 and they stayed in situ until 1660 when they were demolished. Nothing now remains.

Don't miss out Arthur Street, on the corner of which is the half-timbered **Butchers Arms** - one of the oldest inns in the town with a fascinating history. In 1672 a Royal Licence allowed the use of a room for the dissenting independent Church of Sweeney who used it until 1750 when they erected the first non-conformist chapel in Oswestry. The building is now the Kingswell Centre and the chapel is a community and arts centre.

The Heritage Gallery, 1-3 Cross Street, Oswestry Tel: 01691 670323

Visitors to Oswestry will make a real find when they call in at **The Heritage Gallery** on Cross Street. You cant help but be impressed by this splendid black and white timbered building known as Llwyd Mansion, built prior to 1604 as a town house for John Lloyd of Llanforda, a local landowner. An Eagle Crest was awarded to Meurig Lloyd of Llanforda by the Emperor of Austria for Bravery. The fabulous oak beams and daub and wattle construction make this a very special place and is now a listed monument where visitors regularly ask to be shown around. You will no doubt be enticed by the wealth of gifts and mementoes available here, including a vast selection of greeting cards suitable for every occasion, various items of jewellery and watches, a popular range of soft toys, plus a well-known brand of mouthwatering chocolates to tempt the sweet-toothed.

AROUND OSWESTRY
WEST FELTON. A couple of miles from Oswestry on the B5009, you'll discover another wonderful Shropshire public house - **The Punchbowl.** It has a striking newly painted exterior and has been substantially renovated by its tenants Mike and Nadine. They took over the Punchbowl twelve months ago when it was on its last legs and have revived its custom with excellent facilities for all the family and created a wonderful atmosphere. Mike is quite a character and ensures all his customers enjoy themselves and the wonderful food too. Nothing is too much trouble, and food is available at all sensible times. There's a good selection of ales - no keg beer here. Children have a good play area and will find an interest in the animals wandering about.

The Punchbowl, Holyhead Road, West Felton, Oswestry. Tel: 01691 610201.

MELVERLEY.
In **Melverley**, St. Peters Church is the oldest church in Shropshire. It was founded in 1406 and is timber framed and painted black and white on the inside and the outside. At first glance the church makes you wonder how it manages to stay safely in such a precarious position on the banks of the River Severn. It must be incredibly sturdy because time and again it has survived floods. It is a very picturesque building and inside there is an overwhelming sense of serenity.

At the **Tontine Inn** in the village, you'll discover that the Severn used to be navigable as far as Pool Quay, where Offas Dyke joins the river bank. You may have heard of the Tontine Bell at Lloyds but may not have realised that the word tontine derives from a mutual insurance set up by the bargemen who carried the river freight.

The Inn is well-worth making the effort to find, its an exceptional pub and eating place which lies in the lanes between the A5 and B4393 in this picturesque village. Since taking over in early 1996, proprietors Kevin and Anne-Louise Banks have transformed the interior, creating a unique atmosphere filled with a wonderful assortment of bygone memorabilia. The bar and conservatory are hung with model aircraft, hot air balloons, antique sewing machines and cameras, and there is even a pool room with a full-sized pony trap built into the beams. Customers can enjoy a pleasant drink or delicious meal in front of a cosy fire, surrounded by bookshelves and arrangements of dried flowers.

The Tontine Inn, Melverley, Near Shrewsbury, Shropshire
Tel/Fax: 01691-682258

While you are here, you must pay a visit to the Old Oswestry Hill Fort. Its just a mile north of the town and is clearly signposted. Without a doubt it is one of the best examples of an iron age hillfort in the country. It is really huge, with massive earthwork ramparts and salients.

The Tanat Valley offers a great day out - turn right on to the main A483 at **Llynclys** and just wander from village to village along this beautiful valley. The valley runs from **Llanyblodwel** and follows the erratic course of the River Tanat up to the Berwyn Mountains. The spectacular Llanrhead Waterfall, one of the seven wonders of Wales is just off the valley. It is an incredible sight.

Its easy to spend a day just doing nothing except picnicking and enjoying the wonderful views at a local beauty spot, Racecourse Common, signposted on the B4850 road to Llansilin. It ceased being a racecourse in 1850 and is now open to the public. The figure of eight circuit is about one and a half miles long, and offers spectacular views over Shropshire and Wales. If you feel like walking, a series of footpaths will take you down into Candy Woods along Offas Dyke.

This area of the Welsh borders has many historic sites and ancient churches - one notable example being the restored 6th century church of Pennant Melangell near Blaen Cwm.

LLANSILIN.

A little known village in this area, and just the sort of place that this book is all about. Steeped in history and wonderfully unspoilt by modernisation or tourist paraphernalia, it nestles in the Afon Cynllaiths valleys. Protected by steep hills interspersed by rocky outlets, yet heavily wooded, the green of the trees creates a superb setting. The peacefulness spills down into the village of Llansilin, which can boast a beautiful church dating back to the 13th century. Although it was destroyed by fire it was rebuilt in the 15th century and much of the original materials were used in rebuilding. In the chancel the high, barrel, vaulted ceiling is made of carved oak and is quite lovely.

SELATTYN.

A picturesque village, three miles from Oswestry. **The Old Rectory** is at the beginning of the village and is approached via a long gravel drive which is bordered by a variety of magnificent mature trees, including one believed to be the oldest and tallest in the village. The sweeping drive leads to a large stone-built period residence that dates back to the 17th century. This lovely building has an old wisteria, fragrant roses and japonica climbing its walls. Facing the house is a magnificent bank of azaleas and rhododendrons. Bill and Maggie Barns will greet you at the door and what a charming couple they are; they are excellent hosts and in no time at all will have a good old pot of English tea, ready to refresh you. With such a warm welcome it seems certain your visit will be enjoyable.

The Old Rectory

The spacious but welcoming entrance hall has a large wood burning stove and pictures of wild flowers on its walls. The Dining room looks out across the fields down onto the Shropshire plain, while the bedrooms also have beautiful views. An evening meal, including delicious homemade soups, fresh vegetables and old fashioned sweets, is available on request. Breakfast is a real treat with a variety of options including vegetarian. For those who prefer self-catering there is a delightful two storey cottage attached to the house. It has a wealth of natural wood beams and enjoys lovely views of the Shropshire countryside. In its fully equipped modern kitchen the old bread oven is retained as a feature. This cosy cottage provides excellent accommodation for a couple or a young family.

The Old Rectory, Selattyn, Oswestry, Shropshire. Tel: 01691 659708

WHITTINGTON.
The parish is centred on Whittington Village, said to be derived from 'White Town' - named after the tufts of cotton and marsh grass that is said to have once blanketed the area.

A short distance from the village is Halston Hall, once the home to a local eccentric by the name of Mad Jack Mytton about whom many stories circulate. Said to have lived a life of excess, he died in a debtors' prison.

Ye Olde Boote Inn - Whittington

One place that is guaranteed to provide an entertaining family day out is **Park Hall Working Farm Museum**, which is situated between Oswestry Showground and the Roberts Jones and Agnes Hunt Orthopaedic Hospital. Set in 40 acres the farm is centred around Shire horses and you can watch these gentle giants in action, working just as they would have done 100 years ago. There is a vast display of bygone farm implements and a visit to the Shafting House shows where the process for chopping up produce for animal feed begins. There are other animals including some unusual and rare breeds, plus seasonal demonstrations of sheep shearing, sheep dogs and various craft displays, with the gift shop providing ideal mementoes of your visit here.

Park Hall Working Farm Museum, Whittington, Oswestry
Tel: 01691 652175

ELLESMERE.

This town is one of those small market towns with a friendly personality and a warm welcome for all visitors. Although no major historical buildings are to be found in here, the town has many interesting and attractive ones. Among those are the Old Town Hall, presented to the town by the Countess of Bridgwater in 1833. It stands in the Square and dominates every other building with its massive roof. Underneath it are fine, brick, vaulted cellars, now transformed into a pleasant restaurant.

Shopping in Ellesmere is an experience too. Many shops are family owned, and makes this a very pleasant place to do ones leisurely shopping.

The Square used to be the home of the weekly market but that has been moved to the Market Hall further up Scotland Street. Inside, the hall not only has masses of stalls, but quite recently some fine murals have been painted by local artists. Ellesmere has had a market continuously since 1212 and it is now open each Tuesday morning.

Another building which catches the eye is the Old Railway Station, an impressive Victorian structure that was intended to be the head office of the Oswestry, Ellesmere and Whitchurch Railway. However, the company only operated for two days before it was absorbed by Cambrian Railways.

There are several pubs in the town and each has its own virtues. The White Hart is, reputedly the oldest pub in the county. The Bridgewater Arms Hotel is named after the Duke of Bridgewater, to whom Ellesmere owes its canal, and The Red Lion Hotel, situated next to an old churchyard, offers the traveller comfortable respite.

Another of the towns old hostelries is **The Ellesmere Hotel** which has been developed and restored to a very high standard with a transformed interior which has carefully chosen furnishings, redesigned restaurant and bars recreating the luxury of former days and the Hotels association with the Duke of Bridgewater. In essence, this is a high class country town hotel providing all modern up to date facilities for holiday guests and business visitors. The Bridgewater restaurant serves generous meals all week with good value specials on Sunday. Tasty wholesome food is also served in the bar where there is enough room for drinkers and diners to mix without intruding on each other. Main dishes are prepared to order using local produce whenever possible and all tastes are catered for including vegetarian. The twelve refurbished en-suite bedrooms and one suite have colour televisions, telephones and all facilities to make your stay comfortable and complete. The hotel also has a separate residents lounge adjoining the public area and an elegant banqueting suite where many types of functions are catered for. The Ellesmere is one of the select hotels owned by Honeycombe Leisure Group.

The Ellesmere Hotel, The High Street, Ellesmere, Shropshire.
Tel: 01691 622055.

There was once a castle in Ellesmere, which stood high above the town and it was in the first line of defence against the Welsh before the more westerly castles at Whittington, Chirk and Oswestry were built. Now nothing remains except a mound which is used as a crown bowling green, believed to be the oldest in the county.

Without doubt the most impressive building is the Parish Church of St. Mary the Virgin and there has been a church on the site overlooking The Mere since before the Norman Conquest. If you happen to hear the fine peal of eight bells ring out on a Sunday morning calling all to worship then do try and go. The church is quite beautiful inside with a magnificent panelled roof.

Cremorne Gardens lie between the town and lake and stretch around half the Meres circumference. It is a lovely waterside park with well-kept lawns and avenues of trees, the gentle waters of The Mere are always in sight and wildbirds can frequently be seen. Water plays a great part in Ellesmere, which calls itself Shropshire's Lakeland. The Mere is the most important, although there are eight smaller lakes. It is paradise for boating enthusiasts as well as fishermen and bird-watchers.

Overlooking Shropshire's largest Mere, famous for its renowned heronry, Canada geese and Swans, **The Boathouse** enjoys a most spectacular Mereside location. Built by Lord Brownlow in the 1930s, it was recently refurbished to a very high standard retaining all its original character, with polished wood floors, oak beams, gardens to the waters edge and its own rowing boat in the rafters! Helen and Nick are your hosts, responsible for all the work and the success of The Boathouse which, from its colourful frontage and gardens to the interior decor and furnishing, benefits much from the professional touch.

The Boathouse

The Brownlow Room restaurant looks out across the Mere where diners can enjoy watching the abundant wildlife. The extensive menu caters to a variety of tastes and guests will surely find something to satisfy their palate. The Boat Room caters for less formal meal and offers food and drink throughout the day starting with Morning coffee from 11am., followed by Lunch, Afternoon tea and High tea. Sunday lunch is very popular and you are well advised to book rather than be disappointed. The Boathouse is licensed and displays an interesting selection of wines and cold bottled beers. The service is wonderful and the smiles on the faces of the staff gives one the impression that this is an enjoyable place to work. Above all, there is a wonderful ambience and relaxed feel about the place where you may play chess, read the newspaper or admire the birds and the view. The Boathouse has extremely good wheelchair access and can seat around 80 inside, plus extra seating on the Terrace and in the Garden. Open everyday until 6pm April - October. Closed Mondays, November and March, and Mondays and Tuesdays - December to February. Spring 1997 will see The Boathouse open in the evenings, so do ring and check precise opening times. Situated between the A528 Wrexham to Shrewsbury and A495 Whitchurch to Oswestry roads.

The Boathouse, Mereside, Ellesmere, Shropshire. Tel: 01691 623828

The Shropshire Union Canal also passes this way and has played a great part in the history of Ellesmere. The Old Wharf with its warehouses and crane is a reminder of a prosperous period for the development of the town, when it was at the centre of plans for a link to the River Mersey, at what was to become Ellesmere Port. It is almost two hundred years since this plan was first mooted and the outcome is the attractive canal from Llangollen's Horseshoe Falls to Hurleston Junction near Nantwich and there is a thoroughly enjoyable walk along the towpath. Another place you can join the canal is by the junction of the Whitchurch and Shrewsbury roads, east of Ellesmere. The junction stands above one of the earliest tunnels to carry a towpath through it so do have a good look if you are interested in canal archaeology.

To the east of here, is Blakemere, a lake left by the glaciers some twelve thousand years ago. In autumn, the trees on the opposite bank cry out for a landscape painter, while a variety of birds can usually be found on and around it.

DUDLESTON HEATH.

A little distance from Ellesmere on the B5068 is **Dudleston Heath** and **The Fox Inn** which offers the traveller comfortable respite. Two and a half years ago, Reg and Gill took a big gamble when they accepted the tenancy of **The Fox Inn** at Dudleston Heath - it had been closed and boarded-up for two years and they knew a great deal of effort would be needed to get it back on its feet. Now the Fox is again a successful and excellent country inn.

The Fox Inn and Reg and Gill have come a long way in those two and a half years and the place really is a credit to them. With its roaring fire on colder days, there is a cosy and comfortable atmosphere welcoming you in. The inn is open everyday, all day, with food available at all times except on Sunday evenings.

A varied menu is available and Gill will try and cater for your special needs. The dining rooms seats around forty people and it is advisable to book for the popular Sunday lunch. Children are welcome if eating. Good access for wheelchairs. Well kept ales include Marsdens Traditional and Pedigree, Guinness, Strongbow and a selection of lagers. Situated in the village of Dudleston Heath and found a mile or so out of Ellesmere towards St. Martins.

The Fox Inn, Dudleston Heath, Ellesmere, Shropshire. Tel: 01691 690636.

WELSHAMPTON.

On the way to Whitchurch you will pass through **Welshampton**, not a particularly remarkable place but it does have an unusual church built by Sir George Gilbert Scott in 1863. It has a rounded apse and stands out because of its curious yellow colouring. Inside it is pretty ordinary but you may wonder why there is a memorial window dedicated to a Basuto chieftain. He had been a student of theology studying at Canterbury. Part of his education brought him to the vicarage at Welshampton, where he stayed with the vicar. Sadly he was taken ill and died in the same year that the church was completed.

WHITCHURCH.

From here taking the A495 brings you into **Whitchurch** which is a lovely town. The Romans were the first people to develop it back in AD55, calling it Mediolanum, meaning the place in the mid-plain. At one time there was a castle guarding the Welsh Marches, but that has gone and all that you can see now is an earthwork. As far back as medieval times Whitchurch became famous for its cheese making and this has never changed.

Tucked away in Pepper Street, one of the oldest streets in Whitchurch, is the **Anchor Inn**. Hosts Sheila and Alex have only recently acquired the tenancy here but have 30 years experience in the licensed trade and know well how to look after the needs of their customers. Since their arrival they have been steadily building their clientele and the Anchor is proving a popular venue for lunch and evening meals and booking is advisable for peak times. The menu is based on generally popular pub food offering a good selection at reasonable prices. The Inn caters for bed and breakfast guests with accommodation for children and help for the less-abled. There's a good selection of keg beers and real ales. Special evening are arranged linked to Medieval, Halloween and other occasions.

The Anchor, Pepper Street, Whitchurch, Shropshire. Tel: 01948 662184

In the heart of Whitchurch, hidden away off the main street in St. Mary's Street, is the lovely **Old Town Hall Vaults**. This 18th century building was the birthplace of Edward German, composer of such classical pieces as Merry England and Tom Jones who was knighted by King George V in 1928 and died in London in 1936. Formerly known as The Black Dog, the inn has character and a display of interesting memorabilia from bygone days. Renowned for its delicious food and excellent ales, it is also open from 10am for morning coffee. There is a cosy dining area seating fifty people and a small outdoor enclosed patio. Hosts and tenants Colin and Pauline have been resident here for eleven years. They are closed on Wednesday from 3.00pm.

The Old Town Hall Vaults, St. Mary's Street, Whitchurch, Shropshire.
Tel: 01948 662251

High Street, Whitchurch

Whitchurch is dominated by the outstanding Queen Anne parish church, which was built between 1712 and 1713 after the previous one collapsed in 1711. The semi-circular porch, dainty balustrades and pinnacles, the Earl of Bridgewater's arms and the clock on the south side of the majestic sandstone tower, make it very attractive. Inside it feels very grand. There are superb classical columns and a splendid 18th century organ case on the top of which stands a trumpeting angel. Sir John Talbot, the first Earl of Shrewsbury, was killed at the Battle of Castillon, near Bordeaux in 1453 and at his request his heart was brought back to Whitchurch and is buried under the porch of the Parish church. Later his body too was interred in the church and now lies in the Egerton Chapel. The church is normally open on most days.

To the north of the church there are some fine Georgian houses and to the south, the High Street leads to the remarkably unspoilt town centre. Here the architecture produces infinite variety and its a joy to wander around. It is clearly a lively, thriving market centre. If you take the trouble to explore the narrow streets you will find not only Georgian houses but 15th century half-timbered and Edwardian shop fronts.

Walkers is a celebrated family-bakery with a coffee shop attached which occupies one of the oldest and most attractive buildings in Whitchurch. This superb timber-framed structure dates from the 16th-century and can be found on the High Street in the centre of town. Proprietor John Huxley is a third generation baker who is renowned for his mouthwatering crusty bread, savouries, cakes and pastries. In 1995, he added a delightful first-floor coffee shop which offers an appetising range of lunches and all-day snacks, including filled baked potatoes, baguettes, salads and Danish open sandwiches, together with a selection of tempting sweets, pastries and beverages.

Walkers Bakery Coffee Shop, 21-23 High Street, Whitchurch, Shropshire
Tel: 01948 664687

Also to be found on the High Street is the historic **Victoria Hotel,** formerly a Coaching and Post inn, stands on Whitchurch's High Street and has been offering food, drink and accommodation for over 300 years. Its external old world appearance gives an indication of the character within. The hotel has seven varied letting rooms and is open all year. The stylish dining area caters for forty people and food is available at lunchtimes and in the evening from a set menu supplemented by a specials board. Burtonwood ales, Stella and Carlsberg Lagers compliment an otherwise good selection of bottled beers, wines and spirits. Open all day. Area for children.

Victoria Hotel, High Street, Whitchurch, Shropshire. Tel: 01948 662031

AROUND WHITCHURCH

Moving first to Grindley Brook - **The Horse and Jockey** is a handsome traditional inn which was built in the 1780s to serve the busy road, and later canal, traffic; it stands beside the busy A41 Chester road, two miles from the centre of Whitchurch. Landlord Bill Barton offers a warm welcome, a fine selection of traditional ales, and an excellent range of bar food, including ploughman's lunches, basket meals, fish, steaks and vegetarian dishes; there is also a special menu for children. The lounge is relaxed and comfortable, and furnished with an interesting collection of canal paintings, antique brasses, and a set of tables adapted from sewing machine bases. Outside, there is a safe fenced playground, and at the rear of the inn, an attractive caravan and camping site. The Horse and Jockey stands at the southern end of the Sandstone Trail, a thirty-mile long-distance footpath ending at Frodsham in Cheshire which passes many of the prominent sandstone outcrops that occur in this part of the country. Less strenuous is the two-mile circular walk which starts and ends at the inn, taking in the Grindley Locks; on busy weekends, this can provide an unexpected spectacle as the barges and motorcraft ascend and descend this famous flight of locks.

Horse and Jockey, Grindley Brook, Whitchurch, Shropshire
Tel: 01948 662723

PREES.

Just south of Whitchurch lies **The Holly Farm Nurseries** at Prees, situated on the main A49 Shrewsbury to Whitchurch road, two miles from its junction with the A41. Founded in 1978 by Tim and Helen Noble, over the years they have built up a thriving concern which offers a comprehensive range of goods and services for the amateur or professional gardener. The majority of shrubs and plants on sale are grown here, and there is also a full range of garden accessories, all expertly laid out on a level site which is suitable for wheelchairs. Pick-your-own fruit and vegetables are offered in season, and a helpful and knowledgeable staff are always on hand to deal with enquiries.

Holly Farm Nurseries, Prees, Whitchurch, Shropshire
Tel/Fax: 01948 840630

Returning to the B5476 Whitchurch to Wem road, we discovered the attractive half-timbered Bull and Dog. Built in 1568 as a coaching inn, it served as a staging post on the Cheltenham-Liverpool run. John and Claire have been tenants here for eighteen years and offer a really interesting and comprehensive menu featuring dishes chosen from around the world. Don't miss the traditional Roast served every Sunday lunchtime. Children welcome. Good wheelchair access. Great atmosphere!

The Bull and Dog, Coton, Nr. Whitchurch, Shropshire. Tel: 01948 880559.

CHAPTER TWO

Much Wenlock, Ironbridge and Shrewsbury

Ironbridge

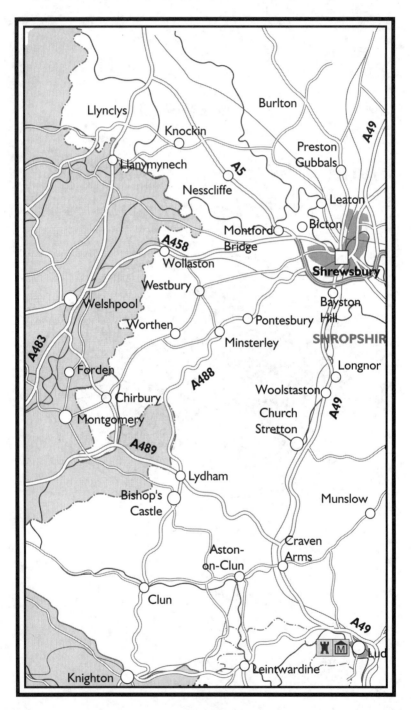

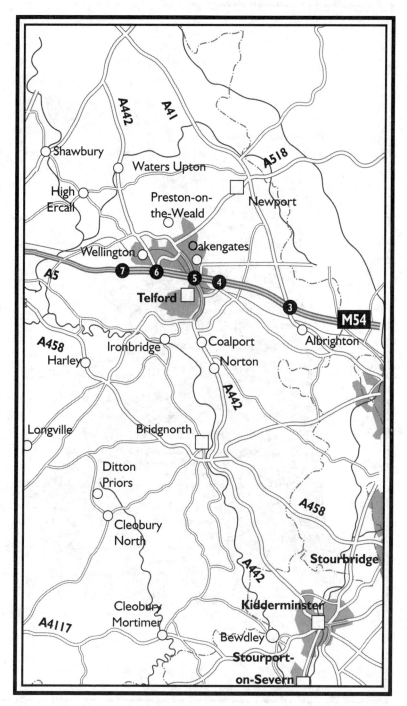

Guildhall & Church - Much Wenlock

CHAPTER TWO

Much Wenlock, Ironbridge and Shrewsbury.

MUCH WENLOCK.

The narrow streets of the medieval town of **Much Wenlock** will have no trouble keeping you enthralled, or possibly lost, as you wander around. It is well worth doing so though, to have the chance to admire the mellow buildings of stone and timber and the glorious black and white Guildhall. This is one of the most striking buildings here and the panelling and carving of the interior are superb.

Bourton Manor is a superb country house hotel which stands in six acres of beautiful grounds near the village of Bourton. Easily reached from the B4378 Much Wenlock to Shipton road, this impressive part 16th-century manor house commands spectacular views of Wenlock Edge and Corve Dale. The interior is sumptuously appointed, with oak-panelled walls, antique furniture and an elegant Queen Anne staircase, and the guest rooms are all equipped with en suite facilities, radios, colour TVs and direct-dial telephones. Open to non-residents, the dining room provides the finest traditional English-style cuisine and also hosts occasional gourmet and murder mystery evenings.

Bourton Manor, Bourton, Much Wenlock, Near Telford, Shropshire
Tel: 01746 785531 Fax: 01746 785683

The large Norman church is wonderful too, with additions made in medieval times including the impressive 13th century doorways in the porch. The 14th century chapel has decorated tracery of such intricacy in the windows that you wonder how it was ever achieved and by whom. On the Jacobean pulpit, there are some impertinent and rather incongruous Mermen with two tails apiece. The church is open from 9am to dusk, daily.

Stokes Barn is the ideal place to stay for groups who come to enjoy the beautiful Shropshire countryside around Wenlock Edge. This superb development has been tastefully-converted from an old stone threshing barn and outbuildings to provide well-appointed and inexpensive bunkhouse accommodation for families, clubs and colleges. Lying off the A458 Shrewsbury road one mile to the northwest of Much Wenlock, the five dormitories and self-contained cottage can sleep up to forty people. The surrounding area offers magnificent opportunities for walking, pony trekking, canoeing and orienteering, and breakfasts, packed lunches and evening meals are available by arrangement.

Stokes Barn, Newtown House Farm, Much Wenlock, Shropshire   Tel: 01952 727293 Fax: 01952 728130

Another 17th century building made of timber frame and plaster, is just across the High Street from Barclays Bank. The building is Ramrods Mansions, which has three bays with a second storey balcony. Almost next door is the Corn Exchange, not quite so old but still impressive. It dates back to Victorian times. Just down the road near the car park is one of the earliest buildings in the town, Ashfield Hall. It was once an inn, dating back to the 15th century and was reputedly visited by Charles I.
  The Talbot Inn is a charming black and white timbered building on

the High Street. Dating from 1360 the inn boasts a wealth of beams and log fires, enhancing the lovely Olde Worlde atmosphere. Here you can savour a fine selection of ales and excellent homecooked food recommended by Egon Ronay and the Good Food Guide. Each lunchtime and evening there is a wide choice of food including homemade dishes prepared from fresh local produce. The 18th century malthouse in a central medieval courtyard has been converted to provide excellent en-suite accommodation in six attractively appointed bedrooms, all furnished with antique pine. There is a quiet resident's lounge and full English breakfast is enjoyed overlooks the courtyard, a scene which remains virtually unchanged over the centuries.

The Talbot Inn, Much Wenlock, Shropshire. Tel: 01952 728436.
Fax: 01952 728436.

In spite of all these wonderful places, it is the ruins of The Priory of St. Milburga which make Much Wenlock so special. The priory was originally a nunnery in the 7th century, founded by the Mercian princess, St. Milburga, and ranked high in the monastic orders of Mercia. It did not last all that long - some two hundred years later it was destroyed, probably by the Danes. Leofic, Earl of Mercia and husband of Lady Godiva, rebuilt it as a priory in 1050, encouraged by his wife. In later years, Roger de Montgomery re-established it as a Cluniac priory, subject to French allegiance. However, this was not popular with the Kings of England, who resented anyone having such an allegiance. They penalised the priory until it was eventually forced to sever its ties with France in 1395.

All went well with the priory until, at the time of the dissolution, Henry VIII destroyed most of the buildings and looted the valuables. He must have gained immensely from this, because the priory held considerable lands and had coal mining and iron founding interests.

The best remaining features of the spectacular ruins are the carvings on the wall head in the cloisters, and the Norman interlacing of arches and doorways in the Chapter House. Particularly impressive is the restored Prior's Lodge, dating from about 1500, which has a steeply pitched roof of Hoar Edge sandstone tiles above its rows of mullioned windows.

Wenlock Pottery is located at the heart of Wenlock in the old Methodist Chapel, which was built back in 1825. The owner and resident potter is Mike Fletcher, who produces a staggering range of unique, hand crafted oven to tableware, all of which have been handthrown in traditional stoneware. You can visit Wenlock Pottery 7 days a week, from 8.00a.m.-6.00p.m. on weekdays and from 9.00a.m.-5.00p.m. on the weekends.

Wenlock Pottery, Shineton Street, Much Wenlock, Shropshire
Tel: 01952 727600

HARLEY.

A real gem set in the heart of the Shropshire countryside, the **Plume of Feathers** at Harley stands on the main A458 Shrewsbury road, two miles northwest of Much Wenlock.

Plume of Feathers

The lounge bar of this magnificent part-17th-century inn, restaurant and place to stay has some outstanding period features, including a full-sized cider press, inglenook fireplace and rare Charles I oak bar back. An impressive range of fine wines and traditional ales is served here, along with a superb à la carte menu, with all dishes being freshly prepared to order by the French chef and his skilled team. There is also an attractive

90-seater restaurant for diners wishing to enjoy their meal at leisure. The inn also offers excellent accommodation in nine recently-constructed guest rooms. ETB 3 crown commended and AA 3 Qs recommended, all rooms have en suite bathrooms, colour TVs and tea/coffee making facilities.

Plume of Feathers, Harley, Much Wenlock, Near Telford, Shropshire
Tel: 01952 727360

BROSELEY

Situated midway between the spectacular Ironbridge Gorge and Much Wenlock is **Broseley**. and **The Lawns**, a house that was built in 1727, the year that George II came to the throne. The following year John Wilkinson - known as Iron-mad-Wilkinson - moved in. He was probably the greatest of the Ironmasters, and made Broseley the headquarters of his industrial empire for the next thirty years.

During this time John Wilkinson rose to the height of his power, and it was while he was living at The Lawns that he commissioned the Shrewsbury Architect, Thomas Farnols Pritchard, to design the world's first iron bridge. He also launched the world's first commercial iron boat, 'The Trial' on the Severn in 1787. He was an extraordinary man and such a fanatic about iron that he left instructions that he was to be buried in a cast-iron coffin!

In 1800, Wilkinson leased The Lawns to John Rose, the founder of Coalport, who was then rising to a position of eminence as a manufacturer of fine porcelain.

Today, The Lawns is a private house.

An interesting story in more modern times concerns Clive Maiden who took a derelict shop property, little more than a heap of rubble, and transformed it into the very classy **Old Butchers Shop Bar** in Broseley High Street. It's a real picture inside and out with hand painted decoration on the windows and a variety of memorabilia items which have been linked into the decor; one such item is an outstanding pair of bellows that somehow have been fashioned into a feature table. Good ale, good conversation, and a great atmosphere in excellent surroundings is what Clive has achieved since opening in 1994. Good quality background music supplied by CD's makes for a relaxing setting. Food is not served in The Old Butchers Shop Bar but a wide selection of ales, interesting wines and other drinks are the speciality of this establishment.

The Old Butchers Shop Bar, 69-70 High Street, Broseley, Shropshire.
Tel: 01952 884410.

Situated just a mile from Ironbridge and a mile from Broseley, **Benthall Hall** is an attractive mellow stone house which, although home to the Benthall family, comes under the care of the National Trust. Mullioned windows and moulded brick chimneys enhance its impressive outer appearance and inside a major feature is the intricately carved oak staircase which is beautifully complemented by an elaborately decorated plaster ceiling and fine oak panelling. Outside the house is surrounded by a lovely plantsman's garden which is a joy to walk in. The house is open from April to the end of September on Wednesdays, Sundays and Bank Holiday Mondays from 1.30 - 5.30pm. Please ring to check opening times.

Benthall Hall, Broseley Tel: 01952 882159

Ironbridge

Broseley Pipeworks Clay Tobacco Pipe Museum is a brand new museum set in a unique Victorian factory with all its original equipment. Demonstrations of pipe making are given and there's a shop to browse in. Open March to October.

IRONBRIDGE.

Driving to the next destination you will cross the first iron bridge ever constructed. The village you are entering is **Ironbridge**, one of the most extraordinary areas in the world. This remarkable valley was the cradle of the Industrial Revolution and is a living record of Man's industrial achievements. Here you will find a unique series of industrial monuments and several fascinating museums which together make up the Ironbridge Gorge Museum. For full visitor information ring 01952 453522/452751.

In 1986, the supreme historical importance of the Gorge was recognised internationally, with its designation as a World Heritage Site - ranking it alongside the Pyramids, the Grand Canyon and the Taj Mahal in an elite group of less then two hundred and fifty sites worldwide. World Heritage sites are designated by UNESCO (United Nations Educational, Scientific, and Cultural Organisation) and are defined as places of such exceptional interest and value that their protection is a concern for all nations. The Ironbridge Gorge was the first British site on the World Heritage list.

The uniquely preserved landscape of the Gorge recalls the atmosphere of the pioneer days. It does not take much to imagine the stench of smoke belching from the blast furnaces, the fierce fiery glow illuminating the steep-sided valley and the lives of those who lived and worked there.

Visiting all the museums located here in the Ironbridge Gorge, may seem a slightly daunting task, but is richly rewarding non the less.

The Museum of Iron is our first stop, because this is where the whole industry began. It was here in the village of Coalbrookdale, back in 1709 that Abraham Darby invented the revolutionary technique which enabled the mass production of cheap cast iron. The smelting furnace used by him is still here, the centrepiece of a collection that traces the history of ironmaking and the achievements of the Darby Dynasty.

Nearby is the **Great Warehouse**, built in 1838, and which contains a fascinating series of displays, models and exhibits; from cooking pots and boilers to the magnificent 'Boy and Swan Fountain' cast for the Great Exhibition of 1851.

Riverside Park, is tranquil and pretty, ideal for a picnic lunch, and handy for **The Museum of the River**, which is situated in a Victorian-Gothic warehouse on the bank of the River Severn. Here an audio-visual programme presents the history of the Gorge. The whole museum has some wonderful displays which tell of river history and the use of water in the gorge.

MUCH WENLOCK, IRONBRIDGE AND SHREWSBURY

At the **Jackfield Tile Museum**, the large scale, hand painted pictorial designs on the tiles are nothing short of spectacular. Jackfield was once the centre of the decorative tile industry, and it was here that this distinctive and colourful ceramic art form reached its peak. The collection is quite unique and traces the development of the art, which includes strikingly patterned wall and floor tiles and the brilliant colours and elaborate designs of a huge variety of glazed tiles, used for walls, porches, fireplaces and washstands.

Coalport china is famous the world over and the **Coalport Museum** naturally houses a superb collection of typical Coalport ware and examples of special commissions created for Victorian state occasions. The visitor is taken on a lively and informative tour through Coalport's history, and the use of intricate techniques used in the manufacture of porcelain, as well as seeing live demonstrations of these traditional skills.

Coalport Bottle Oven

If you are tempted to stay in the area -

The Valley Hotel is a beautifully refurbished Georgian listed ilding (originally an 18th century country house) set in its own spacious and secluded grounds and situated in the Worlds Heritage Site of Ironbridge in the stunning Severn Gorge. Less than ten minutes walk away is the now world famous Iron Bridge itself. The Valley Hotel's unique and sympathetic refurbishment blends ideally with the hotels historic location. One-time servants quarters and stables have been 'absorbed' by the main hotel to provide 'mews style' accommodation, accessed by glass covered walkways. All the bedrooms have en-suite facilities and are furnished with antique-style pine furniture, some with four poster Beds. Each room is luxuriously equipped and includes free satellite video reception. The Chez Maw Restaurant offer a truly superb selection of imaginatively prepared food with full a`la Carte menu, a vegetarian selection and a daily changed Table d'hôte menu. The hotel caters for all major functions including Wedding receptions and banquets and is conveniently located to Telford town centre and the M54 motorway. E.T.B. 4 - Crown Commended. A.A. 3 Star.

The Valley Hotel, Ironbridge, Telford, Shropshire. Tel: 01952 432247 Fax: 01952 432308.

Another Museum worth a visit is **Blists Hill Open Air Museum,** a unique recreation of a living, working industrial community of the 1890's where you can literally watch the past at work. The museum is a series of 19th century buildings which have been carefully reconstructed in their original condition on a forty acre site, and here history literally comes to life. The candlemaker, the blacksmith, the cobbler and the carpenter still practise their traditional crafts, using the tools and equipment of a hundred years ago. You can see the spectacle of iron castings being made in the foundry, and witness the only working wrought ironworks in the Western world.

Strolling along the main street you feel like you have all the time in the world, visiting first the Victorian sweetshop, and then the chemist and butcher. The local inn serves good ale, and should you want to cash a cheque there's a bank too. In fact, with a bakery, a doctor's surgery and a school, there is everything you would expect to find in a small, thriving Victorian town.

Wander along the canal wharf, taking a look at the moored tub boats and the extraordinary Hay Inclined Plane, an astonishing feat of canal engineering, designed to lift the boats up the steep banks of the Gorge to the Shropshire Canal.

With the same imaginative brilliance **The Shelton Tollhouse**, designed by the great road builder, Thomas Telford, has been rebuilt, and together with the tiny Squatters' Cottage, which housed a family of ten, you can see exactly how ordinary people of the period would have lived.

AROUND IRONBRIDGE.

Two miles west of Ironbridge, on an unclassified road off the B4378, you'll find **Buildwas Abbey**, one of the finest ruined abbeys in England. After eight hundred and fifty years the church is virtually complete, except for the roof. It is a compelling place situated in a meadow by the River Severn, against a backdrop of wooded grounds. The bluntly pointed arches of the church nave, which frame the surrounding countryside are quite dramatic.

Time has spared Buildwas from much of the destruction handed out to so many other medieval churches and abbeys. It really is a place of simple grandeur, completely in keeping with the dignified austerity in which the Cistercian monks lived. It is a joy to wander around and you constantly come across something of interest like the lead-glazed tiles depicting animals and birds in the chapter house. They are purely decorative and are thought to date from the abbey's construction in about 1200. It is quite likely that the floor of the nave and transepts were once covered with such tiles. It is an odd coincidence when you realise how famous this same part of Shropshire became for tiles, centuries later. The abbey is open all the year round and there is easy wheelchair access.

Coming from Ironbridge towards Much Wenlock, on the B4380, and taking a right turn at the petrol station delivers you to the All Labour in Vain pub; an unusual name with a story behind it. Apparently in the days when coloured people of any race or creed were rare in this country, a woman spied a small boy who was as black as could be. She was horrified and took him home in order to give him a bath and get him clean! When this didn't work she apparently held up her hands in horror and cried, 'All my labour is in vain'.

NORTON.

Back on the main A442 road between Kidderminster/Bridgnorth

and Telford, is the village of **Norton** and for somewhere that is a little bit different, treat yourself to a break at **The Hundred House Hotel.** This is one of those very rare gems, unusual, idiosyncratic and yet luxurious. After all there can be few places to stay that offer not only four poster beds, but swings in some of the bedrooms! The hotel's name stems from medieval days when subdivisions of the Shires of England were known as 'hundreds'. The oldest remaining part of this Hundred House is the delightful 14th century half-timbered, thatched courthouse barn in the hotel courtyard. Wood panelling, red quarry tiles, open log fires and bunches of dried flowers and herbs all serve to enhance the unique character and welcoming ambience of this super establishment. Dining is an absolute delight, with a bar menu far above average and an a` la carte restaurant offering "real food in the modern English and Continental style". Home made stocks, pies and pasta; real mayonnaise, first pressing olive oil, wine vinegar and freshly grated Parmesan are just some of the special ingredients used to create exceptional tastes for the most discerning gastronome. With all this and more, staying at The Hundred House is truly a memorable experience. A wonderful place!

The Hundred House, Hotel, Restaurant & Country Inn, Bridgnorth Road (A442), Norton, Nr. Telford, Shropshire TF11 9EE. Tel: 01952 730353 Fax: 01952 730355

COALPORT

It is no distance from here straight up the maid road to Telford, but it's worth making a mini detour to the left onto a small road that leads to **Coalport,** where John Rose had been employed as an apprentice at the Caughley porcelain factory. Thomas Turner had been making fine porcelain there since 1772 and John Rose, having learnt all he could from him, set up his own business and in 1795 bought out his former employer's factory as well. Poor Thomas Turner spawned another rebel in Thomas

Minton, who also branched out on his own to found another famous name in fine china.

The Caughley factory should be famous for originating the famous Willow pattern, which has since been credited to Thomas Minton. Meanwhile, at Coalport, the famous Indian Tree pattern had been introduced. By 1820 the Coalport factory was winning awards, one came from the Royal Society of Arts for its introduction of a feldspathic glaze. Before this workers in the industry had suffered from a health hazard known as 'potter's rot', caused by the lead glaze previously used.

The Coalport factory is no longer located here, but has moved to Staffordshire. John Rose died in 1841 and it was his nephew who nurtured the company and brought it to even greater heights. They became known rapidly for the fine quality of the decoration and lavish gilding, reaching its peak when the painter William Billingsley worked for the company. He was an absolute ace at flower painting and introduced new techniques which put Coalport way ahead of its rivals. Queen Victoria had a great penchant for it, commissioning a Coalport dessert service for Czar Nicholas I in 1845.

The Brewery Inn in the High Street, Coalport, is an impressive pub and eating place which once brewed its own beer. A handsome 18th-century brick building which backs onto the River Severn, it has fishing rights over 700 yards of the riverbank. The inn is renowned for its excellent pub food and offers an extensive range of popular dishes, all freshly prepared and offered at surprisingly low prices; there is also an excellent value choice for children. The landlord since 1980, Roger Hotchkiss is a friendly and popular host who is also the licensee of the nearby Shakespeare Inn and the Huntsman at Little Wenlock.

Brewery Inn, High Street, Coalport, Near Telford, Shropshire
Tel: 01952 581225

The extraordinary **Tar Tunnel**, a hidden spring of natural bitumen, has its entrance in Coalport. It was a popular attraction for tourists in the 18th century, and it is still possible to visit it, one of the most interesting geological phenomena in Britain.

You have to have great respect for the miners who were dedicated and brave enough to drive a tunnel through this unstable strata, leaving something which is still fundamentally sound nearly two hundred years later. It is the only place in the Gorge where a visitor can venture any distance under the surface, and to see what one distinguished visitor once described as 'the most manic and fantastic of all those early confrontations between technology and geology'.

It was as long ago as October 1786, under the direction of the ironmaster William Reynolds, that miners began to drive a tunnel into the side of the Severn Gorge from a riverside meadow in Madeley. About three quarters of a mile away on Blists Hill, Reynolds had recently sunk shafts to the coal seams, which lay between 440 and 600 ft below the surface. He intended that the tunnel should be used for a canal, which would reach the shafts about 150 ft below the ground. The distance which coal had to be lifted was thus greatly reduced, and it could be conveyed to the riverside on the level by boat, rather than down a steep hill by cart or waggon.

After they had driven the tunnel about three hundred yards the miners struck a spring of natural bitumen. William Reynolds immediately recognised the scientific interest of the discovery and sent samples of the bitumen for analysis to various scientists who found that the properties of the bitumen were superior to those of tar made from coal. The tunnel was visited by several eminent scientists, among them Erasmus Darwin, Robert Townson and Charles Hatchett, and it became to be regarded as one of the many wonders of the Severn Gorge.

The Tar Tunnel was almost forgotten over the years. The outlines of its history were known to people interested in the industrial past of the Ironbridge Gorge but few imagined that it could possibly still be accessible. In 1965, after exhaustive enquiries in the neighbourhood, the Shropshire Mining Club persuaded the then owner of the village shop in Coalport to allow them to explore the darkness which lay beyond a door opening out of his cellar. They discovered it was the Tar Tunnel.

It was for the most part, brick lined. There were large piles of rocks and clay along the left-hand side, while tar could be seen seeping through the mortar joints of the lining, and in the water which ran along a gulley on the right hand side. From the roof of the tunnel hung multitudes of straw stalactites, one of which was over four feet long. A bit further in they found a spectacular section where flowstone, coloured red, blue, black and orange by the iron and other chemicals in the surrounding strata, covered the walls, while the roof was adorned by a profusion of stalactites, and the floor dotted with pools of tar. It must have been a fantastic sight.

It was another eighteen years before visitors were regularly allowed and still you are only able to see the first hundred yards of its length, a section which is defined by a locked iron gate. If money becomes available it is hoped that the safety precautions can be improved sufficiently to allow visitors to see the brilliantly coloured section three hundred yards in.

Overlooking Thomas Telford's famous iron bridge, **The Woodbridge Inn** at Coalport stands in a superb riverside position. One of the oldest public houses in Shropshire, this imposing white-painted building stands within attractive grounds which slope down to the banks of the Severn. Judi and Paul Symington have built up an enviable reputation for providing a warm welcome and some of the finest food and drink in the area. They also offer comfortable accommodation in four well-appointed guest rooms, one of which has a four-poster bed. Spring 1997 sees the opening of a sanctuary for birds of prey at the rear of the inn. Here, visitors have the opportunity to watch flying displays and observe these wonderful birds, and other animals, at close quarters.

Woodbridge Inn, Coalport, Near Telford, Shropshire   Tel: 01952 882054

TELFORD.

Leaving behind the industrial heritage of Ironbridge our journey takes us to **Telford**. The developers have linked together several existing towns by means of creating a modern purpose-designed town centre.

Care has been taken to make sure it is a green and pleasant place and a million trees and shrubs were planted to achieve this. Certainly Telford Town Park, which is right in the centre, is an expansive area of landscaped countryside featuring a miniature steam railway, lakeside amphitheatre, sports arena and children's fortress. You can walk here for quite a while along footpaths which follow the routes of old railway lines and canals, providing links with wilder areas of woodland, marsh, ponds and meadows in the south of the park.

AROUND TELFORD

SHIFNAL. On Church Street is the **Old Bell Hotel,** many parts of it date back to the 16th century and during its lifetime it has been an alehouse, a coaching inn, pub and perhaps other things too. When Sally and Mark purchased the property in 1992 it had been boarded up for over a year and both the inside and outside was in a dreadful state, relates Sally. So began the task of renovation and a lot of hard work. Today, The Old Bell is a shining example of what can be achieved given time and determination. The atmosphere is superb, there's plenty of character retained in the old beams and flagstone floors; the rear bar and seating area is housed in the old cellar with its arched brick ceiling a real feature. The restaurant is excellent both in decoration and its cuisine. Open everyday except Sunday evening, it is advisable to book to avoid disappointment. The a'la carte and bar menus are listed on blackboards and the selection is extensive. Sally and Mark keep a fine selection of ever changing real ales. Six attractive en-suite bedrooms are available throughout the year and complete the first class facilities of The Old Bell.

The Old Bell Hotel, Church Street, Shifnal, Shropshire. Tel: 01952 417777

OAKENGATES.

Just to the north of Telford is **Oakengates** which, if you are a horse racing buff, you will know is the birthplace of the incomparable jockey and trainer Sir Gordon Richards. He first learned to ride on pit ponies because his father was a miner. It must have been the right sort of training, for when he retired after thirty-three years he had four thousand, eight hundred and seventy wins to his credit and had been champion jockey for twenty years.

The Duke of York on the main street in Oakengates is a lively and popular public house which is situated off the A442 ring road on the eastern outskirts of Telford. This handsome 16th-century former coaching inn has been owned and personally-run since 1991 by Patricia and Ian Barton, friendly and attentive hosts who have successfully created an atmosphere which is welcoming to visitors and locals alike. Along with a good selection of real ales, live entertainment is offered on Thursday, Friday and Saturday evenings.

Duke of York, Oakengates, Near Telford, Shropshire   Tel: 01952 612741

Ian Barton is also the licensee of the **Blue Pig**, a popular traditional inn which is situated in Capewell Road in the nearby village of **Trench.** Their telephone number is: 01952 676026.

PRESTON-ON-THE-WEALD.

Situated in the lanes to the north of Telford and easily reached from junction 6 on the M54, **Hoo Farm Animal Kingdom** and Christmas Tree Farm at Preston-on-the-Weald Moors provides an interesting day out for all the family. The attractions here vary with the seasons, beginning with lambing in mid-March and ending when the Christmas tree farm closes for business in late December.

Hoo Farm

One of the most unusual events are the sheep steeplechases, ewe-nique races founded by proprietors Carolyn and Edward Dorrell as a way of employing their tame orphan lambs. Christmas World opens in mid-November, with Father Christmas taking up residence a couple of weeks later.

Hoo Farm, Preston-on-the-Weald Moors, Near Telford, Shropshire
Tel/Fax: 01952 677917

WATERS UPTON.

Standing on the main A road through Waters Upton is the stylish **Swan** public house, personally run for the past five and half years by Mike and Sarah Price. Its attractive outdoor appearance is mainly due to the outstanding hanging baskets and window boxes that fill the air with their heady perfume in the long summer months. The interior is warm and welcoming with a cosy rear dining/lounge area which is heavily beamed and lavishly decorated with a large collection of colourful plates and stylish prints and photographs. The Swan is renowned for its hospitality and well kept collection of real ales including Worthington, Tetley and Banks plus a regular guest bitter. A varied and delicious selection of home-cooked food is available each evening (except Monday) and on Saturday and Sunday lunchtimes, throughout the Summer - Friday and Saturday evenings and Saturday and Sunday lunchtimes during the winter, though it is preferable to book to avoid disappointments. There is a smashing beer garden to the rear of the Inn with children being always welcome and plenty of off road parking with good access for the disabled. A warm welcome is guaranteed at The Swan, and I am sure that if this will be your first visit, it will not be your last!.

The Swan , Waters Upton, Telford, Shropshire TF6 6NP. Tel: 01952 54122
Fax: 01952 541842

MUXTON.

The Shropshire is an impressive golfing development lying on the north-eastern outskirts of Telford which incorporates a stylish wine bar and Brasserie. Prior to 1992, this magnificent 250-acre site was a working farm which once formed part of the Duke of Sutherland's estate. Today, it boasts two scenic golf courses (one 18-hole, one 9-hole), a golf shop, and a popular bar and restaurant. A 'pay and play' course where everyone is welcome, lessons are available from the course professional, if required. Delicious food and drink is available all day, every day in the beautifully furnished 60-seater Brasserie, a delightful oasis for golfers and visitors alike.

The Shropshire, Muxton Lane, Muxton, Near Telford, Shropshire
Tel: 01952 677800 Fax: 01952 677622

It is difficult in this part of Shropshire to ignore the insidious disruption of county life by the creeping motorway. Not many places escape some intrusion into what was once a peaceful existence in glorious countryside.

TONG.

Tong is one place that has escaped both the motorways and the coal fields and is a very attractive village. The wizard Merlin is credited with the origin of its castle, which no longer exists, and it was he who helped Hengist to include Tong in his domain. His wizardry could not save the castle from an ignoble end and it was blown up in 1954.

The Vernons and the Durants were the lords of the manor here in Tong for many years and in the elevated 15th century church of St. Bartholomew there are monuments to many of them; especially the Vernons, who in one way and another had distinguished careers. One was a Speaker of the House of Commons and another was Lord High Constable to Henry V. In the Golden Chapel, which has a superb gilded fan vaulted ceiling, there is a rare 16th century bust of Arthur Vernon, a revered Cambridge Don.

Exploring the church further and you'll find not only a lovely timber roof ornamented with bosses in the nave, but the choir stalls will also reveal delightful carvings.

The Durants were not quite so notable, nor so respected. You have only to look at the bare breasted woman mourning George Durant on one monument to accept that they were perhaps a little eccentric.

Dickens is thought to have had Tong church in mind when he wrote The Old Curiosity Shop - Little Nell's home was right by the church porch, and some say she is buried in the churchyard.

At the turn of the 17th century Venetia Stanley made her appearance on an unsuspecting world. Her father was the agent for the owner of Tong Castle. She was descended from both the Vernons and the Earls of Derby and as she grew up her beauty became apparent. Poets sang her praises, every artist wanted her as a model and she was courted by a bevy of admirers. She revelled in the admiration and became a noted courtesan counting Ben Jonson, Van Dyck and the Earl of Dorset among her paramours.

In 1625 she married Sir Kenelm Digby, whose father, Everard, had been executed for his part in the Gunpowder plot. Digby adored his beautiful wife but was insanely jealous. When she died at the very young age of thirty-three it was suggested that death was caused by drinking viper-wine to preserve her beauty, but it was also whispered that Sir Kenelm poisoned her.

From Tong you do not have far to go to visit **Boscobel House**, which lies just four miles to the north-east. After Charles II was defeated by the Roundheads at the Battle of Worcester in 1651, he was compelled to run for his life, and this was how he came to Boscobel. Cromwell's soldiers were close behind him, and Charles was advised by his friends to seek refuge at this remote hunting lodge, already known as a safe house for Royal fugitives. Together with William Careless, one of his most trusted officers, Charles hid during the day in the branches of an old oak tree and then under cover of darkness crept into the house, where they hid for the night in an attic. As we know from the history books, he eventually escaped and nine years later was restored to the throne.

The name of Boscobel House has a very romantic ring to it, not surprising, since it comes from the Italian 'bosco bello' meaning beautiful wood. The house really is beautiful too, although the buildings Charles II would have known have changed considerably. The house has the romantic character of a Victorian historical novel and its great chimney is still painted with curious devices. There are panelled rooms and secret

Much Wenlock Priory

hiding places including the 'sacred hole' in the attic where the future king of England apparently spent the night.

There is a pretty garden, with knots of lavender laid out in the 17th century manner, a summer house on a mount, where Charles II is said to have rested, and a Victorian farmyard complete with farm implements, a working forge and a display of butter churns, pats and stamps from the turn of the century, when Boscobel was still a working farm.

An exhibition gives a vivid account of the fugitive king's perilous adventures and the delightful tea room is an ideal place to relax, and enjoy a hot cup of tea and some excellent fruit cake.

No one comes to Boscobel without wanting to look at the Royal Oak in which Charles once hid. Sadly the original is no longer standing - it was destroyed by enthusiastic loyalists who wanted souvenirs, hacking away the branches and roots until nothing was left. Today's tree is a direct descendant of the famous oak and is itself nearly three hundred years old.

Just south of Tong and off the A41 road heading towards Albrighton is something totally different. In beautiful Royal Oak Country, the **Aerospace Museum** at Royal Air Force Cosford is one of the largest Aviation collections in the United Kingdom. There are over sixty aircraft on display with missiles, engines, uniforms, aviation memorabilia and models. The museum houses collections of Military and Civil Transport aircraft, which include the oldest surviving Comet Mk 1 jet airliner, Viking and Britannia passenger aircraft and a 1930s German Junkers JU52. There is a collection of Research and Development aircraft like the ill-fated TSR2 and test pilot Neville Duke's sound barrier breaking Hawker Hunter and World War II aircraft include a Spitfire, Mosquito, Liberator, Dakota, Lincoln, and post war military aircraft include the Canberra and the awesome Vulcan and Victor 'V' bombers.

It's hard to believe that there have been so many missiles, but in the collection they have here, which is the largest in the world, you realise just how many varieties of these deadly weapons there are. Slightly less menacing is the Aircraft Engine Exhibition which ranges from the early piston engines to the modern jet, some of which are sectioned to show their internal components. It is overall a very impressive museum, and one which kids and would-be fighter pilots of all ages will really enjoy.

Folklore accounts for many things, and Shropshire folk would have us all believe that the lonely hill which is undoubtedly the county's best known landmark - the Wrekin - owes its site to the malicious giant who was carrying a huge load of earth to dam the Severn and flood Shrewsbury simply because he did not like the people. It is a strange story and is attributed not only to The Wrekin but also to Gloucestershire, the same river but a different location. The devil is supposed to have met a cobbler who dissuaded him from this evil act, and so he dropped the earth where he stood and that is how the Wrekin came to be where it is.

The Wrekin's Iron Age hill-fort was there before the Roman invasion and true Salopians consider that anyone not born within sight of it are foreigners! It's quite a climb to the top, up a path which leads from Forest Glen through gaps known as Hell's Gate and Heaven's Gate. It is worth the climb and when you reach the top you realise why it is a natural site for warning beacons. The panoramic view covers miles on a clear day. There have been beacons here to tell of the coming of the Spanish Armada, and centuries later to celebrate Queen Victoria's Jubilee. Today there is a vast transmitting mast which beams television over a wide area.

The village of **Longdon-on-Tern**, situated on the B5063 Shrewsbury to Telford road, is probably best known for the aqueduct built by Thomas Telford in 1796 as a pilot scheme for the Ironbridge itself.

WROXETER.

Heading towards Shrewsbury brings you to Wroxeter, and the vast ruined Roman city of Viriconium, Britain's fourth largest. It began as a garrison for the Fourteenth Legion, who built Watling Street, now more famous as the A5. When the army moved out it became a civil city of around 4000 people, complete with public baths and gymnasium. Many of the fascinating artefacts from the site are on display there and at the Rowley's House Museum in Shrewsbury.

ATCHAM

Where the River Severn is crossed by the Roman road is the village of **Atcham**. There is a splendid seven arched bridge here which was built in 1769. Alongside it is the new bridge, the architecture isn't quite the same and who knows if it will still be standing in two hundred years? The old bridge was designed by John Gwynne, who was a founder member of the Royal Academy and responsible for the design of the delightful Magdalen Bridge at Oxford.

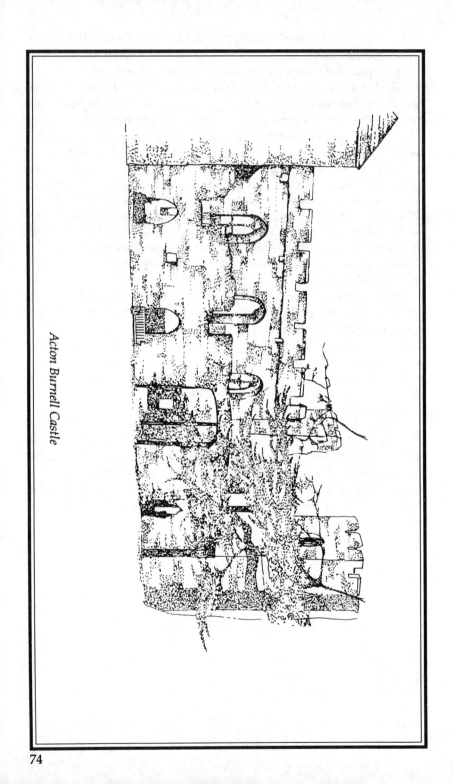

Acton Burnell Castle

MUCH WENLOCK, IRONBRIDGE AND SHREWSBURY

Here in Atcham you will also find **Attingham Park**, built in 1785 for the 1st Lord Berwick, encasing an earlier building known as Tern Hall. It is a magnificent mansion, set in 230 acres of superb parkland. Fortunately the 8th Lord Berwick bequeathed the house and the park to the National Trust in 1947 and it now serves as the head office for their Mercia region.

It's easy to pass an afternoon here drinking in the beauty of the fine staterooms, all full of wonderful objects. The Regency interiors are rich and colourful and must be much as they were in the days of the 1st Lord Berwick, who desired his mansion to show all who saw it that he had arrived in society.

There is a fine collection of French and Italian paintings and furniture brought to England by the 2nd Lord Berwick and his brother, the 3rd Lord Berwick. It was the latter who acquired the spectacular collection of Regency Silver - over three hundred pieces in all - during the course of his career as a diplomat in Italy.

The incomparable Humphrey Repton was commissioned by the 2nd Lord Berwick to advise on the park. He wrote in his Red Book - a book he produced for every task he undertook - 'Although there is no very romantic or uneven ground within the park at Attingham, there are few places which possess so many different features to interest in the course of its walks or drives; and it is my duty to bring these features properly into notice'. This he certainly achieved, and the National Trust work unceasingly to keep the walks beautiful, with a constant planting scheme to ensure that future generations will not be deprived of trees. A visit will leave you both refreshed and enriched. The Hall is open Saturday to Wednesday, afternoons only, between April and October and weekend afternoons from October onwards.

Attingham Park, Atcham, Shrewsbury Tel: 01743 709203

From Attingham Park it is worth taking a gentle drive around the countryside before making tracks for Shrewsbury. Just three miles south of the town on the Acton Burnell Road is Cantlop Bridge, which is the last survivor of a type designed by Thomas Telford, spanning the Cound Brook, where there is a small attractive picnic site. Following the road all the way to **Acton Burnell** will bring you to the ruins of the castle there. Stricly being a fortified house, it has some significance in the history of England. It was built at the end of the 13th century of red sandstone from the quarries at Grinshill, and was among the earliest of such fortified houses in the country. Close by are two stone gables which are presumed to be the end walls of the 'great barn' in which the king held a properly constituted parliament in 1283. The roofless ruins are attractive and interesting, and the battlemented walls and angle-towers are surprisingly intact.

Travelling a little further west and you join the A49, which leads you to Lyth Hill, another lovely spot with around seventy acres of grassland, scrub and woodland on a relatively narrow steep slope. There are absolutely marvellous views from here and it is alive with wildlife.

SHREWSBURY.

The River Severn winds around the lively, beautiful county town of **Shrewsbury** in a horseshoe bend, making it almost an island site. It would be hard not to love this town as it is so rich in picturesque half-timbered houses of the 16th century and the later, more elegant Queen Anne, Georgian and Victorian architecture. Wherever you walk in the narrow streets and by-ways you see superb examples of Tudor architecture, with quaint overhanging upper storeys and beautiful carved beams. One of the finest is Ireland's Mansion in the High Street, a four gabled Elizabethan masterpiece with variegated oriel windows. There is also an interesting Visitors Centre at Shrewsbury Abbey.

A sense of history follows you everywhere. Several of the houses are associated with famous figures in history, like the house where Queen Mary Tudor lodged, or a few steps away you can look up to the window of the room where Henry Tudor, Earl of Richmond, slept a night while on his way to London.

The Lion and Pheasant, an old Coaching Inn complete with entrance arch and, no doubt, a considerable history, stands in the centre of Shrewsbury. This 16th century hotel has been tastefully renovated and retains a great charm and character with many exposed beams and an inglenook fireplace. Notable as the last place in Shrewsbury to be raided where persons were arrested for cock-fighting. The character of the hotel is fully reflected in its warm and intimate restaurant and its menu is deserving of particular attention for the unusual combinations it suggests, the imaginative presentation of the hotel's proprietors Rachael and

Andrew Griffiths. The restaurant is open to non-residents and food is also served in the bar accompanied by real ales. The bedrooms each retain the character of the building, no two rooms are the same. Many have private facilities whilst all rooms are provided with television, beverage tray and telephone. The hotel is beautifully presented and the owners' personal touch is always evident. E.T.B.-3 Crowns Commended.

Lion and Pheasant Hotel, Wyle Cop, Shrewsbury. Tel: 01743 236288
Fax: 01743 244475

The street names are fascinating in themselves, let alone the buildings. There is Butchers Row, Mardol, Grope Lane, Wyloe Cop, Dogpole, Murivance and Fish Street. Fish Street is cobbled and full of centuries-old houses, which make a marvellous frame for the pinnacled tower of St. Julian's Church which is now a craft centre.

The outstanding **Carnival Crafts**, owned and run by Gill Mason for the past three years, is somewhere that every passer-by should visit at least once. The displays of crafts are truly International, from Italy there are wooden music boxes and pottery, Africa displays some traditional carvings in stone and wood and from Thailand there is a wonderful selection of hand-painted fans, butterflies and intricate carvings. Also on show you will find Carvings from Bali, unusual leather products from Morocco, exquisite perfume bottles from Egypt and many, many more, including Gill's own individual glassware. All of the goods on display have come directly from the artists and with Gill knowing each person that she deals with personally, so you can guarantee that each piece is authentic. The full range of unique and unusual gifts and crafts is truly remarkable, Gill has managed to bring the whole world to your doorstep, giving you the opportunity to purchase items that you would never have seen without the benefit of an expensive plane fare!. Open 9.00am -

The Shrewsbury Quest & Shrewsbury Abbey

5.00pm six days a week, visit Carnival Crafts for a guaranteed cultural experience.

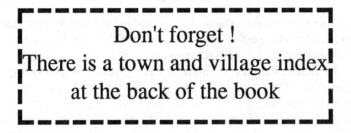

There are thirty churches in Shrewsbury, all of which seem to have some feature of architectural or historical interest. The great parish church of St. Mary's is wonderful. It was built in Norman times and has a marvellous octagonal spire which dominates the town. A memorable place, not least because of the superb medieval stained glass. Shrewsbury is blessed with some stunning churches including St. Alkmunds, with a magnificent chancel window and the Georgian round church of St. Chads.

Holy Trinity Church, Meole Brace, is a must for anyone who admires stained glass. Here William Morris is responsible and the glass is superb. Pugin designed and built the Cathedral of Our Lady on Town Walls in 1856, and very impressive it is too with tall proportions of nave and aisle and steep gable with a big bell-cote.

Perhaps the town's favourite, though, is **Holy Cross Abbey**. The west front is superb with a great Perpendicular window, sumptuously traceried and extended by a crocketed ogee gable up to the statue of Edward III, in whose reign the building of the tower began. The Norman interior with its massive nave pillars was restored in the 19th century. Towards the back are the remains of a shrine to St. Winifred, part of the former abbey.

Outside, and to the south, there is an exquisite 14th century stone pulpit, shaped like a lantern, which was once inside the abbey refectory and from which the lessons were read while the monks ate. It has a vaulted roof with a beautiful boss of the Crucifixion.

Courtyard Coffee House is definitely the place to rest yourself during your shopping or explorations around Shrewsbury. Hidden away in Gullet Passage off the Main Square it offers a refuge for morning coffee and tasty homemade scones and cakes or a light meal or snack. With 30 years experience, the owner Barry Irving knows his business well, and you will surely enjoy your visit. The building dates from the 17th century and once was used as the holding cells for Shrewsbury Gaol - now there's something to think about as you bite into your cream cake!

Courtyard Coffee House, Gullet Passage, Shrewsbury. Tel: 01743 367242

The architectural and historical interest of the town and the county of Shropshire is reflected in its museums, which cover both natural and human history from fossils to firearms.

The first is **Rowley's House** in Barker Street, which is a glorious timber-framed building of the late 16th century, and an adjoining brick and stone mansion of 1618. Housed here is the largest collection of material from the Roman city of Viroconium at Wroxeter. There are some other spectacular displays too, of costume and accessories, natural history, local history and a geological display emphasising the rich nature of Shropshire's geology.

Five minutes walk from Rowley's House brings you to **Clive House**, in the Georgian area of the town. Clive of India lived here in 1762 while he was Mayor of Shrewsbury and there are one or two mementoes of this great man to be seen. The house is built of 18th century brick and is quite splendid. Several of the rooms show period settings, mostly as backgrounds to the Borough's magnificent collection of Shropshire ceramics, which includes one of the finest groups of Coalport and Caughley in the country.

Charles Darwin was born and educated in the town and as a celebration of his life and work, new displays can now be seen in Clive House Museum.

Don't miss taking a stroll in the pleasant, well kept gardens, leading up to **Laura's Tower**, an untouched example of Telford's skill as architect and interior designer.

You cannot get into **Shrewsbury** by land other than by using one of the ten bridges which cross the river, enabling pedestrians, road and rail traffic to reach the town centre. The earliest one is the English Bridge which was designed by John Gwynn and opened in 1774, but in fact it was totally rebuilt, stone by stone in 1925. That was followed by the Welsh bridge in 1795, others having been built as they were needed, with the latest Frankwell Footbridge opened in 1979.

The Sheldon Hall Hotel is an impressive, yet intimate, country house hotel which offers the finest food, hospitality and accommodation. Located off the old A5 (now the B4380) on the north-western outskirts of

Shrewsbury, this handsome residence stands within three-and-a-half acres of beautiful tree-filled grounds. The nine individually-decorated guest bedrooms are equipped with en suite facilities and an array of thoughtful extras, and most also have fine views of the garden. The delightful Cedar Suite restaurant serves the finest English and continental cuisine and is also open to non-residents. Rated 2 star by the AA and RAC, recommended by Les Routiers and ETB 4 crown highly-commended, the Shelton Hall Hotel is ideal for a relaxing country break.

Shelton Hall Hotel, Shelton, Near Shrewsbury, Shropshire, SY3 8BH
Tel: 01743 343982 Fax: 01743 241515

Shrewsbury is known as 'The Town of Flowers'. It has more than two hundred and fifty acres of parks and open spaces with marvellous riverside walks. Quarry Park at the opposite end of the town from the castle sits on the banks of the River Severn. Its centrepiece is 'The Dingle', which has wonderful displays in the spring, summer and autumn. As you wander you'll come across little nooks and side paths and may discover the statue of Sabrina - Goddess of the Severn.

Sunbeams Guest House

Situated in a quiet residential area about half a mile from Shrewsbury town centre and near Brother Cadfel Trails, **Sunbeams Guest House** is

The Abbots House, Shrewsbury

the ideal place for an overnight stay or short break. Your friendly hostess is Dorothy Smith who enjoys sharing her large Victorian home with her many guests. There are five individually furnished guest rooms providing very comfortable and homely accommodation enabling her guests to relax and enjoy their stay. Dorothy provides an excellent home cooked breakfast and is happy to cater for evening meals by prior arrangement. A short walk or car journey will take you into the historic town of Shrewsbury which has a wide choice of restaurants.

Sunbeams Guest House, 1 Bishop Street, Cherry Orchard, Shrewsbury.
Tel: 01743 357495

The Coach and Horses is a hidden gem which can be found in Swan Hill on the edge of Shrewsbury town centre. Owned and run by Roger Goodall and Linda Chambers, this delightful free house and restaurant occupies a handsome white-painted building dating from the 17th-century. A mecca for lovers of fine ales, around eight are normally on offer, including 'Goodall's Gold', a beer brewed locally to Roger's own recipe. In 1995, the adjacent yard and outbuildings were tastefully transformed into a superb new dining area seating up to 60. Here, diners can enjoy a first-class meal in an atmosphere which pleasantly in tune with the rest of the inn.

Coach and Horses, Swan Hill, Shrewsbury, Shropshire   Tel: 01743 365661

Shrewsbury Castle, dating from 1083, was built by the Norman, Earl Roger de Montgomery and last saw action during the Civil War. It was later converted into a private residence by Telford, the great engineer. It now houses the regimental collections of the Kings Shropshire Yeomanry Cavalry and the Shropshire Royal Horse Artillery. It is a fascinating place and you can almost feel you are fighting the battles which won an empire in Canada, America, India, Egypt, Africa and Europe. There are relics on display from the last War and uniforms dating back to the Napoleonic invasion scare at the beginning of the nineteenth century.

The splendid **Three Fishes** public house stands adjacent to St Alkmund's church in the heart of the town. The only no smoking licensed premises in the town, this impressive Grade II listed half-timbered building has a characteristic white stuccoed façade and overhanging upper floor. Originally owned by Lillieshall Abbey, its unusual sign depicts the salmon, perch and pike, fish that can be found in the nearby River Severn. Licensee John Sims offers an impressive range of cask-conditioned ales in an atmosphere which is friendly, smoke free and full of traditional character and charm.

The Three Fishes

Never lacking in imaginative use of beautiful buildings, Shrewsbury has produced The Parade Shopping Centre in St. Mary's Place, where in the restored historic building of the Royal Salop Infirmary with its fine terrace looking out over the River Severn, there are many town centre shops, a restaurant and a coffee shop. It is a delightful place in which to browse, eat or just stand on the terrace and watch the activity on the river.

TheThree Fishes, Sish Street, Shrewsbury, Shropshire Tel: 01743 344793

The superb **Pierre Victoire Restaurant** is housed in a Grade 11 listed building. It has in its lifetime had many uses; a private house, bakery. tea-rooms and now a successful restaurant. After visiting a Franchise Exhibition in London, Gail Ramsay decided this was the thing for her, and so the Restaurant was opened in 1994. What a splendid place it is too, Old World and full of character and style with an intimate feel. The Pierre Victoire Restaurant provides exciting French Provincial food, all fresh and cooked to order, served in a relaxed and friendly atmosphere and accompanied by an extensive and affordable wine list. Gail prepares special menus to order and arranges Gastronomique and Wine Tasting Evenings. The regular live piano music is a nice touch. Open every day for Lunch 12 - 3pm and Dinner 6- 11pm. Bon Appetit!

Pierre Victoire, St. Mary's Street, Shrewsbury. Tel: 01743 344744
Fax: 01743 344422

From May 1st to the end of September you can go on a full general sightseeing tour of Shrewsbury every day at 2.30pm, lasting about one and a half hours, accompanied by an official town guide. It seems that no matter how much you explore every nook and cranny for yourselves, you always learn just that bit more from guides who obviously love their job and are a mine of information, not only about the buildings but about the famous people who have taken part in the history of the town. A variety of tours take place throughout the year; further details are available from the Tourist Information Office.

Sir Philip Sydney in the 16th century and Charles Darwin in the 19th century both attended Shrewsbury School for example. Admiral Benbow was born here in 1653 and Lord Hill, Shrewsbury's most distinguished soldier, is yet another famous name.

Lord Hill was the Duke of Wellington's right hand man in the Peninsular Wars and at the Battle of Waterloo. He succeeded Wellington as Commander in Chief of the army in 1828. He died in 1842 and a column in his memory is still to be seen at the top of Abbey Foregate. It is 133 ft high, the highest Greek Doric column in the world.

Ideal for those with an appetite for good home cooking, **The Pantry** is a delightful eating place which is situated off the High Street. Housed in a handsome Grade II listed building in Golden Cross Passage, this charming establishment has been owned and personally-run since 1987 by Jane Evans. Her wide-ranging menu includes sandwiches, quiche,

Fish Street & St. Julian's Church, Shrewsbury

filled croissants and jacket potatoes, along with a selection of daily specials, both sweet and savoury. The atmosphere could be described as a 'cookery theatre', with all food being prepared on the premises in front of customers. The choice of beverages includes filter coffee, speciality and herbal teas, lager and wines. Open Monday to Saturday, 8.30am to 3.15pm (3pm Saturdays).

The Pantry, 2 Golden Cross Passage, off High Street, Shrewsbury, Shropshire   Tel: 01743 344929

AROUND SHREWSBURY
MONTFORD.

Montford Church is worth taking a look at. Charles Darwin was buried here, but his body was apparently moved at a later date. Not far away are the impressive ruins of Shrawardine Castle.

All around Shrewsbury is lovely settled countryside. All the time there are discoveries to be made, castles to be seen and monastic buildings appearing half hidden by the glorious trees. It is a sort of chain of defence which produced strongholds to quell the turbulent Welsh along the Marches.

Just off the B5062, north-east of Shrewsbury, is Haughmond Abbey, founded in 1135 for Augustinian monks and rebuilt fifty years later. Of the church only the foundation remains but there is still much to see such as the 15th century oriel window, a Norman doorway and the chapter house with ornamental entrance.

FRANKWELL.

A Trail with a difference is the one on offer at nearby **Frankwell**. It has elements of both a Town and Nature Trail, but it differs from either in attempting to describe the interwoven fabric of tree-lined meadows and terraced streets which is part of the charm of Shrewsbury.

The Trail is not designed for those who want to see famous buildings or battlefields, rare birds or flowers; it deals with the ordinary features of the landscape where the town and country meet. Its linking theme is the River Severn, whose changing course has shaped the growth of Shrewsbury over the centuries.

Floating on the River Tern, near the Welsh Bridge on the border of Shrewsbury, is the **Floating Thai Restaurant.** Owned and personally run by Ken Lao since 1993 but who has been a Restaurateur for the past fifteen years. Occupying a lovely position in the river it enjoys a scenic view and looks a picture, especially floodlit in the evening. As you an imagine, this is a popular venue and booking is recommended at weekends. Here you can enjoy an oriental taste with a difference - perhaps many of the dishes on the menu will not be familiar, but once you get started and discover the intricate tastes of Dara Rhai Spare Ribs, Pla Toadlardprig, Ped Yang (Roast Duck topped with a very tasty herb sauce) or perhaps Pad gratiam Prigthai (shallow fried chicken or pork with garlic, pepper corns and herbs, you'll be on your way to a really enjoyable and different night out. Open every evening from 6pm - last orders 10.30pm. Try something different.

Floating Thai Restaurant, Welsh Bridge, Frankwell, Shrewsbury.
Tel: 01743 243123 Fax: 01743 343788.

Atmosphere, hospitality and facilities, that's what you can guarantee when you visit **The Swan Inn** at **Frankwell.** Owned and personally run by Veronica, Mike and son Brian for the past four years, the Inn dates back to the late 18th century when it was originally known as The Black Swan. A very lively pub, The Swan's atmosphere is a warm and welcoming one with good ale and good food served throughout the day and some excellent live folk music on the first Thursday of every month.

The Swan Inn, Frankwell, Shrewsbury, Shropshire SY3 8JR.
Tel: 01743 364923

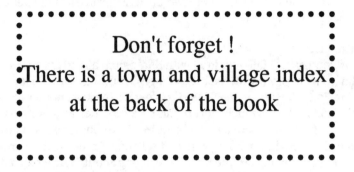

:: Don't forget !
:There is a town and village index:
:: at the back of the book

NOBOLD

The Day House in Nobold is a very grand and elegant 17th century farmhouse owned by Tom and Patricia Roberts who offer a warm welcome to their many guests. Somewhat 'hidden', this charming house can be found by taking the road to Nobold off the A488 where you will see the private drive for The Day House signposted. Once here it is hard to believe Shrewsbury is only two miles away. The large pool in the beautifully kept gardens is a haven for a variety of bird and wildlife and the countryside views are superb. Within the house, the atmosphere is homely and relaxed and there are three lovely guest rooms, all with private facilities, providing very comfortable overnight accommodation.

The Day House, Nobold, Shrewsbury SY5 8NL. Tel: 01743 860212

To the south west of the town are the awesome **Stiperstones.** From a height of 1762 ft these jagged rocks overlook abandoned lead mines said to have been worked by the Romans. Most striking is the Devil's Chair, so called because of its shape. Legend has it that when England's safety is threatened the ghost of Wild Edric, a Saxon earl who defied the Normans, rides the hills.

BICTON.

If you haven't fallen in love with Shropshire already, you certainly will do after exploring all the little villages around this area. Don't pass by **The Four Crosses** on the B4380 thinking it to be just another roadside public house, there's much more to this Hotel and Restaurant than meets the eye. Jeffrey and Carol Blundell acquired The Four Crosses in January 1996 in a somewhat derelict state and set about its renovation creating their own interior design and features bringing about the transformation. They opened in May, since when they have seen their efforts rewarded. The Brasserie Restaurant is cosy and intimate with seating for 32 diners. "Nice and simple" food is served at the bar and wherever you choose, the food is freshly prepared and of excellent quality. There's plenty of variety and the Sunday Carvery has proved very popular too. In 1997 six en-suite bedrooms are scheduled for completion and the owners will be pleased to accept bookings for the Restaurant and future accommodation.

The Four Crosses Hotel, Holyhead Road, Bicton, Nr. Shrewsbury.
Tel: 01743 850258

WOOLASTON.

Further to the west at **Wollaston** you'll find the church which has a memorial to Thomas Parr who, it is claimed, died at the age of a hundred and fifty two years and was the longest lived Englishman in history. Although his age has never been authenticated, he is buried in Westminster

Abbey, giving the story some credence. He was born during the War of the Roses and managed to live through ten reigns, dying in the reign of Charles I. He remained a bachelor until he was eighty-eight when he married and produced two children and then, believe it or not, he married for the second time when he was 122!

WESTBURY.

A couple of miles south of Wollaston brings you to **Westbury.** There has been a **Lion Inn** in Westbury for over 200 years although the original was demolished in the 1960's to make way for a new Lion Inn. Robert Briscoe is The licensee and leaseholder, a local man who came here in 1991. His well stocked bar includes Burtonwood ales, plus Worthington Mild, Lager and Guinness. Belinda is the expert in the kitchen, her dishes are home cooked and are available at all times, although you need to book for Saturday evening and Sunday lunch. The menu and 'specials board' cater for the popular traditional food ranging from Scampi, Chicken, Fish and Grills and well as Curry, Salads and Vegetarian dishes. Good atmosphere - give it a try.

The Lion Inn, Westbury, Shrewsbury, Shropshire. Tel: 01743 884446

Also to be seen in Westbury are the massive earthworks, which is all that remains of Caus Castle. It was built in Norman times by the FitzCorbets, and was strategically important. A town was created within its outer walls but the Corbets were always fighting on the borders and the town was burnt down during Owain Glyndwr's rebellion. Some records say that the final destruction came during the Civil War and Cromwell was blamed, but unfairly so, the town was in ruins by the 16th century.

Many families fled from Caus, one, the Thynnes family, moved to

Minsterley, a pretty little place, where they built both the church and the hall towards the end of the 17th century. The hall is delightfully timbered, while the brick church has a small timber top to its tower. Here you'll find many maidens' garlands - wreaths of paper flowers and ribbons in a wooden frame - which were carried at the funerals of virgins and then hung in the church in remembrance.

To the west, **Worthen** has a grisly story to tell. During restoration work in its very old church, parts of which date from the 12th century, a vault was discovered and in it were thirteen skeletons. To this day, no one knows who they were.

Lord Herbert, brother of the poet George Herbert, lived at **Chirbury**. He left the village a wonderful library of chained books but sadly these are considered to be so valuable that they are kept in the county archives at Shrewsbury. It is an odd village, with a half-timbered school built in 1675 partly in the churchyard. The Vicar was not a bit popular with the village for choosing such an unseemly site, but he carried on in spite of their displeasure.

At the foot of Stapeley Hill is the even smaller village of **Middleton-in-Chirbury**, which has some fascinating wood carvings on the bench ends of the little Victorian church. The vicar, Mr Brewster used his parishioners for his models!

On a hill above the village is a Bronze Age circle known as **'Mitchell's Fold'**. A curious name with an interesting story. Apparently there was a famine in the area and the good fairy was called upon to see what she could do about it. She conjured up a white cow, which had an unending supply of milk. This was splendid until a witch appeared and milked the cow until it fell dead from exhaustion. The good fairy got to hear about this and promptly returned. She turned the wicked witch into stone, where she can be seen today surrounded by other stones. When you look at the circle you can almost believe it to be true!

WELSHPOOL.

At this point we make a diversion across the border to Welshpool to visit the **Golfa Hall Hotel**. Set in eight acres of gardens, with commanding views to the south, Golfa Hall Hotel is a beautiful Country House with a Restaurant. The hall offers a really warm welcome throughout the year with excellent comfort, hospitality, quality fare and imaginative wines. All this is owned and run by Sean and Leanne and offers a relaxed and informal atmosphere for the discerning guest. The spacious accommodation is elegantly furnished throughout with all 14 bedrooms being en-suite with complimentary tea/coffee facilities. Also included is a colour television, hairdryer, trouser press and direct dial telephone, as well as many thoughtful extras. There is a good choice of twin, double or family rooms, including some single accommodation which is also en-suite. The Drawing room with its high ceilings and original cornice offers a perfect retreat in which to read, whilst the south facing Sitting room is a delightful spot in which to relax in a large, comfortable arm chair and appreciate the wooded-hill views. Vegetarian dishes are always on the menu at Golfa Hall Hotel, and are created by Sean, a Chef of some 16 years who only uses the finest and freshest ingredients to create a wide and varied menu. After your delicious meal why not help yourself to the wide range of Welsh Cheeses (plus Stilton of course!) and limitless after-dinner coffee. The Wine list has been carefully selected to include familiar favourites as well and some interesting and more unusual wines for you to explore. Dinner is served nightly in the Dining room where the selection is one of imaginative country cooking in plentiful supply. The large Entrance Lounge with its log fire also has a bar which is fully licensed for residents and diners only.

Golfa Hall Hotel Welshpool Montgomeryshire Powys SY21 9AF
Tel: 01938 553399 Fax: 01938 554777

PONTESBURY.

Tobie's Cafe Bar is a great meeting place in the village of Pontesbury. On a bright sunny day there's room to sit outside and enjoy morning coffee or a lunch break. Ex-licensees David and Margaret Phillips, together with their daughters Katie and Lucie run this successful business catering throughout day and evening. The choice of food is extensive and surprising. In the morning you can take breakfast from 8.30am, morning croissants, pastries and coffee, fresh sandwiches and a variety of beverages. At lunchtime there is a huge selection of dishes; salads, hot jacket potatoes, appetisers and full lunch menu including Pizzas made in a traditional stone oven. Meet a friend for afternoon tea or call in for a glass of wine with friends in the early evening. A full range of excellent traditional and oriental meals are served in the evening. The quality and popularity of Tobie's is such that you should book at weekends. Children are welcome and facilities are provided for disabled customers. Full take away service.

Tobie's Cafe Bar, Main Road, Pontesbury, Shrewsbury. Tel: 01743 792955.

Situated beside the A488 seven miles southwest of Shrewsbury, the **Red Lion** at **Pontesbury** is one of the finest pubs in the area. This handsome former stables building first became an inn around 1750 and today, it is run by Alison and Derek Brookes, friendly and experienced hosts who provide a warm welcome and first-class food and drink. Delicious home-cooked meals are served at lunchtimes and in the evening, including steaks, fish and vegetarian dishes, along with a variety of daily specials. The bars contain a number of glass display cabinets, one of which houses an unusual collection of miniature brewery vehicles, over 200 in all.

Red Lion, Main Road, Pontesbury, Near Shrewsbury, Shropshire
Tel: 01743 790321

BAYSTON HILL.

The Compasses Inn at Bayston Hill is an inviting roadside pub which stands beside the A49, two miles south of Shrewsbury town centre. Originally a row of cottages, this handsome white-painted building first became an inn in 1851. Since then, it has had only eight licensees, the present incumbents being Pam and Ken Williams, charming hosts who purchased the property in 1991 after having been tenants for six years. The bar is filled with a wonderful array of bygone memorabilia, including model ships, old propellers and diving helmets, and is a wonderful atmosphere in which to enjoy a pint, a chat and a bite to eat.

Compasses Inn, Hereford Road, Bayston Hill, Near Shrewsbury, Shropshire
Tel: 01743 872921

CHAPTER THREE

South Shropshire and Bridgnorth

Thatched Church

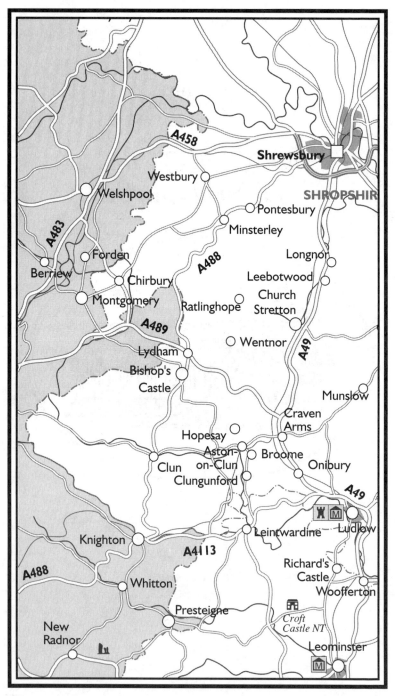

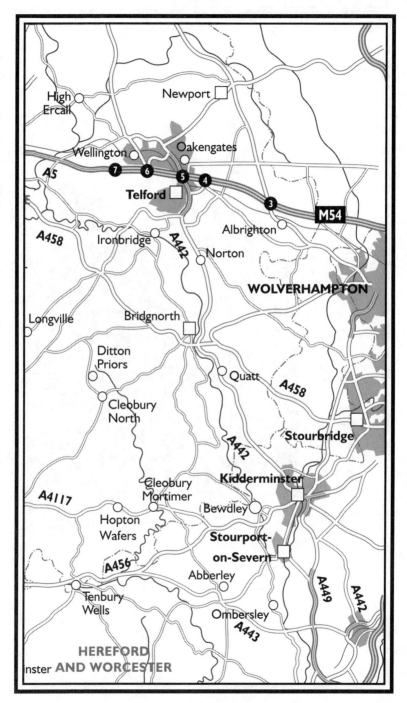

The Buttercross, Ludlow

CHAPTER THREE

South Shropshire and Bridgnorth

Travelling from the densely populated area of The Black Country and the West Midlands to the very large rural area that is South Shropshire is quite a change. There are less people in the whole of this area than there are in one Birmingham suburb.

For the most part, this sparsely populated area consists of small villages and hamlets, with life centred around the larger market towns as it has for centuries.

LUDLOW.

Ludlow is one of the most beautiful country towns in England, and an ideal starting point for this chapter.

It was from here that the Welsh were administered, taxed and tried. It was a great place for lawyers, who grew rich from the pickings and almost equalled the number of local textile merchants whose broadcloth was hugely popular in the Low Countries.

The fine Norman Castle was the home of the Lord President of the Council of the Marches of Wales, and it was a regular occurrence for the English monarch to take up residence at the Castle as well. Indeed, the people of Ludlow treated the arrival of the Monarch as a perfectly normal happening.

The castle was built between 1086 and 1094 by a Norman knight named Roger de Lacy. The outer bailey is the size of a sports field and may well have been used as a place of refuge for the townspeople when the Welsh were marauding. The massive keep was built up from the original gatehouse tower in the early 12th century and the domestic buildings were added in the late 13th and early 14th centuries, mainly by the Mortimer family who inherited the castle from the de Lacys. The Elizabethan buildings came when the castle became the seat of the Council of the Marches, set up to govern Wales and its wild borderlands.

The Mortimers were an ambitious family; one managed to get himself made Duke of York and another became Edward IV. The doomed 'Little Princes' grew up here, and it was probably the happiest time of their short young lives. Prince Arthur brought his bride, Catherine of Aragon here for their honeymoon, but it ended sadly in his death from pneumonia. The poet John Milton attended the first performance of his masque 'Comus' in the Castle. It was based on the real life adventure of three of a Lord President's sons who were lost and then found in Ludlow forest.

In the summer, Ludlow holds a festival of music, drama and art. Among its highlights is an open air production of a Shakespeare play staged in the castle for a two week period from the end of June.

It is almost unfair that one small town should have so many things of great beauty, one of which is the wonderful, spacious church of St. Laurence with its 135 ft tower. Built mostly in the 15th century, it is one of the largest parish churches in England and has the most glorious misericords in the chancel.

Next to the church in the Garden of Rest, is the Reader's House. It got its name because it was the home of the Rector's chief assistant, known in the 18th century as The Reader. To the west of the church stand Hosier's Almshouses, they were originally built in 1486 by a rich local wool merchant, John Hosier, but the present buildings date from 1758. A great place for a stroll, there are a number of good places to eat and drink.

One of the finest eating places in Ludlow can be found opposite the tourist information centre in Church Street, close to its junction with Market Square. Housed in a handsome 15th-century building, **Aragon's Restaurant** is a delightful licensed bistro which is owned and personally-run by Tim Gaudin and his sister-in-law Debbie. The menu includes an impressive variety of meat, chicken and vegetarian dishes, fresh pizzas, and the speciality of the house, homemade pasta. There is also a good range of snacks, including sandwiches and baked potatoes. Aragon's is open until 7pm on Sundays to Thursdays, and 10pm on Fridays and Saturdays.

Aragon's Restaurant, 5 Church Street, Ludlow, Shropshire
Tel: 01584 873282

The classically designed 18th century stone building, The Buttercross, lies in the heart of the market place. It once was a school, but is now the offices of Ludlow Town Council.

Ludlow Museum re-opened in 1995 at a new site with completely new and fully wheelchair accesible displays covering the history of the Ludlow area from 450 million years ago to the present day. Visitors enter the museum through "Reading the Rocks" an exhibition about local rocks and fossils, moving on through prehistoric times the visitor is invited to explore "Ludlow, a fine planned town" before exiting via the final gallery that currently contains changing natural history displays.

Throughout the museum there are plenty of hands-on activities, such as Civil War helmets to try on, a video microscope to zoom onto fossils and timber joints to construct.There's lots of things to see in draws, books and bats. Open April until October, Monday to Saturday 10-30 - 1-00, 2.00-5.00 and also bank holiday Sundays and Sundays in June, July and August. Also the home of the Tourist Information Offices.

Ludlow Museum, Castle Street, Ludlow. Tel: 01584 875384

Just across from The Bull Ring, at the top of the hill in Ludlow is **Victoria's Tea Rooms and Antiques.** It's a traditional English Tearoom in a most attractive 16th century wood-framed building - an attractive part of our heritage which we all too frequently take for granted.

It is run by Pam Alcock Brown and her grand-daughter Victoria. Here you can sit down to morning coffee, enjoy a light lunch, toasted whatever, or an oozing cream cake. All the meals are home-cooked and there's lots to enjoy. Perhaps you might even join in the gossip of the day! Victoria's also sell antiques and miniature dolls house furniture - so browse around and treat yourself.

Victoria's Tearooms & Antiques, Tower Street, Ludlow. Tel: 01584 874789

The historic **Oaks Restaurant** is to be found in Corve Street in Ludlow. A seventeenth century coaching inn, it was once known as the Eagle and Child and earlier as the Eagle inn. There is still evidence of the cobblestone blacksmith's yard and tethering rings for horses.

The entrance hall has some handsome oak timbers with wattle and daub plastering, a small portion being exposed for the interest of the visitors. The Restaurant with its original beams and old stone fireplace has been skilfully panelled with oak from Acton Scott Hall and Bitterly Court, two local country houses.

This beautiful 17th century panelling gives examples of Norman Arches Raised Mouldings and Cartouche carving with Coboschen centres. The Lounge above is equally rich in old oak timbers which recently have been exposed, again there is evidence of wattle and daub construction.

The Restaurant is now owned and run by Ken and Isabel Adams who delight in preparing beautifully cooked quality produce, selected from local farms and specialist suppliers for their guests. With a fine discerning wine list and a choice of aperitifs, brandies and liqueurs to compliment your meal. Relaxing with unpretentious service from Isabel and her friendly team, you are invited to linger in the cosy bar with small "hors d'oeuvres" and a glass of wine or fine sherry while selecting from the menu.

In the kitchen Ken, the chef-proprietor, creates interesting dishes to the highest standard; menus change regularly as Ken likes to make allowance for the seasons. Seafood and game are a speciality with locally smoked fish proving a favourite with patrons. Featured in all major guides including Egon Ronay, Michelin and AA-Two Rosettes. Open for Dinner Tuesday to Sunday - six night from 7.00pm.

Oaks Restaurant, 17 Corve Street, Ludlow. Tel: 01584 872325

At one time in the last century, the making of gloves was the main occupation of the people of the town. There were something like nine master glovers, who in turn employed some seven hundred women and children who were required to turn out ten pairs each a week, for the American market. Today the economy is more broadly based and an increasingly popular centre for tourists.

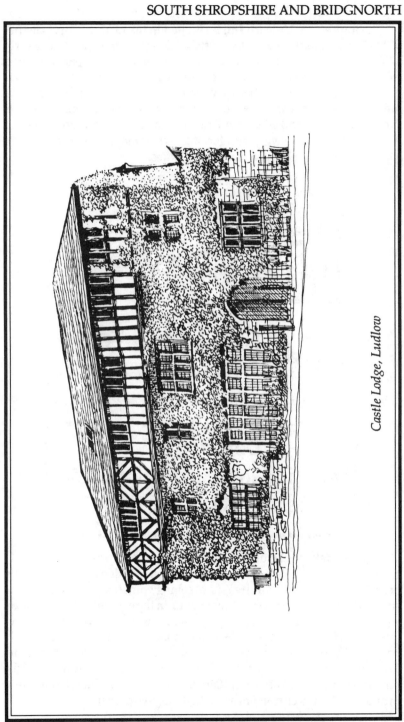

Castle Lodge, Ludlow

The impressive **Unicorn Inn** is situated in the historic Corve district of Ludlow, a quarter sprinkled with buildings dating back to the early 17th-century. Full of character and charm, the inn has a part-timbered exterior, beamed ceilings and roaring log fires in winter. The bar provides the ideal atmosphere in which to enjoy a relaxing drink or light meal, and there is also a restaurant serving the finest English cuisine. Proprietors Alan and Elisabeth Ditchburn and their son Jon provide a warm welcome and very comfortable accommodation in five guest rooms, three of which have en suite facilities.

Unicorn Inn, Lower Corve Street, Ludlow, Shropshire   Tel: 01584 873555

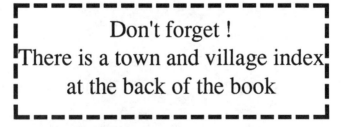

Don't forget !
There is a town and village index
at the back of the book

The Old Bakehouse, one of Ludlow's oldest bakeries was delightlfully transformed by Lisa Brown into an old fashioned eating place. Originally described by Lisa as a 'little tea shop' selling homemade cakes and light snacks during the day, with a fuller menu in the evening. It has come on a pace since then and The Old Bakehouse now offers a wider variety of food, which is all homemade. The homely interior is very nicely presented and the atmosphere warm and friendly. Opening hours are: 9am - 5pm Monday to Thursday. 9am - 9pm Friday and Saturday whilst on Sunday the hours are from 10am until 6pm. The Old Bakehouse is proud to offer it's customers a smoke-free environment.

106

The Old Bakehouse, Tower Street, Ludlow, Shropshire. Tel: 01584 872645

Without doubt one of the most interesting streets to explore has to be Broad Street. There is an excellent book that has been written about the street, its houses and residents through eight centuries, produced by the Ludlow Historical Research Group.

Their devotion to the detailed reconstruction of the past means that today anyone taking a walk from one end of the street to the other can savour the different styles of architecture that sit so happily together. Even the intrusion of Victorian buildings here and there does not impair the overall beauty.

There has always been a cross-section of the community living here, although Broad Street has long enjoyed the reputation of being the most fashionable street in the town.

In the Middle Ages, merchants and clothiers were the most influential groups, but the 17th century brought a change and landed gentry moved in. In the 18th and 19th century it was the turn of the professions - mainly doctors and lawyers.

Ludlow was very much the social centre of Shropshire in the 18th century, and families used to move from their country homes to houses in Broad Street so that their daughters might be introduced to Ludlow society. These privileged families met at houses such as Number 40, where one Lady Boyne had built a ballroom.

Walking up the street brings you to Broad Gate. The last remaining of seven town gates, it was built in the 13th century, and is an important feature of this castle town. The Ludlow Historical Research Group book mentions nine pubs below the Broad Gate, but there is only a sole survivor. However, when you take a walk up Broad Street, look at numbers 37 and 39 which were once The Old Stag's Head, The Dial at 49 and 50, The Vineyard at 63 and The Mermaid at 68. Tucked in the shelter of the mellow walls of Broad Gate is that sole survivor, **The Wheatsheaf Inn**.

A superb hostelry, it was built in 1688 and first licensed in 1753. The historic **Wheatsheaf Inn** stands beside the medieval Broad Gate at the lower end of Broad Street. Its interior is full of genuine character, with exposed stone walls, timber beams, and two open fireplaces to provide a warm welcome on colder days. Owned and personally-run by Carol and Sam Loxton with the assistance of son Gareth and daughter Karen, The Wheatsheaf is renowned for its superb food and impressive range of cask-conditioned ales, including the unique Broadgate Bitter. There are also five beautifully-furnished guest rooms equipped with en suite facilities, colour TVs, direct-dial telephones, and a number of thoughtful extras.

Wheatsheaf Inn, Lower Broad Street, Ludlow, Shropshire   Tel: 01584 872980   Fax: 01584 877990

Visitors to Ludlow would be well advised to spare a few hours for a tour around the **Dinham House Exhibition Centre**. This impressive 18th century mansion house has a rich and fascinating history with many notable residents over the years, not least of which was Lucien Bonaparte, brother of Napoleon, who stayed here as a prisoner on parole during 1810.

Privately owned and funded, there is a nominal entrance fee to the house where there are various exhibitions, one of which details all the various residents and their time of occupancy here. There are also craft studios where you can watch amongst others, a potter, sugarcraft artist and stained glass maker at work, creating a wealth of potential gifts and mementoes. After strolling through the beautiful gardens and grounds, relax with some refreshment in the coffee shop before making your way home.

Dinham House Exhibition Centre, Ludlow Tel: 01584 874240

STOKESAY

Seven miles north of Ludlow on the A49 is **Stokesay Castle**. From the road you will catch a glimpse of the castle rising up behind the trees and there is a narrow lane which leads up to it. From here, you can see the lovely Elizabethan Gatehouse, with the crenellations of the medieval garrison tower in sharp contrast beyond.

Stokesay is the oldest surviving fortified manor house in England and probably the only one of its age virtually complete. It does not take a great imagination to feel what life must have been like here hundreds of years ago. Conjuring up images of a great Tudor banquets; of which there must have been many in the fine great hall.

Stokesay is called a castle but was never meant to be more than a family home, and as you go through the Gatehouse archway door into the courtyard garden you can understand this. This lovely place has so many unique features that it will appeal to everyone of whatever age.

CRAVEN ARMS

The village of **Craven Arms** can be found just a mile from Stokesay. It got its name from the hotel and pub that were built here by the Earl of Craven. Standing at this once important junction of roads, the village became an ideal market centre for farmers over a wide area. One of the largest sheep auctions in Britain used to be held here. The place would really come alive each autumn when on an ordinary day over twenty thousand sheep would be sold by relays of auctioneers!

It would be hard to imagine a more picturesque or tranquil setting for a self-catering holiday than in the tiny village of **Hopesay** which lies in an area of outstanding natural beauty in the Shropshire hills. Hesterworth, the location of **Hesterworth Holidays**, stands on a rise, surrounded by its own 12 acres of trees, fields, stream, pond and garden. The resident proprietors Sheila and Roger Davies extend an invitation to "come and share the delightful situation". They comment "we truly believe that there is no better centre in Britain for the historian, motorist, walker, bird watcher or simply for people who love the countryside'. This is certainly a lovely part of the world with many popular places to visit nearby. The Cottages and flats are named after local hills and each has its own character; they are comfortably furnished and well-equipped. If you prefer, stay bed and breakfast. All guests have the option of an evening meal. Licensed. E.T.B.- 3 Keys up to Commended.

Hesterworth Holidays, Hesterworth, Hopesay, Craven Arms, Shropshire.
Tel: 01588 660487

Heading back towards Craven Arms we arrive at **The Engine and Tender** at **Broome,** an impressive pub and eating place which lies hidden in the minor roads between the B4367 and B4368. An imposing white-painted building, its interior is filled with a wonderful assortment of memorabilia, including old railway signs, water jugs and horse brasses.

It has been owned and personally-run since 1986 by Marie and Walter Rossler, charming hosts who provide a warm welcome, fine ale, and delicious food ranging from sandwiches to succulent steaks. There is also a self-contained games room and a small caravan and camping park to the rear with room for sixteen touring caravans, with one well-appointed static caravan being available to let throughout the year.

Engine and Tender, Broome, Near Craven Arms, Shropshire
Tel: 01588 660275

Between Stokesay and Ludlow you may spot signs for **The Wernlas Collection** at **Onibury**. It is the most extensive collection of large fowl in the United Kingdom, displayed in spectacular countryside with other rare farm animals. 'I didn't know chickens could be so beautiful' proclaims their guide book and it's perfectly true. It's amazing what a multitude of colours and patterns there are to be seen among the many rare breeds of large fowl which are kept in a traditional manner on this attractive smallholding.

The Wernlas Collection

The chickens have rather fun names too - there are punk headed Polands, feathered legged Cochins and exquisite Seabrights, as well as the common or garden farmyard hens that we've all known since our childhood days. The Collection is sited on a ridge above Onibury, and even if you do not enjoy looking at the chickens you cannot fail to enjoy the superb views of the South Shropshire Hills.

In addition to our feathered friends, there are rare breed goats, sheep and pigs, the young of which can be seen at most times during the season. Nobody minds you getting close to the animals, who love having a fuss made of them. Small children will delight in being allowed to hold the fluffy chicks.

You can get light refreshments here, or if you take a picnic with you, 'The Dingle' is a wonderful place to sit and eat, surrounded by a semi-wild area of natural beauty and tranquillity where wild flowers, birds and animals can frequently be seen. The Wernlas Collection opens daily from Good Friday to October 29th from 10.30am - 5.30pm, but they are closed on Mondays except for Bank Holidays.

CLEEDOWNTON.

Clee St. Margaret is a quiet and pretty place with an attractive church. Nearby and enjoying a lovely rural location in the picturesque village of Cleedownton is **The Moor Hall.** Built in 1789, it is a splendid example of the Georgian Palladian style and enjoys breathtaking views over miles of unspoilt countryside. The atmosphere is relaxed and friendly, combining all the comforts of the twentieth century with the traditional qualities of the English country house lifestyle. The gardens which extend to five acres provide a perfect setting in which to idle away a few hours, whilst the hills beyond offer wonderful discoveries for the more energetic. The Moor Hall is splendidly presented and guests will be reluctant to leave this beautiful home and tranquil setting. To enjoy your visit to the full, make arrangements to dine here. Travel along the B4364 towards Bridgenorth and The Moor Hall is two and a half miles beyond the village of Middleton.

The Moor Hall, Cleedownton, Nr. Ludlow.   *Tel: 01584 823209*
Fax: 01584 823387

BROMDON AND WHEATHILL.

Just a miles east is **Bromdon**. It has been mentioned in history as far back as Saxon times, but because it has no church of its own (no village was a proper village unless it had a church) it has always appeared in the records as subservient to nearby **Wheathill** with a wonderful old church dating back to the 11th century. Thus it has remained a hamlet and part of Wheathill, and would probably have never made much of a stir in the history books if it had not been for the persecution in central Europe, which led to the Second World War.

When the impact came it was dramatic, and now Bromdon will never be forgotten. One hundred men, women and children fled from Nazi oppression to this little backwater hamlet. This number of people would have been an invasion in itself, but it became sensational when it was realised that they belonged to a commune, living a totally unfamiliar lifestyle and speaking an unfamiliar language. They were joined by others as time went by, including many English people who were attracted to their simple life with its doctrine of All for One and One for All.

The origin of this movement came from as far back as 1920 when, under the leadership and example of Doctor Eberard Arnold, a group of men, disenchanted and disillusioned with post war society in Germany, established a religious commune which they called a Brotherhood. The rules were strict and it was a deeply religious life, in which they worked for the good of the whole commune, with no competition and no financial reward. There were no winners or losers - the only reward was the joy of service to God and the community.

In 1937, they found themselves expelled from Germany by Adolf Hitler and found temporary homes in Wiltshire and Gloucestershire. This was a temporary sanctuary, for the main body had established a commune in Paraguay. Sadly, the war made them technically enemies of this country even though they were refugees, and the two 'Bruderhofs' were closed down and the brothers and sisters all emigrated to Paraguay where they established three new settlements.

Back at Bromdon, three members had been left behind to wind up their affairs, with the intention of joining the others in Paraguay. But the same longing for a return to their old roots and to the simple life which had brought the original group together was still alive in England, and as more and more men and women were led to join these three in a search for that life style, it was decided that they would stay, and so it was that they purchased Bromdon Farm and established the Wheathill Bruderhof.

From then on it grew. An influx of war orphans, displaced and lost children, survivors of the Concentration camps and who knows what other horrors, came in the post war years to the tranquillity of Bromdon so that by 1951 there were one hundred adults and seventy-four children. It was a life of simplicity and frequently hardship for them all, supporting themselves entirely on the produce of their three farms, Upper and Lower Bromdon and Cleeton Court - a total of five hundred and forty five acres. Most of the land was at a height of one thousand feet or more, which meant that it was not easy to work.

You can imagine that their arrival in the area was not greeted enthusiastically and in fact there was some hostility, but it soon passed and they continued living here until 1963. By this time they had earned nothing but respect from the local people for their high integrity and conducting themselves, and their affairs, in an unyielding and unbending Christian principle, which nothing could compromise.

There are many Bruderhofs today throughout the New World, in South America, the USA and Canada, where they live freely, away from the traditional European prejudices and rivalries. Over the last twenty-five years or so, the farms have reverted to conventional farming. The building that the Brethren constructed as a dining hall is now the village hall.

One final interesting point is that because the rules of the Brotherhood demanded that they did everything for themselves in death as in life, so they had their own cemetery, which is still cared for at Little Bromdon and is regularly visited by members or relatives of the community. Before the establishment of this cemetery there was one death, that of a little boy, who is buried in a corner of Egerton Meadow, just outside the house platforms. No one seems to know why they abandoned this peaceful spot when they made their cemetery, for this was the only burial there. However, it is still maintained and enclosed so that the farm animals cannot despoil it. If you would like to know more about the Bruderhofs, their history and aims, you can always write to; The Hutterian Society of Brothers, Rifton 12471, New York, USA.

NEEN SOLARS.

Almost by the River Rea, hidden in the lanes between the A456 and A4117, eight miles west of Bewdley, is the curiously named - **The Live And Let Live Inn** at **Neen Sollars**; it's a real gem.

Live and Let Live

This striking part-medieval building stands in an elevated position with magnificent views all around. Inside, it is full of genuine character with oak-beamed ceilings, panelled walls, intricate wood carvings, and stained glass. There is also a fine array of memorabilia, including an unusual collection of miniature whiskies. Partners Chris and Ian Ferguson and Sue and Steve Painter serve an excellent selection of traditional ales and some of the finest home-cooked food in the district. Open every evening, and for lunch on Saturdays and Sundays.

Live and Let Live Inn, Neen Sollars, Near Kidderminster, Shropshire
Tel: 01299 832391

CLEOBURY MORTIMER.

To **Cleobury Mortimer** next, to investigate the legend of Maisie Bloomer. It was the birthplace of Maisie, a witch, in the 18th century.

Curses and love-potions were her specialities, and the villagers had no doubt that she was in league with the devil. A lady who was much feared and also sought after. The town is well worth visiting to see the famous crooked steeple of St. Mary's church. Also well worth a visit is

The Royal Fountain, an impressive inn and restaurant which stands on Church Street in the heart of the village This handsome white-painted building dates back to the 15th-century and is adorned with hanging flowers in summer. A popular oasis for visitors and locals alike, it offers a wonderful selection of traditional ales and some of the finest cuisine in the area. Diners can eat in the bar or in the restaurant, with its intimate atmosphere and friendly waitress service. The menu features a variety of steaks, fish, meat and poultry dishes, along with a selection of daily specials from the chalkboard.

Royal Fountain, 13 Church Street, Cleobury Mortimer, Near Kidderminster,
Shropshire Tel: 01299 270177

Whilst in this area, don't miss a visit to **The Gobbett Rare Breeds**

Centre and Nursery where a collection of rare waterfowl and farm animals can be seen.

At **Hopton Wafers,** you'll find **The Crown Inn,** is an outstanding pub, restaurant and place to stay which stands beside the A4117, midway between Ludlow and Cleobury Mortimer. Originally part of the Hopton Court estate, this handsome part-16th-century inn was the place where workers were paid and rents were collected; indeed, the bar is still known as the Rent Room. The atmosphere throughout is welcoming and full of character, with open log fires and exposed timber beams. The restaurant offers a varied and imaginative menu, and is the perfect setting for that special meal. There are also eight beautifully-appointed guest bedrooms, each different in style and equipped with en suite facilities and an array of thoughtful extras.

Crown Inn, Hopton Wafers, Cleobury Mortimer, Near Kidderminster, Shropshire   Tel: 01299 270372 Fax: 01299 271127

Wandering the lanes north and crossing the B4364 brings you to **Chetton** and up a lane, near **Brown Clee Hill,** you'll discover a church said to have been founded by Lady Godiva but is now mostly 18th century. Brown Clee Hill, incidentally, is eighteen hundred feet tall and the highest hill in the county.

EARDINGTON.

Another few miles and along more peaceful lanes and you'll arrive in **Eardington.** There is an ancient custom here connected with Moor Ridding Farm. Edward I granted the land to the Earl of Shrewsbury in return for a bodyguard to protect him when he hunted in the area. The annual fee for this was an 'item of war', which is still paid today at Michaelmas in 'the Quit-Rent Ceremony', when the Queen's Remembrancer receives the fee from the senior aldermen of the City of London at the Law Courts in the Strand. Once, the weapons of war would have been swords and knives, but they are now represented by a billhook and a hatchet.

CHELMARSH.

The village has been lucky enough to escape industrial development, and is delightful, with a church built of sandstone with a saddleback roof. Situated on the B4555 in the village, it seems the **Bulls Head Inn** has everything the passing traveller could wish for. With its superb atmosphere and fine views across the Severn Valley, the Bull's Head Inn at Chelmarsh provides the ideal holiday base.

The Bulls head

Perfect too for an enjoyable drink or meal, the three bar areas have a wonderful traditional ambience, with wood-burning stoves, exposed stone walls and old timber beams.

The intimate restaurant serves an extensive range of top class dishes, and there are nine beautifully-appointed en- suite guest rooms, all with colour televisions and a number of thoughtful extras, with guests having access to a jacuzzi. Proprietors Sue and David Baxter also have three superbly-furnished self-catering holiday cottages available close by, each sleeping up to seven, and for guests with disabilities, they offer both self-catering or bed and breakfast in recently-constructed ramped accommodation on the ground floor.

Bull's Head Inn, Chelmarsh, Near Bridgnorth, Shropshire
Tel: 01746 861469 Fax: 01746 862646

HAMPTON LOADE.

Situated between the River Severn on the one side and the Severn Valley Railway on the other, **The Unicorn Inn** at **Hampton Loade** is a pleasant family-orientated pub and eating place, with caravan and camping park attached, which occupies an impressive 7-acre site between the River Severn and the Severn Valley Railway. The inn is renowned for its food and offers an extensive range of popular dishes, including chicken and chips, burgers and daily specials such as baltis and casseroles; there is also a special children's menu.

First-rate bed and breakfast accommodation is available at the inn, and there are also a number of well-appointed self-catering flats and static caravans for hire. There is also plenty of room for touring caravans.

Unicorn Inn, Hampton Loade, Chelmarsh, Near Bridgnorth, Shropshire
Tel: 01746 861515

QUATT.

The middle years of the twentieth century, so disastrous for many country houses, have been the most fruitful in **Dudmaston**'s long history. To see this unique house, now owned by the National Trust, take the A442 Kidderminster - Bridgnorth Road and you will find it just four miles south east of Bridgnorth, in the little village of **Quatt**.

Why is it so special? Firstly, for 850 years the Dudmaston estate has always passed by descent or devise and has never been offered for sale. It has had periods of uncertainty, when the estate was heavily encumbered and the house stripped of most of its contents. In recent years, however, Dudmaston has enjoyed a period of unusual enrichment, with the introduction by Sir George and Lady Labouchere of 18th century Dutch flower pictures, fine Continental and English furniture and an important collection of contemporary paintings and sculpture.

The present house, attributed to the architect Francis Smith of Warwick, was probably begun by Sir Thomas Wolryche in 1695 and largely built by the time of his early death in 1701. In the 1820's the roof-line was altered and pediments and a parapet were added. Dudmaston was given to the National Trust in 1978

Stokesay Castle

The rooms in the main house are mostly small and filled with Sir George and Lady Labouchere's personal possessions. It is precisely this intimacy of scale which makes this house so attractive. There is a ramp to the front door which makes most of the house accessible for the disabled and a wheelchair is available if it is needed. A pleasant afternoon at Dudmaston can be rounded off with a cup of tea in the tearoom, situated in the Old Stables alongside the car park.

Dudmaston, Quatt, Bridgnorth Tel: 01746 780866

The church at Quatt does not hold great appeal outwardly but a look inside is rewarded by the sight of a place of worship that is obviously loved. There are some splendid monuments and memorials to the Wolryche family and one in particular may take your fancy. Lady Mary Wolryche died in 1678 and you can only hope she is made more comfortable in heaven than she is depicted here. It would seem that even as a child she rebelled at playing a musical instrument, and certainly she does not look happy with the lute she holds in her left hand.

WOOTTON GREEN.

One of the first of its kind in Britain, **The Cider House** is a hugely-popular licensed establishment which is dedicated to West Country cider. It can be found 3 miles southwest of Bridgnorth, in the lanes between the A458 and A442 in the lovely old hamlet of **Wootton Green**. Since coming here 1983, proprietors Kath and Brian Jervis have built up a thriving concern which is visited from all over the region. Instead of beer and lager, they offer around 15 types of cider, from familiar brands to those made by small producers, along with a range of appetising snacks. The four bars are full of character and atmosphere, and there is also a large patio garden to enjoy in summer.

The Cider House, Wootton Green, Near Bridgnorth, Shropshire
Tel: 01746 780285 Fax: 01746 780199

ALVERLEY.

The history of American Civil War General Robert E. Lee and his family, is an entertaining one. The Lee family can be traced as far back as the Knights of the Round Table. **Coton Hall** in **Alverley**, where the Lee family lived for three hundred years can still be seen although the Lees themselves are long gone.

There is a lot of modern development in Alverley, but just a little way north of the village, there is an old sandstone cross which has withstood the test of time and still has a Maltese cross on either side of its round head. It is possible that it has associations with those famous knights, the Knights Hospitalers.

CLAVERLEY.

The excellent **Plough Inn** is situated in the lanes between the A454 and A458 in the lovely old village of Claverley. Constructed in the 18th-century from reclaimed ship's timbers, this handsome former farmhouse first became an inn in the 1840s.

Plough Inn

Today, it retains its delightful character, with beamed ceilings, open fires, old horse brasses, and an unusual collection of foreign bank notes. The Plough is renowned throughout the area for its food. Irene and David O'Gorman and son James serve a superb selection of home-cooked dishes, such as tasty beef and Guinness pie, along with a wide range of succulent steaks, vegetarian dishes and lighter meals.

Plough Inn, Claverley, Near Bridgnorth, Shropshire Tel: 01746 710365

BRIDGNORTH.

The main part of the town of **Bridgnorth** stands on a high ridge above the River Severn and is known as High Town while below the ridge and across the river is it known as Low Town. The two 'towns' are linked by a six arched road bridge, built in 1823. The only other way to go between the two is either by steep flights of steps or by the cliff railway of which there are only two left in the whole country. The other is in Devon and joins Lynton to Lynmouth. The fare is worth every penny for the superb views that unfold before you as you rise nearly five hundred feet.

Situated on the B4364 on the edge of the town is an historic inn of great appeal. Unlike some historical inns which have been modernised and have lost their aged appearance, **Ye Olde Punch Bowl Inn** has retained its old architecture with interesting shapes and sizes; cobbled walls, old windows, beams, lamps and ironwork.

Ye Olde Punch Bowl Inn

This is a building with great character and charm reflecting its 500 year history. The records show that in 1785 it became an inn, which at some time acquired a tunnel across the road leading to a cellar, now a private house. Today, this traditionally run family establishment provides excellent facilities including a top class, non-smoking restaurant (book early not to be disappointed) and bar food. All the food is prepared fresh daily by the hotel chefs and a wide choice of meals and bar snacks are offered. If staying-over, there are five comfortable guest bedrooms, one of which is a family room. The owners pride themselves on a good cellar with well kept ales in top condition and there's an excellent array of bottled beers, wines and spirits.

Ye Olde Punch Bowl Inn, Ludlow Road, Bridgnorth, Shropshire.
Tel: 01746 763304 Fax: 01746 764021.

Many of the shops and pubs are in the High Town, and it is very pleasant to walk along, looking at the quaint cottages that make Bridgnorth such a lovely place. The Castle Walk, adjoining the Castle grounds, provides the loveliest views of this delightful town. Near to the Castle grounds is the church of **St. Mary Magdalene**, which is the third church to be built on the site. It was designed by Thomas Telford and built in 1792, although most people connect him with bridges and canals, rather than church design, he has certainly created a lovely building in the Italianate style.

The sturdy supporting columns of Bridgnorth's lovely **Town Hall** have stood since 1652. Made of sandstone and then covered in brick, they show no signs of wear and tear. The Town Hall is a wonderful building, built from the proceeds of a nationwide appeal after most of the town was burnt down in the Civil War. Charles II took a great interest in it and when improvements were needed some ten years later, he saw to it that money was available from his own purse and from a collection he ordered from every parish in England.

Bishop Percy's House is Bridgnorth's oldest house. It is an attractive timbered building of 1580, and was later the birthplace of Thomas Percy, who became Bishop of Dromore. The house stands on Cartway, which leads down from the High Street to the river and has caves along its sides cut into the sandstone which were used as dwellings in Victorian times. One, The Hermitage, is said to have been the home of Ethelred, brother of King Athelstan, in the 10th century.

Little remains of **Bridgnorth Castle**, but the ruined Norman keep is still standing - just! It leans at seventeen degrees from the perpendicular because it was undermined during the Civil War. If you have ever seen the Leaning Tower of Pisa, you may be interested to know that this is leaning at an angle three times greater!

Castle Tea Rooms, 1 East Castle Street, Bridgnorth, Shropshire.
Tel: 01746 763161.

Situated on the site of the old castle walls and just outside that of the Postern Gate, which was also demolished, the delightful **Castle Tea Rooms** owned and personally run by David and Kay is a very appealing rest stop at any time of day. Originally Tea Rooms in the 1860's, though a building put to many other uses over the years, it is refurbished in the Victorian style, and as in those genteel days, offers a waitress service. It is tastefully decorated with many attractive features and enjoys a 'smoke-free' atmosphere. Daily specials are available between 12 noon and 2pm (exc. Sundays) . The Tea Rooms are open everyday, except Sundays between the end of September and the beginning of March.

The Bridgnorth Museum, Northgate, should be on your list of places to visit. It is well worth spending a couple of hours looking at the relics and curios telling the story of the town and life in Shropshire, all displayed in the rooms alongside the 18th century brick-built gateway. It is open from Easter to mid September on Saturdays and Bank Holidays from 2 - 4pm. Also on Mondays, Tuesdays and Wednesdays at the same times from mid July to the beginning of September.

Guided walks take place from Easter to October and details of these may be obtained from the Tourist Information Centre.

One of the most delightful ways of seeing the beautiful wooded valley of the River Severn is from the **Severn Valley Steam Railway.** This beautifully-preserved railway line runs from Kidderminster to Bridgnorth, and is now one of the premier visitor attractions in the West Midlands. Steam trains run every weekend throughout the year, with a daily service between mid-May and end-September. The wonderful old engines, stately and gloriously noisy, chug their way along the sixteen-mile stretch of track, giving ample opportunity for passengers to admire the view. The train passes over the impressive Victoria Bridge and stops at half-a-dozen stations along the way, including the beautifully-maintained station at Arley which is featured in the popular BBC TV comedy series, Oh, Doctor Beeching!

Opened in 1862, the line originally ran from Shrewsbury to Hartlebury, north of Worcester, connecting towns like Ironbridge, Coalport, Bridgnorth, Bewdley and Stourport-on-Severn for the first time. Then in 1878, a branch from Kidderminster to Bewdley was added so that trains could run from Birmingham and the West Midlands directly into the Severn Valley. These lines survived intact until 1963 when, like so many country branches, they fell under the axe of Dr Beeching.

In July 1965, the Severn Valley Railway Society was formed by a group of enthusiasts who wanted to preserve the line south of Bridgnorth. British Rail accepted the sum of £25,000 for the stretch from Bridgnorth to Alveley, and after much work to repair and restore the stations, locomotives and coaches, the first public passenger train steamed from Bridgnorth to Hampton Loade on 23 May 1970. The society then became a limited company and purchased the line from Alveley to Foley Park following a successful share issue. Passenger services were extended to Bewdley in 1974, then in 1983, the company purchased the remaining line into Kidderminster along with a site for a new station. The following year, steam-hauled passenger trains pulled into Kidderminster Town for the first time.

The Severn Valley Railway

The Severn Valley Railway is now the home of the largest collection of working steam locomotives and restored rolling stock in Britain, a new purpose-built locomotive repair depot and boiler works having been opened at Bridgnorth in the late 1980s. The railway is operated largely by volunteer staff, up to 300 of whom are needed at busy weekends. There is also a growing team of paid staff who deal with essential maintenance and administration.

Severn Valley Railway, Railway Station, Bewdley, Worcestershire
Tel: 01299 403816 Fax: 01299 400839

Our next step takes us from steam trains to fabulous models of cars and motor cycles. **The Midland Motor Museum** on the Stourbridge Road is a fantastic place. It was first opened to the public in 1978 by Bob Roberts and Mike Barker. Both men are keen drivers themselves and enter many competitions. Long before the Motor Museum was even thought about, Bob and Mike had successfully used their cars, and it was always the intention to carry on with an active programme of motor sport after the Museum was opened.

Bob Roberts owns several cars but his favourite is a 1927 Bugatti Type 43 that in recent years has won the fastest vintage sports car award three times at the Shelsley Speed Hill Climb, at a site about twelve miles south west of Kidderminster. The car has also been raced at Silverstone on many occasions, and has competed at other events and venues in vintage meetings.

Bob has also demonstrated his twenty-four litre Napier Railton on several occasions. This is the car that set the fastest ever lap at the Brooklands circuit in Surrey at 143.44 mph, driven by John Cobb. He also owns a 1925 Sunbeam Tiger which held the land speed record for a while in 1926 at 152 mph, driven by Sir Henry Seagrave. It was also a successful Grand Prix car in its day, and was the last Grand Prix-type car to hold the world land speed record.

The Midland Motor Museum, Stanmore Hall, Bridgnorth
Tel: 01746 762992

Mike Barker started motor competition in the early 1950s with a Manx Norton motorcycle and a 1935 Ulster Aston Martin. Since then he has competed in a great variety of vehicles, some of which belong to Bob Roberts. Mike also designed and built his own Jaguar sports racing car in the late 1950s, called the Alton Jaguar. This car won over fifty awards before being partially retired to the museum.

Cars are the lifeblood of these two men, and the display of sports and racing cars and motor cycles in the Motor Museum is fantastic. The Museum has gained national recognition for the quality, and great admiration for the high standards that are maintained. They could not have found a more beautiful site either and the grounds have wonderful views over the Severn Valley towards the Clee Hills. In part of the parklands, and surrounding a lake, is a touring camp site, open all year and catering for many visitors from home and all over the world, who come to see and enjoy the many tourist attractions that this part of Shropshire has to offer.

The villages of **Badger** and **Birdsgreen** have been encroached upon by the inescapable influence of industry but it is not the sudden explosion of factories, but of commuter housing that has caused the problem. Badger has a remarkable Victorian church, which is so full of works by the masters of sculpture, Flaxman, Chantrey and Gibson, that you might be excused if you thought you had stumbled upon an exhibition.

The church at **Worfield**, a little further west and just north of Bridgnorth, with an elegant tall spire, is the parish church for as many as thirty hamlets around and about. Apparently it is one of the largest parishes in the country.

From Worfield, wended your way westwards along some of the smallest lanes in this part of the county, enjoying the countryside and every now and again happening upon an appealing little hamlet. **Astley Abbots** is the first stop, where Frances Pitt, who wrote so well about the environment and added to this talent by taking the most wonderful photographs, once lived. Without the help of television or even the press to any extent, she managed to make people realise the wonders of our natural heritage. She was also Master of the Wheatland Hunt for some twenty years.

There are two attractive Norman churches at **Morville** and **Aston Eyre**. The tympanum over the doorway of the church at Aston Eyres is very special. It represents Christ's entry into Jerusalem and shows him sitting, not astride but sideways. There are two men on either side of him, one with a young ass, the other spreading palm leaves.

If you drop down from here towards Weston and Shipton, you will come to **Corve Dale**, full of lush pasture and with the farms and hamlets nestling along the river or its tributary streams where they have been since Saxon times. Marvellous names these hamlets have too - there is Brockton, Stanton, Long Bourton, Great Oxenbold, Hungerford and Holdgate.

'Thonglands' is a moated house at **Holdgate** which is apparently haunted by a phantom choir. No one seems to have heard them perform recently, but the little village does have an ethereal air about it. Once, it had a castle and the church still has a sheel-na-gig on the south wall.

Sheel-na-gigs are somewhat unusual - being a grotesque sculpted stone figure of a woman, grinning from ear to ear, with legs wide apart. There are only eighteen in the country, four of which are in Shropshire. We believe them to be found, without exception, set in walls of Christian churches and almost always on the outside. The origin is a mystery although the 'sheel' part sounds of Irish extraction. Whatever and wherever they came from they have always been regarded as lucky charms. Many times church leaders have asked for their removal, but the will, or the superstition of the people has always prevailed.

The church in Holdgate is crumbling, but the sheel-na-gig remains beside a window in the outside south wall of the chancel, overlooking the churchyard. She is only about eighteen inches high, so you will have to look hard for her.

Tugford, close by, has two sheel-na-gigs - quite plump ladies looking a bit like Toby Jugs. Church Stretton has one who is far more refined and far more human.

And so to Wenlock Edge, a long, wooded ridge of limestone running north east from Craven Arms and believed to be four hundred million years old. Take your time along the road from Church Stretton to Much Wenlock and you will be rewarded with some wonderful views.

The three hamlets of **Westhope**, **Middlehope** and **Easthope**, quite naturally are to be found in Hope Dale. People do not like going to Easthope at night because it is believed to be haunted by two monks who disliked each other sufficiently to quarrel unto death!

West of Wenlock Edge is Ape Dale, a strange name for such a lovely area. It has many ancient settlements, for example at **Rushbury** there is a castle mound, and the steep road up to the Edge is called 'Roman Bank'.

ACTON SCOTT.

Towards the western end of the dale is **Acton Scott Historic Working Farm** which demonstrates farming and rural life as practised in the South Shropshire hills at the close of the 19th century. It is a living museum with a commitment to preserving both traditional farming techniques and rural craft skills. Visitors can witness the daily workings of the farm as washday gets under way and the bread oven if fired up ready for bread and pies at the Bailiff's Cottage. The Waggoner and his team of heavy horses provide the power to work the land while the stocksperson cares for the farm's livestock including a range of rare breeds. The blacksmith and wheelwright maintain an extensive collection of fully working period implements and machines.

The museum is based in what was once the Home Farm of the Acton Scott estate. The range of buildings grouped around the farmyard provides an unspoilt environment for the museum, with daily demonstrations of farming functions such as handmilking, buttermaking and feed processing machinery fully restored and driven by an iron horse gin. Many special events take place throughout the year including demonstrations and talks with some hand-on opportunities. Children love to get at close quarters with the animals and there is a great variety for them to meet on the farm.. Out in the fields, look out for lambing, shearing, cider making and threshing with steam and flail.

The School House Cafe is located in what was the village school built in the 1860s. It serves a range of light meals, luncheons and afternoon teas which can also be enjoyed in the cottage garden. We are able only to scratch the surface of the many attractions, in the space available here - visitors will find so much to interest them at Acton Farm which offers such an insight and education into our past heritage.

Acton Scott Historic Working Farm, Wenlock Lodge, Acton Scott, Nr. Church Stretton, Shropshire. Tel: 01694 781306.

CHURCH STRETTON.

Church Stretton is a town that looks old, indeed it is, and there has been a market here since King John granted a Charter in 1214. The market is not very big today, but choose a Thursday to visit and the market will be in full swing in the square. Many of the black and white timbered buildings look medieval, but in fact are not. They were built around the turn of the century when the town had ideas of becoming a health resort.

Remains of the medieval town are in High Street, once part of the old Bristol to Chester road, an important coaching route. There are some genuinely old buildings here sitting amidst the 18th and 19th century buildings, which are both half timbered and more conventionally Georgian and Victorian.

The High Street features a box of delights at the quaintly named **Dappled Duck.** This lovely gift shop is owned and run by Anne Halliburton who stocks an amazing selection of quality gifts and crafts all individually selected and beautifully displayed. As the shop name might suggest, there are ducks of every conceivable shape and size, made from wood, porcelain, papier maché and soft fabric. Teddy bears and soft toys are always a popular choice for presents, as are the limited edition prints depicting local scenes. Customers travel a long way just for Anne's superb collection of fine art postcards and greeting cards. A stockist of hard-to-find Okra glass, she also sells items of jewellery, various minerals, rocks and crystals as well as a comprehensive Beatrix Potter range, making this the ideal place to find your holiday and 'occasion' presents. The prices cover a wide range and customers are sure to find something to suit their budget. Telephone enquiries are welcome.

The Dappled Duck, 57 High Street, Church Stretton, Shropshire.
Tel: 01694 723913.

The Church of St. Laurence sits just behind the High Street. Built on a Saxon foundation, it has a Norman nave and a tower that was built about 1200. Above the doorway in the north wall is the sheel-na-gig.

Over the aisle is a memorial to a tragic event that happened in 1968 when three boys died in a hotel fire. The memorial takes the form of a gridiron with twisted flakes of copper simulating flames. The gridiron is the symbol of St. Laurence, who was burnt to death on one in AD258.

The Victorian novelist, Sarah Smith, who wrote under the name 'Hesba Stretton', has a small memorial window in the south transept dedicated to her. She was a constant visitor to All Stretton, and the figure in green on the window represents her book 'Jessica's First Prayer'.

If you like Victorian at its most decorative, then you will love Sandford Avenue. It is wide and spacious and was created by the Reverend Holland Sandford in 1884. It was here in the Crown Inn that the three boys died. It never became a hotel again and most of the building has now been converted into shops and flats, but a pub still called The Hotel does a busy trade.

Tucked away above the Four Seasons shop in the town you will discover a 'hidden gem' called **Acorn Wholefood Restaurant and Coffee Shop.** Specialising in all kinds of wholefoods and vegetarian dishes, visitors here can choose from an imaginative and tasty selection of homecooked fare which on fine days can be enjoyed in the outdoor tea garden. They specialise in many and varied home baked original recipes of cakes and are well known for their selection of more than thirty different flavours of Tea. It is now a totally non-smoking establishment. Chris Bland is the welcoming hostess who, together with her friendly team of staff, offers fast and efficient service in a warm, relaxed atmosphere, ensuring complete satisfaction for her many customers. Open five days a week from 9.30am until 6.00pm - On Sundays and Bank Holidays the hours are 10am to 6pm. - closed on Tuesday and Wednesday (except school holidays).

Acorn Wholefood Restaurant and Coffee Shop, 26 Sandford Avenue, Church Stretton. Tel: 01694 722495.

Town Hall, Bridgnorth

Church Stretton is actually three settlements in one. **Little Stretton** stands one and a half miles south of the town and has a number of fine timber-framed buildings, some genuine and some, like All Saints Church, not what they seem. It is a beautiful church with its trim thatch, Gothic windows and close-set timbers but it was actually built in 1903.

The delightful **Green Dragon Inn** can be found on the southern edge of Little Stretton, on the B4370 close to its junction with the A49. With its exposed oak beams and unusual collection of antique horse brasses, this handsome 250 year-old inn is renowned for its genuine character and charm. It is owned and run by Janet and Bill Reynolds, ably assisted by daughter Marie and son-in-law John, very friendly hosts who provide a warm welcome, a fine selection of cask-conditioned ales and superb food, served either in the bar or in the charming atmosphere of the 40-seater restaurant.

Green Dragon Inn, Ludlow Road, Little Stretton, Shropshire
Tel: 01694 722925

All Stretton is said to have got its name because James I needed to distinguish between the three when he visited. He is supposed to have arrived at Little Stretton, and gave it that name; then he went on to name Church Stretton because of the Norman church, and when he finally reached the village, he remarked, 'It's all Stretton hereabouts.'

Wherever you go you are reminded of the town's growth in the late 19th and early 20th centuries, when it was endeavouring to establish itself as a health resort. It certainly had natural springs of pure water equal to any in the country. The Victorians enjoyed the town more because of its bracing and exhilarating surroundings. The scenery is superb, with Carding Mill Valley between Long Mynd to the west and Caer Caradoc opposite.

Carding Mill Valley, which belongs to the National Trust, is a lovely place about a mile from the town centre, taking its name from an old mill, now demolished. To get to it you walk along an attractive cul-de-sac road that winds its way up the hillside.

AROUND CHURCH STRETTON.

Approximately five miles from Church Stretton in the parish of Rushbury, surrounded by Roman history, lies Gilberries cottage, enjoying views of the famous Wenlock Edge and distant Clee Hills. The cottage is centrally heated, with one large double or family room and one twin bedroom, both with radio and tea making facilities. The lounge and dining room with colour television and log fire is available for guests at any time providing a warm and friendly atmosphere in which to relax. A full English breakfast is served at a time to suit the convenience of guests. The cottage is adjacent to the family farm and features a large lawned garden surrounded by open fields. The local countryside is ideal for walking and motorists are within easy reach of many places of interest. ETB - 1 Crown Commended.

Gilberries Cottage, Wall-under-Heywood, Church Stretton.
Tel: 01694 771400

LEEBOTWOOD.

Travel a few miles north on the A49 to Leebotwood, and there discover The Pound Inn and Restaurant, one of the very few thatched properties in the county. Built circa 1500, it was originally used to 'hold' animals on their journey to market. On becoming an inn in 1804 The Pound started to brew its own ale. It was originally kept by the Dodd family and their relatives between 1806-1916. Having had various owners since then, it has been owned and run by Michael and Joan Ebrey since 1994 and more recently assisted by their son Simon. The Pound Inn is a true 'picture postcard' inn, its white exterior contrasting with the mellow thatch. Inside are old beams in profusion, polished brasses, a glint of copper, old prints and photographs and an old world atmosphere. But the food and real ale is the big attraction at The Pound. Head Chef Mike Shaw, creates a fine and varied selection of traditional and Vegetarian dishes, served either in the Restaurant or bar lounge seven days a week; the Sunday Carvery Lunch being especially popular. All food is freshly prepared and of excellent quality.

The Pound Inn, Leebotwood, Shropshire.   Tel: 01694 751255.

FRODESLEY.

A little further north, turn off the A49 and head towards **Longnor** and on to **Frodesley** which lies on a Roman road just a few miles from the remains of the Roman city of Viroconium. In this village you will find **Meadowlands,** where Ron and Jennie offer bed and breakfast in their comfortable home. It's an ideal location for discovering Shropshire and the Welsh Marshes and lies in an area of Outstanding Natural Beauty in the heart of Cadfael country. Meadowlands lies on a quiet lane adjacent to the church with its 13th century bells (the oldest in Shropshire), the Tithe Barn and Medieval Pound. The accommodation at Meadowlands includes double and family rooms providing for a total of six guests. There are two lounges, one with television. You can enjoy a hearty breakfast and in the evening eat at the local pub. Ron and Jennie are happy to share their knowledge of the local area and can supply maps and guide books as well as arrange itineraries for you. Just a mile and a half away is **Acton Burnell** where Parliament met in King Edward 1's time. It has a small but picturesque castle, while just three miles away lie two outstanding Elizabethan Manor houses - Pichford Hall and Condover Hall..

Meadowlands, Lodge Lane, Frodesley, Nr. Longnor, Shropshire.
Tel: 01694 731350

Before getting to Bishop's Castle, the next destination, you'll get some good views of Long Mynd (pronounced like pinned). Long Mynd is redeemed by the several lovely valleys like Ashes Hollow and Carding Mill Valley where the abundance of dancing hawthorn and bilberries makes it a special place, and the walk along the stream with its little waterfall called Light Spout is a joy.

Church Stretton Golf Course, one of the highest in the country, is just north of the Carding Mill Valley, where Bodbury Hill still has the marks of a circular encampment. If you play the course, when you get to the eleventh tee stop and look at the glorious views across the valley. You almost need oxygen to play the fourteenth hole, because here on the green you will find yourself about twelve hundred feet above sea level.

RATLINGHOPE.

The tranquil hamlet of **Ratlinghope** lies between Long Mynd and The Striperstones and it was here, on a lovely sunny day when the dappled sunlight fell across the picturesque Shropshire country lanes, we came across **Lower Stitt Farm.** Overlooking open rolling countryside, this clean white house with its colourful shrubs and plants is the wonderful home of Brian and Ann who provide outstanding bed and breakfast accommodation. Set in a 209 acre working animal farm, though the visitor will see no evidence of this upon arrival, it makes a delightful stop-off point where you can be assured of a wonderful stay. Once the site of a Hermitage, Ann will be happy to relate its history. The rooms are beautiful and the hospitality excellent. E.T.B. - 1 Crown Commended.

Lower Stitt Farm, Ratlinghope, Shrewsbury, Shropshire SY5 0SN.
Tel: 01588 650640.

The little village of **Asterton** nearby, is a natural home for The Midland Gliding Club. You can watch members taking off from the Mynd's western escarpment, soaring like eagles over the valley between Long Mynd and Stiperstones.

WENTNOR.

You may have to search a little to find **The Inn On The Green;** it's in the little village of **Wentnor** between Shrewsbury and Bishop's Castle which lies adjacent to Asterton. Surrounded on every side by scenic countryside, the inn is owned and personally run by Ian and Sue Butt. Blending well with its surroundings, the 'L' shape design of the building with its smart white exterior walls and neat shrubs and plants gives the inn a welcoming appearance.

The Inn On The Green

Equally well presented inside, there's a real feeling of hospitality as you enter. The Inn On The Green is well known for its good company and excellent selection of food and drink. Saturday night is Country and Western night in the lounge bar and on Sundays there is a very popular Carvery in the restaurant - bookings are advisable. Closed lunchtimes during the winter - October to Easter (except Sundays when open all day).

The Inn On The Green, Wentnor, Nr. Bishop's Castle, Shropshire.
Tel: 01588 650498.

Caught at the right time of year, the hanging baskets and climbing plants and shrubs add a blaze of colour to the 17th century **Crown Inn** in the village. David and Jane Carr are your hosts and offer a full a'la carte menu in their restaurant which is open seven days a week with a good selection of fresh home cooked food. Optional lighter meals and sandwiches are served at the bar at lunchtime if preferred. There is a good choice of food available with availability of lighter snacks if preferred. The four guest bedrooms are large and comfortable and you can expect a peaceful night's sleep in this quiet village. A Free House, the Crown serves Real Ales, ciders, lager and a choice selection of fine wines and malts. Excellent hospitality.

The Crown Inn, Wentnor, Shropshire. Tel: 01588 650436

There are not many village greens in Shropshire, but one is to be found in the pretty village of **Minton** which lies, almost hidden, in the quiet lanes below the eastern slopes of Long Mynd. The village dates back to Saxon times and there is a castle mound still to be seen.

BISHOP'S CASTLE.

Bishop's Castle today, has neither a Bishop nor a castle, but it is a delightful little town at the heart of the Border hill country. It is classed as a conservation area, not because it is full of architectural gems, though there are several, but for the range of façades. There are half-timbered Elizabethan houses, some beautiful Georgian houses, and the elegance of the best of the Victorian era.

The Bishop of Hereford built a castle on a site in 1127, to protect his sheep pastures against raids by Welshmen from across the nearby border. All that is there now is a few stones round a bowling green.

One thing that may strike you forcibly is that chain-stores do not seem to have bothered Bishop's Castle. The town is a haven of family businesses which seem to thrive. The people are friendly and there is a great informality about the place.

In its heyday, it was a 'rotten borough' under the patronage of Clive of India with two Members of Parliament, and though it lost its MPs in 1832, there is still great pride in the 18th century town hall and its neighbouring House on Crutches, both rescued from dereliction by the people of Bishop's Castle. A pretty stalwart effort from a population of less than two thousand. (The House on Crutches is so called because its upper storey is supported by posts).

The Old Brick Guest House, Church Street, Bishop's Castle, Shropshire.
Tel: 01588 638471

In the heart of Bishop's Castle on Main Street is **The Old Brick Guest House.** Here Peter and Phyllis Hutton have offered quality bed and breakfast accommodation for many years. There is a friendly and homely atmosphere in this house, built in the 1720's. The garden produces a good supply of fruit and vegetables, which are used in the kitchen for cooking, and also in home-made preserves and chutney. All the bedrooms are en-

Bridgnorth Castle

suite and have central heating, colour television and hot drinks facilities. Guests have their own lounge with an attractive inglenook fireplace and evening meals can be provided upon request. There's a nice terraced garden and easy parking. For the benefit of walkers and cyclists, the owners will arrange to transfer luggage up to a radius of twenty miles. Children, disabled guests and dogs are welcome.

Should you prefer your food and accommodation in the congenial atmosphere of a 'local', then try **The King's Head,** a friendly pub and eating place standing on Church Street in the heart of Bishop's Castle. Since taking over in 1989, Proprietors Pam and Ken Gardner have created a delightful atmosphere which is welcoming to visitors and locals alike. The front bar is geared to lively socialising, while the rear bar, with its wood-burning stove, exposed stone walls, beamed ceilings and unusual display of antique china, is cosy and intimate. Equally inviting is the Duck 'n' Steak restaurant, a delightful eating place housed in the former stables which offers a varied menu, with steaks and roast duck a speciality. Pam and Ken also have four comfortable letting bedrooms available all year round.

King's Head, Church Street, Bishop's Castle, Shropshire   Tel: 01588 638816

CLUNGUNFORD.

Well know author A.E. Housman is quoted as saying that 'Clunton, Clunbury, Clungunford and Clun are the quietest places under the sun'. The villages have changed since Housman's time but the countryside is still peaceful although it is an area where it is advisable to have your wellies. **Clungunford** sits almost atop of the country borderline in the south. Much of the village has moved towards the main road and to higher ground to get away from the torrent of water that descends from the hillside after heavy rain, or when the snow thaws. The streams get swollen, and it is not unusual for the River Onny and the River Clun to burst their banks and flood the meadows on either side.

A unique establishment well worth making the effort to find is the **Bird on the Rock,** a delightful tearoom, plant nursery and B & B which lies on the B4367 Knighton road out of Clungunford. Owned and personally-run by Sheila and Reece Mytton from their superb 17th-century black and white timbered cottage, the tearoom has a wonderful atmosphere, with stone-flagged floors and antique furnishings. The bed and breakfast room is luxurious, with a large en suite bathroom and romantic half-tester bed. The nursery has a lovely range of traditional garden perennials for sale, many of which can be seen growing around the cottage. Open daily, 10am to 6pm, all year round (closed Mondays, except Bank Holidays).

Bird on the Rock, Clungunfod, Near Craven Arms, Shropshire
Tel: 01588 660631

Clunbury has a delightful church, St. Swithin, with a short, stubby tower and the focal point of this, the quietest of the four villages. Though not one of Housman's Cluns **Aston on Clun** is well worthy of a mention. Their Arbor Tree dressing Ceremony is the last in England and has taken place every year since 1786.

Following the battle of Worcester in 1651, as chronicled, King Charles fleeing from the Roundheads hid in an oak at Boscobel. To commemorate his escape he proclaimed Arbor Day (a day in May) as a national holiday when tree dressing took place. This custom died out but was revived in 1786 in Aston-on-Clun when a local landowner married. As Aston was part of his family estate he revived the custom of dressing the Black Poplar in the centre of the village, a custom which survives to this day.

Clun Castle

Clunton is right on the main road, and has nothing much to offer, except it leads on to **Clun**. Across the river from the modern village is the fine church of St. George, on rising ground. It has a fortress-like tower with the smallest of windows, and whose sturdiness is complemented by the lovely 17th century tiered pyramidal top. There are also some wonderful Norman arcades with circular pillars and scalloped capitals. The 14th century north aisle roof and restored nave roof keep your eyes pointing heavenward for some time - it really is impressive.

There's some wonderful Jacobean woodwork and a marvellous medieval canopy, studded with bosses, over the altar too. G.E. Street restored this lovely church in 1876 and did it supremely well. The church is open most day during daylight hours.

The medieval bridge across the river, takes you to the ruins of the imposing 13th century castle, where only the keep remains standing, but you can see from the earthworks its original extent. It was ruined many times in its history, and rebuilt because Clun was always the centre of the centuries-long tug-of-war between England and Wales.

CHAPTER FOUR

Worcester and the Malverns

Worcester Cathedral

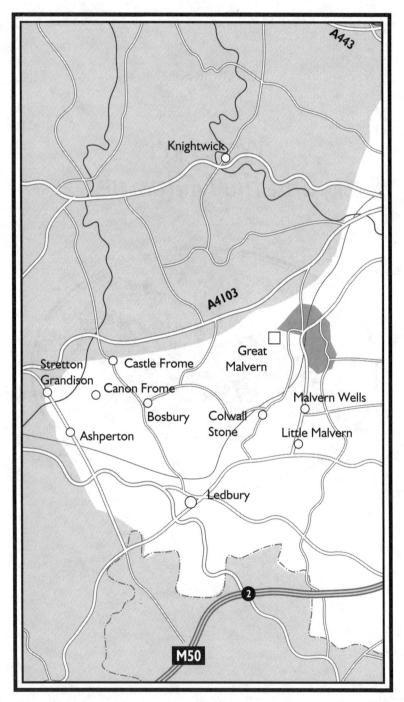

Knightwick

A443

A4103

Stretton
Grandison

Castle Frome

Canon Frome

Bosbury

Ashperton

Great
Malvern

Colwall
Stone

Malvern Wells

Little Malvern

Ledbury

2

M50

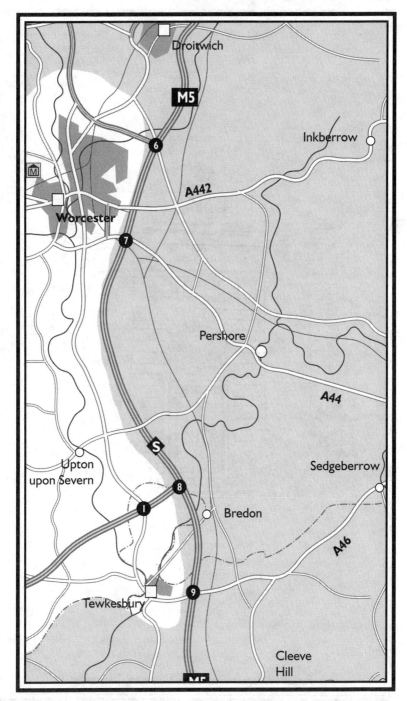

Royal Worcester Porcelain Museum, Worcester

CHAPTER FOUR

Worcester and the Malverns

WORCESTER.

The visitor to Worcester is offered an unending choice of attractions and places of interest to visit. Combining so many fascinating insights into its past with areas for restful interludes such as Spetchley Park Gardens, the City Art Gallery and Elgar's Birthplace, to name but a few.

From Worcestershire County Cricket Club, a superb vista unfolds across the beautiful grounds with fabulous views of Worcester Cathedral in the distance.

Flowing through the heart of the city is the River Severn affording the many delights of the waterside. There are leisurely walks; boat trips and boats for hire. The swans are always a waiting audience seeking their daily bread! For the more adventurous, a balloon trip awaits with spectacular views of the City.

Set on either side of the curving River Severn **Worcester** is a bustling county capital and Cathedral city. The city's architectural ventures span five centuries and there are some marvellous examples of these to be seen.

Standing in the heart of England, this is an area characterised by red earth, apple orchards, hopyards, quiet inns, stone farms and black-and-white timbered houses. As a visible legacy of the ancient forest that once surrounded Worcester, the half-timbered buildings lend colour and variety to the villages surrounding this historic city.

A good place to begin your journey is the **Cathedral**, an obvious starting point when you consider how well it reflects much of the city's early history. The crypt is the oldest surviving building in Worcester, a relic of the cathedral begun in 1084 by St. Wulstan. He was the only English bishop not to be replaced by a Norman after the Conquest, and his church was by no means the first. The masonry from which the crypt was built came originally from St. Oswald's Benedictine priory which was founded in 961 AD, and records show that a church must have existed as early as 680 AD when the first Bishop of Worcester was enthroned.

To many of the local people, it must have seemed that the building work for the present cathedral would never finish - the central tower collapsed in 1175 and a fire destroyed much of the building in 1203. The Cathedral had only just been rededicated after these disasters when Bishop Blois began pulling it down again, only to rebuild it in the fashionable Gothic style.

It wasn't until much later during the 14th century that the nave was rebuilt, under the auspices of Bishop Cobham. The south side was not to be completed until much later, and in a far less elaborate style.

Prior to his death in 1216, King John requested that he be buried in the choir, and his tomb is to be found before the High Altar. It is a masterpiece of medieval sculpture, showing the King flanked by the Bishops Oswald and Wulstan. This magnificent piece of craftsmanship is reputed to be the oldest Royal effigy in England.

The choir stalls are equally impressive. Designed by Sir George Gilbert Scott, they incorporate the misericords from the original stalls of 1397, a superb collection of scenes from scripture and fable, rich in detail and depicting scenes from everyday life. A visit to the cloisters will reveal further examples of carvings, and the quietness here enables visitors to imagine how once upon a time, the monks would sit on the stone benches waiting to receive their visitors. The north range, which leads to the Chapter House, was built around 1120. It is, along with the crypt, the most complete example of Norman architecture to have survived here.

Having wandered around the awe inspiring Cathedral for some time, you may then decide to investigate a few of Worcester's many other attractions. The town centre and shopping precinct have a wealth of interesting features and attractive shops. Accessed from The Shambles, Mealcheapen Street and New Street, Reindeer Court offers quality shopping with many designer shops and is a delightful place to browse. A marvellous bronze statue of one of Worcester's most respected citizens, Edward Elgar, stands tall and proud, serving as a reminder that the town is synonymous with the sound of classical and choir music. The Elgar Trail is a route which should not be forgotten, and we will go into a little more detail about this famous composer further on in the chapter.

The King Charles 11 Restaurant is one of Worcester's most historic houses. It was from this house that King Charles made his escape through the back door closely pursued by Cromwell's forces to exile in France, after being defeated at the battle of Worcester in 1651. The Restaurant itself boasts a dungeon on the ground floor and in the upstairs bar, reputed to have been the King's bedchamber, you may relax and order over a drink.

Meals are presented in the ground floor restaurant with full silver service. Open fires in winter, lace tablecloths, crystal glasses and candles at dinner all add to the excellent atmosphere of this restaurant. International dishes are served and there's an excellent value table d'hôte luncheon menu. Mrs Buckley is the owner of this fine restaurant which is open from 12 noon until 2.00 p.m. & 6.30pm until 9.30pm. Closed on Sundays.

King Charles II Restaurant

The King Charles 11 Restaurant, New Street, Worcester. Tel: 01905 22449

Friar Street has many lovely old timber houses that over the years have been sensitively restored. **Greyfriars** and the **Tudor House** are museums definitely worth a visit, and they are situated in a fine example of a 16th century street. Greyfriars is a medieval house that has managed to survive right in the heart of the town and passing through its archway, visitors will be enchanted by the carefully restored house and pretty walled garden beyond. The Tudor House also enables visitors to glimpse, through its static displays, aspects of domestic and social life in Worcester from Elizabethan times.

The next port of call is to the **City Museum and Art Gallery** in Foregate Street. Exhibited here is contemporary art and displays of archaeology, natural history and the military collections of the Worcestershire Regiment and Worcestershire Yeomanry. Newly opened, there is also a café serving light refreshments for visitors to enjoy. After leaving the Museum and Art Gallery, we recommend you pay a visit to **The Cornmarket** in New Street, and discover the well established and colourful open air market, with a huge range of merchandise for sale.

Dominating the High Street is the imposing **Guildhall**, a marvellous example of Queen Anne architecture designed by a local man Thomas White. Built between 1721 and 1723, at a cost of £3727, the Guildhall is a handsome building of brick with elaborate and extensive stone dressings. Two large Corinthian pillars support a splendid carving which includes the Hanoverian coat of arms.

A sumptuous interior which contains an elegant Assembly Room complements the outside and is well worth a visit. Entrance is free.

The Guildhall, High Street, Worcester

The Commandery Civil War Centre, in the City, is a delightful 15th century timber-framed building containing a dramatic museum, dedicated to England's turbulent Civil War history. The Commandery was established as the Hospital of St. Wulstan in the late 11th century and it contained a monastic order who ministered to the sick and poor of the City. The monks also provided shelter for those who had the misfortune to be shut outside the city gates at night.

After the dissolution of the monasteries, the hospital was suppressed and then sold to the Royalist Wylde family who made The Commandery their home for 200 years. It was subsequently a school for the blind and a printing works, until it was finally purchased by the City Council in 1973

Worcester witnessed the final battle of the Civil War between Charles II and Oliver Cromwell in 1651. The Commandery became the Royalists' headquarters and so was ideally suited as the location for a museum entirely dedicated to telling the fascinating tale of England's traumatic civil war. There are numerous dramatic displays within the Civil War Centre, including interactive video screens coupled with plenty of 'hands on' opportunities in the magnificent Great Hall, and a reconstruction of Charles I's trial, where members of the public become jurors and seal the King's fate. The displays culminate in a hauntingly realistic video presentation of the Battle of Worcester.

The Commandery also has its own Civil War soldiers, The Worcester

Militia, who assist with some of the many special events that take place every year. A gift shop, on site tea rooms and attractive grounds further help make The Commandery a fascinating venue to visit. Open all year except Christmas Day and Boxing Day from 10.00 until 5.00, Monday to Saturday, and from 1.30 until 5.30 on Sundays.

The Commandery, Civil War Centre, Sidbury, Worcester
Tel: 01905 355071

One place that visitors must visit is the **Royal Worcester Porcelain and The Dyson Perrins Museum**. Royal Worcester is Britain's oldest continuous producer of porcelain, and they are world famous for their exquisite Fine Bone China. The factory was founded in 1751 by Dr John Wall with the intention 'to create a ware of a form so precise as to be easily distinguished from other English porcelain'. Today this tradition still flourishes and Royal Worcester's unique range of fine china and porcelain remains unsurpassed throughout the world.

In the magnificent collection at the Dyson Perrins Museum you can see some of the finest treasures from this unique artistic heritage, including the celebrated Wigornia cream jug made in 1751, and the 1893 Chicago Exhibition Vase, at 4' 6" high the largest piece of porcelain ever made at Worcester and which took over a year to produce. The museum is open from 9.30am to 5pm Monday to Friday and from 10am to 5pm on Saturdays.

After seeing the museum it is well worth taking a factory tour, which gives an opportunity to learn some of the secrets of Royal Worcester's success. You will see skilled hands shaping and moulding, painting and finishing - a delight to watch. Helpful guides take you through the many processes and enjoy answering questions. Tours take about 45 minutes and are at regular intervals throughout the day and it is recommended you telephone ahead to ensure your place. There is also a connoisseurs

Worcester Guildhall

tour that last two hours to cater for more specialist interests, and which includes morning coffee or afternoon tea. There are two factory shops, one offers the complete range of current designs and the other contains many items that have failed to meet the factory's exacting standards. After all this there is the restaurant, open throughout the day and the perfect place to take break.

Royal Worcester Porcelain Ltd, Severn Street, Worcester
Tel: 01905 23221

Reindeer Court Shopping Centre, Worcester

AROUND WORCESTER.
LOWER BROADHEATH.

From Worcester, taking the A443, then turning onto the B4204, you will reach **Lower Broadheath**. Edward William Elgar was born here in 1857 in the cottage that is now his museum. He was the son of Roman Catholic parents, his father being the organist at St. George's Catholic Church in Worcester and the family also had a music shop in Worcester High Street.

In the latter part of the 19th century, Elgar earned his living teaching the unwilling daughters of gentlefolk to play the fiddle and the piano. Elgar's wife, Caroline, was a source of great inspiration to him - she believed in his work implicitly and encouraged him throughout their life together.

By the time Elgar had reached the age of 72, he had composed his greatest works - Enigma Variations, The Dream of Gerontius, The Kingdom and The Apostles, two symphonies, the Introduction and Allegro and Serenade for Strings, the concertos for violin and cello and the chamber works. With these went the Pomp and Ceremony Marches

No's 1 to 5 and many other smaller pieces. Elgar's beloved wife died in 1919 and after that he did not write anything of significance again.

As he lay dying in 1934, this incredible man supervised the recording of his works with the aid of a telephone. It is these recordings which enable us to gauge the interpretive genius of a man whose compositions were to play such an important role in classical, choral and chamber music both in this country and in Europe as a whole. Today, Elgar's life and works are remembered, through the many music festivals that take place across the region.

The 'Elgar Trail', is a specially produced cassette that guides you around Elgar's Worcestershire, visiting the peaceful spots where he sought inspiration, the houses where he lived and the buildings which shaped his musical life. Sixty-three special signposts lead visitors around the 45 mile trail which the composer himself once enjoyed while cycling.

GREAT MALVERN.

Heading south, passing through some charming little villages and hamlets, brings you to **Great Malvern**. As you approach the town, in the distance you will be able to see the Malvern Hills. At the northern end of the chain, Worcestershire Beacon at 1,394ft above sea level is the Malverns' highest point. Paths of pinkish gravel lead steeply up from the edge of Great Malvern through a valley which is lightly wooded with birch. A vast panorama can be seen from the summit, extending westwards to the Black Mountains, north to the Wrekin, east to Edge Hill and south to the Herefordshire Beacon. Far beyond, the Mendips in Somerset can be seen.

Scattered outcrops of rock pierce the turf at the highest point, and date back 600 million years. The geology of this formation is hard crystalline and impossible to dissolve by rainwater, this accounts for the local springs, synonymous with the internationally renowned and ever healthy Malvern Spring Water.

One of the most attractive hotels in the area can be found nestling beneath the Malvern Hills in the heart of Great Malvern. Originally built around 1730 and now a listed building, the **Mount Pleasant Hotel** is an elegant example of early Georgian redbrick architecture. It was first converted to a hotel in the 1850s when Malvern became a fashionable spa town and the home of the infamous 'cold water cure'. Now tastefully modernised, its fifteen guest bedrooms are equipped with en suite bathrooms, colour televisions, direct-dial telephones and several thoughtful extras. Owned and personally-run by Sol and Geoff Payne, the Mount Pleasant has an informal atmosphere with an emphasis on relaxation, comfort and personal attention. The lounge bar offers an extensive food menu and a range of traditional ales, and there is also an intimate coffee shop and an elegant restaurant serving a selection of

Spanish, international and traditional English dishes. English Tourist Board 4 crown commended, the Mount Pleasant is set within one-and-a-half acres of attractive terraced gardens which offer some of the most scenic views in the area. Photographs of the hotel and its grounds have been chosen for tourist publications of every type, from Ordnance Survey maps to national tourist guides.

Mount Pleasant Hotel, Belle Vue Terrace, Great Malvern, Worcestershire
Tel: 01684 561837 Fax: 01684 569968

The importance of the Malverns can best be summed up by using the local authorities planning jargon: "a valuable asset and recreational source" - they attract casual walkers as well as veterans of the northern fells. Young guides, scouts and cadets receive their first taste of adventure on the slopes and pilgrims mix with sponsored walkers and marathon trainees. Artists come to paint the outstanding views and hang-gliding enthusiasts float across the horizon. Langland once stated: "They are gentle hills, perfect for the reluctant mountaineer who likes to feel up on top of the world, but doubts his abilities to tackle more challenging peaks."

Beneath the northern slopes of the hills, **Great Malvern** is renowned for its annual music and drama festivals, Boehm Porcelain and, of course, Morgan cars. Close to the start of the Malvern walking trail, in the town, is a Regency cottage housing one source of the famous Malvern water - St. Annes Well - which was built in 1815 to dispense water to thirsty visitors. During the 19th century, Great Malvern owed its prosperity to the vogue for taking medicinal waters and water cures. Today, it is a fine example of a former Victorian spa town, with handsome buildings and leafy evergreens. Priory Park was once a familiar favourite for the nobility and gentry, who would promenade in their finery after taking the waters.

The Malvern Festival Theatre and Winter Gardens Complex is an entertainment complex which attracts plenty of big name stars to the area. It is well supported by the local community and is an extremely popular venue. The programme of events is varied, so if you're staying in town, why not ring ahead and get tickets for a show.

At the beautifully restored Great Malvern Railway Station, you will find Lady Foley's Tea Room and the Brief Encounter Restaurant. Lady Emily Foley was a local landowner and Lady of the Manor of Malvern in the mid-1800s. She was largely responsible for the planning of Great Malvern, and by insisting on large prestigious houses and landscaped gardens, created the unique townscape that you see today. The Brief Encounter restaurant, has a more obvious origin, named after the famous film of the same name. Amusingly, some of the dishes are named after the characters, so why not try Trevor's Treat or Celia's Downfall!

A visit to **Boehm of Malvern** is essential when in the area, and it can be found in Tanhouse Lane. They have earned worldwide acclaim for the very fine porcelain that the Boehm craftsmen have been creating for over thirty years. Edward Marshall Boehm (pronounced 'Beam') founded the studios, and has without doubt poured his passion of the world of nature into porcelain and brought it to life.

While here, you learn the fascinating history of this American, a former veterinarian's assistant, turned artist and naturalist, also about his remarkable wife, who was the backbone of his successful career; with good business sense and great enthusiasm, she has succeeded in keeping his memory alive.

It's an absolutely fascinating day and most visitors would return without hesitation. It is definitely worth a visit for anyone who appreciates the beauty of craftsmanship.

Boehm of Malvern, Great Malvern

Situated within the shadow of Malvern Abbey and just outside the Abbey gates, is a fascinating historic building reflecting the architecture of the Abbey and housing **Cridlan's Licensed Brasserie and Restaurant.** Established in 1830 as a butchers shop when Mr Cridlan from London and Mr. Walker, a local man, became partners. It remained a Butchers shop until quite recently "supplying families on most reasonable terms" which included in its earlier days, Princess Victoria, the then future Queen, who took supplies quite regularly.

The exterior has hardly changed since the 1880's and even retains its original signboard. The Chef Patron of Cridlan's is Trevor Hodgetts who maintains this well established business location in its new form. During the day, the Brasserie provides an extensive menu from speciality sandwiches to Cordon Bleu Continental and British style dishes. From 5.30pm the Restaurant serves a Pre-Theatre Dinner Menu and a full a'la Carte Menu. Whenever you visit Cridlan's you will find a most agreeable ambience and it offers a real change of quality and cuisine from the norm. Start with a glass of wine at one of the outside tables and let the flavour and imagination of Cridlan's carry you along.

Cridlan's, 23 Abbey Road, Malvern, Worcs. Tel: 01684 562676.

COLWALL.

Following the road south brings you to **Colwall** on the west side of the Malverns. Its chief claim to fame being the enormous lump of limestone which stands in the centre of the village. No one seems quite sure who or what was responsible for leaving it there, but it has been variously blamed on the Devil and on a giant from the Malvern Hills with matrimonial problems. He solved these, apparently, by stoning his wife to death in the village!

In the centre of the village of Colwall, and quite unmissable, is a splendid piece of Edwardian architecture in the form of the **Colwall Park Hotel**. It appears odd at first that such an impressive building should be found in this small community, but apparently the hotel was built at the time when Colwall had its own National Hunt Racecourse and was used by the owners and trainers. Nowadays there is no racecourse, but interestingly enough there is a railway station adjacent to the hotel with direct lines to Birmingham and London Paddington.

Beneath the red tiled roof which provides a vivid splash of colour amidst the greenery, this is a 4 Crown Highly Commended Hotel with 23 quality en-suite bedrooms in which careful attention has given to re-creating an overall theme of an English country house. Much of the period detail has been retained, while providing guests with every modern convenience. There are delightful, well tended gardens to enjoy, and for those wishing to venture further afield, the Western Malvern Hills are outside your door. The food is best English fare, well cooked and presented with a good choice for Vegetarians. This is a high quality establishment ideal as a base from which so much wonderful countryside is easily reached. Egon Ronay recommended. AA & RAC - Three Star.

The Colwall Park Hotel, Walwyn Road, Colwall, Malvern, Worcs.
Tel: 01684 540206 Fax: 540847.

East of Colwall is the village of Malvern Wells, where the first medicinal wells were discovered in the 17th century. St. Peter's church was built in 1836 and some of the stained glass still remaining is of this date. Also of interest is the William Morris stained glass window of 1885.

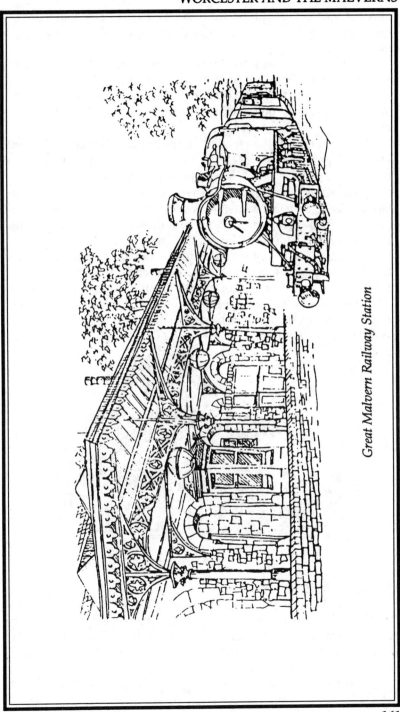

Great Malvern Railway Station

Lovers of the game of golf will also be interested to note that there is a very adequate golf course in the village as well, so don't forget your golf clubs!

The next stop is to be **Little Malvern** due south. This is where, in the **Roman Catholic Church of St. Wulstan**, Sir Edward Elgar and his wife Caroline are buried. It's a popular little church and receives many visitors. Just a little further along the road is 'Craiglea', which was Elgar's home between 1899 and 1904.

Nestling amongst the wooded slopes of the hills behind the Little Malvern Priory is **Little Malvern Court**. Since the Dissolution, the Berington Coat of Arms has remained in the hatchments, and the Berington family have continued to live here although the house is open to the public on certain days in the summer. During the 17th century, the house provided refuge for Catholic priests, and it contains concealed rooms which were ideal for the priests to hide in.

The village of **Bosbury** can be found just four miles north of Ledbury. The wide main street separates the church on one side from several early timber framed houses on the other, including the 15th century hall house with cross wings directly opposite the church. A pretty village, and a picture during the spring when blossom is on the trees as it emerges from a cold and dreary winter.

Ledbury

THE FROMES.

North of here there is a small group of villages clustered together in the Frome Valley, collectively known as **The Fromes** and in **Canon Frome** lies **Mill Cottage**, set in the most beautiful tranquil setting surrounded by established trees of variety and in a delightful situation alongside the River Frome in Herefordshire.

Away from the main roads, though within easy reach of Ledbury,

Hereford and the Malvern Hills, the 16th century home of Julian and Lorna Rutherford is many peoples' dream of a country home and is a lovely spot to enjoy bed and breakfast. There are two en-suite rooms, one with twin beds and the other with four-poster, both with television and hot drinks facilities.

A spacious wing contains a guest lounge with log fire and views towards the river. The five-acre water gardens are bisected by the River Frome. There are further streams and a mill pool. Footpaths, stepping stones and bridges lead one around an interesting, wooded garden with an abundance of wildlife. Facilities include trout and salmon fishing in the river. Two delightful self-catering cottages, one a Swiss Chalet style overlooking a waterfall, are situated in different parts of the garden.

The Swiss Cottage was built in 1838 and has recently been restored and modernised whilst Lime cottage has its own character with exposed beams and looks out over fields and a pool. The area has a number of pubs which serve good food and a grocery shop three miles away stocks a good range of provisions whilst Ledbury offers a greater selection. Book early here for your idyllic holiday setting. Swiss Cottage awarded 3 - Keys Highly Commended.

Riverside Cottages, Mill Cottage, Canon Frome, Ledbury, Herefordshire.
Tel: 01531 670506.

Castle Frome, has a fascinating church containing one of the masterpieces of the Hereford School of Norman Architecture. Its font was one of several outstanding pieces that formed part of the Haggard Gallery's English Romanesque Art Exhibition. This bold and accomplished work depicts the Baptism of Christ. Castle Frome receives a steady stream of visitors throughout the year, including many Mormons from America.

A prominent member of the Mormon community, John Benbow, emigrated from here to America in 1840. He used to live at nearby Hill Farm, and in the pond that can still be seen there, he would baptise children whose families had come to join him in the Church of Jesus Christ of Latter-Day Saints. Apparently, Mormon children are still baptised here on occasion.

ASHPERTON.

On the A417 is the tiny village of **Ashperton** and here we have a traditional country pub set in the heart of the Herefordshire countryside. **The Hopton Arms** was originally built as a Gamekeepers Lodge and was later used as an abattoir for the Manor of Ashperton. A newly converted coach house at the rear of the Hopton has five double bedrooms and one single room, all with private facilities, for bed and breakfast accommodation.

The pub has a very cosy lounge and the bar has a homely touch to it. There is an extensive bar menu as well as a Restaurant offering a wide choice of steaks and fish with any special dietary requirements catered for. To the rear of the coach house there is a two and a half acre field, ideal for ball and field games. All the equipment including a children's play area with swings, scramble net and climbing frames are supplied; enough to keep them happy for hours!

A caravan and camping site is also owned by the Hopton Arms who will happily supply further details. Situated on the A417 close to the junction of the A438 between Hereford and Malvern, which along with Worcester and Gloucester are within an easy twenty mile radius. Trout and Coarse fishing can be arranged at local fisheries. Disabled guests can be accommodated.

The Hopton Arms, Ashperton, Near Ledbury, Herefordshire. Tel: 01531 670520.

You might understandably dismiss this as a sleepy little place where nothing of any consequence could possibly occur, but you should never be fooled by appearances! A daughter of the village was instrumental in founding England's highest order of chivalry, the Order of the Garter, or so is locally claimed. It is said that Katherine Grandison, who was born in Ashperton, dropped her garter at a court ball in 1349 and was saved from her embarrassment by none other than Edward III. He picked up the garter and strapped it on his own royal leg, saying "Shame on anybody who thinks evil of this", or words to that effect.

In those days a garter was considered to be the mark of a witch, so it could be that the King's gallantry saved Katherine from more than embarrassment!

LEDBURY.

The town of **Ledbury** is midway between Great Malvern, but is much more than somewhere to be by-passed. The main street stretches for almost half a mile and is lined with quaint buildings with much character. Many of them date from the 16th century when the townspeople who worked with cloth and leather were enjoying an era of prosperity. The centre of the town is dominated by the Barrett Browning Institute of 1892, which was built in memory of Elizabeth Barrett Browning whose family lived at nearby Colwall. Alongside it are the almshouses of St. Katherine's hospital, founded in 1232 for wayfarers and the poor.

The Old Grammar School (Heritage Centre)

The Market Hall is said to have been built by the architect carpenter John Abel. It is now home to the weekly market and the October Hop Fair.

If you have not already been enchanted by Ledbury, a walk down the little narrow street that leads to the church should do the trick. The old half-timbered houses almost meet overhead, just leaving room for sight of the elegant tall spire. Looking up the narrow Church lane in Ledbury, you have a wonderful little picture-view of black and white timber-framed houses with their quaint windows on both sides of the cobbled lane, and hanging baskets and creeper flowing over walls and the church and steeple framing the picture at the end of the lane. Well worth finding to admire, as is **Mrs Muffin's Tea Shop,** found halfway along this picturesque lane. It is a 17th century house complete with original beamed ceiling. Once inside, you will take in the aroma of blends of coffees; Fresh Colombian - well rounded and mellow, Costa Rican, Kenyan, Old Java - mature and full bodied. You may be tempted by that deliciously naughty Hot Chocolate served with whipped cream and flake. Mrs Muffin's also has half a dozen different flavours of tea plus a selection of herbal teas. So far, we haven't got past the drinks! But while you sip on your chosen drink, choose from a selection of sandwiches, toasties - such as Apple and Stilton, a variety of home made cakes or if it's later in the day there's Cream Tea. You are sure to enjoy this interlude in your day. Open from mid-morning until around 5pm. Open 7 days a week from March 1st until October.

Mrs Muffin's Tea Shop, 1 Church Lane, Ledbury. Tel: 01531 633579.

Just two and a half miles outside Ledbury on the A438 Tewkesbury road, is **Eastnor Castle,** overlooking the Malvern Hills. You could be forgiven for thinking that you are looking at a medieval fortress, though Eastnor was built between 1812 and 1824 and is a major example of the great Norman and Gothic architectural revival of that time.

The first Earl Somers commissioned the building and had the courage to give the undertaking to an original and inspired young architect, Robert Smirke. The Earl wanted a magnificent baronial castle, and in Smirke's creation this is exactly what he got. The combination of inherited wealth and a judicious marriage enabled him to build a family home to impress his contemporaries and place his family firmly in the ranks of the aristocracy. An audacious and breathtaking example of 19th century 'keeping up with the Jones's'. In the first six years, 250 men working day and night used four thousand tons of stone, sixteen thousand tons of mortar and six hundred tons of timber alone.

The castle is as dramatic inside and out. A sleeping beauty for many years, unlived in and unloved, with its many treasures hidden in attics and cellars, it has been restored with grants, family money and no small measure of determination and now all its wondrous arts, furniture and decor can be viewed and enjoyed by all.

The interior is excitingly beautiful on a massive scale. A vast sixty foot high hall leads into a series of state rooms. The Gothic drawing room is spectacular-Pugin designed it and he must have relished the task. The library is totally different; here the style of the Italian Renaissance dominates and allows one to stand and take in the stunning views across the lake. On display are portraits by Van Dyck, Kneller, Romney and Watts, French and Flemish tapestries and a collection of early Victorian photographs by Julia Margaret Cameron.

In the grounds there is much to see as well. The Arboretum's trees are wonderful and include mature cedars, one variety of which was introduced by the Third Earl into the UK in the 19th century. Across the lake is a three hundred acre deer park, where you may be lucky to see the fine herd of red deer feeding contentedly, not appearing to be put out by the visitors' presence. Unsurprisingly the park has been designated a Site of Special Scientific Interest on account of its unspoilt flora and fauna. If the weather is fine, you are welcome to take advantage of the opportunity to picnic in the grounds, although if you wish you can have a delicious home-made tea served in the Old Kitchen.

Eastnor Castle, Eastnor, Ledbury. Tel: 01531 633160 Fax: 01531 631776.

Part of the park is a fine and popular caravan and camping site, and it is easy to understand why this lovely setting is much sought after for caravan rallies. Throughout the year there are many special events and the castle has been frequently used by film makers and television companies, as well as by Land Rover to test and demonstrate their vehicles.

The castle has undergone a triumphant renaissance in recent years but however grand Eastnor is, it is a house which still retains the tangible atmosphere of a home, something that leaves a lasting impression on all its many visitors and is a credit to Earl Somers' descendants, the Hervey-Bathurst family. Do discover it for yourself.

TEWKESBURY.

The old town of **Tewkesbury** lies just over the border in Gloucestershire and is theoretically outside the parameters of this book, but near enough to pay it a visit.

From the 13th to the 15th centuries, **Tewkesbury Abbey** was one of England's biggest landowners, with estates stretching as far as Fairford. This magnificent church survived because of its townsfolk, who paid Henry VIII £453 in 1539.

The medieval street plan has fortunately survived in good order. The wharfs and warehouses of a thriving inland port were built near the convergence of the Rivers Severn and Avon, and a side stream diverted to the town in the 12th century provided the power for several flour mills. One of these, the 19th century Borough Mill in Quay Street, still operates. Today, a good deal of recreation is centred around the rivers, with boat trips from the centre, sailing, fishing, and a recently built marina. While the Severn Salmon are caught in Wales, Tewkesbury plays host to the salmon before they run the weir, and for fishermen seeking something new, the little known Twaite enjoy a brief season in early summer. This herring-like shad breeds nowhere else in Britain. A little further downstream, the elver catch is huge business and not only provides good sport but income as well.

In Church Street, you'll find the **Museum of John Moore**, a local and esteemed naturalist. The Museum has been cleverly furnished in the manner of a merchant's house. Tewkesbury is also a town of festivals and fairs. Occasionally, the local people re-enact the decisive Battle of Tewkesbury, fought in what is still called Bloody Meadow. It is worth visiting and a lot of fun. In October, the streets are closed in order to celebrate Mop Fair. Originally a hiring fair when labourers and domestic servants would carry mops or tools of their trade, it is looked forward to all year long and great celebrations are held in honour of this tradition.

Upton-upon-Severn

UPTON UPON SEVERN.

North of Tewkesbury on the A4104 is the old market town of **Upton upon Severn**. It is a great favourite with those who appreciate walking along the banks of the beautiful waters of the river, which runs through the town. Picnic areas are specially designated by the riverside and you can also take a relaxing river cruise from the old quay.

The old church, which is situated by the cast-iron bridge which spans the river, has earned itself the nickname of the 'pepper pot'. This is due to its handsome tower with a distinctive copper covered cupola. This former place of worship is now a heritage centre, telling of the Civil War battles and describing the history of Upton upon Severn in its former days as a busy port.

The first records indicate that Upton was a Roman station, and the town features in the Domesday Book of 1086. It became an important medieval port, and Upton thrived and expanded when the river traffic peaked in the second half of the eighteenth century. Numerous inns, taverns & alehouses opened and closed in the old town, and in 1840 there were some 20.

From Upton upon Severn back to Worcester taking the A38, you will see the River Severn runs almost parallel to this busy main road. In Roman times, the River Severn was referred to as 'Sabrina', who was the guardian goddess of the great vale that now stretches from the Black Country to Wales.

Today, the river provides many hours of enjoyment for walkers and fishermen alike. Practically every species of British fish can be caught in the river, and the proprietors of hotels and leisure facilities are able to earn a healthy living from playing host to the many fishing associations and clubs who come here. Many of the hotels and clubs allow permits to visitors, as do the farmers who have retained their fishing rights.

And so you arrive at Worcester once again. A few attractions which must be mentioned before closing the chapter are the **Worcester County Cricket Ground**, and of course, for lovers of racing, the **Racecourse**. The fixture list runs from April until December and meetings are held on a regular basis. Cricket lovers will be familiar with the famous County Cricket Ground, and there can be few more relaxing ways to pass a summer's afternoon than watching a first class game of cricket.

Elgar's Birthplace, Lower Broadheath, Nr. Worcester

Ledbury

CHAPTER FIVE

VALE OF EVESHAM

Evesham

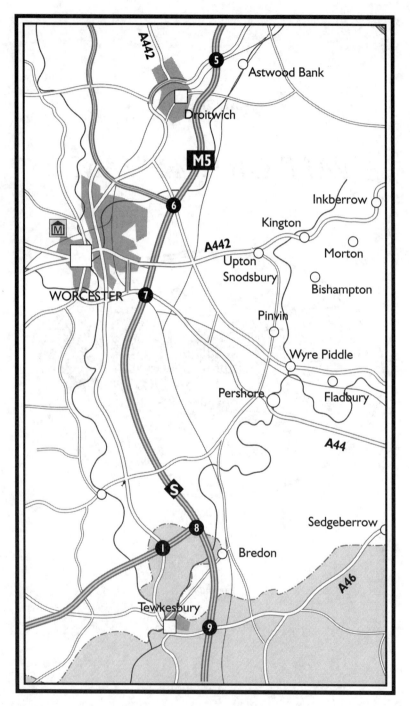

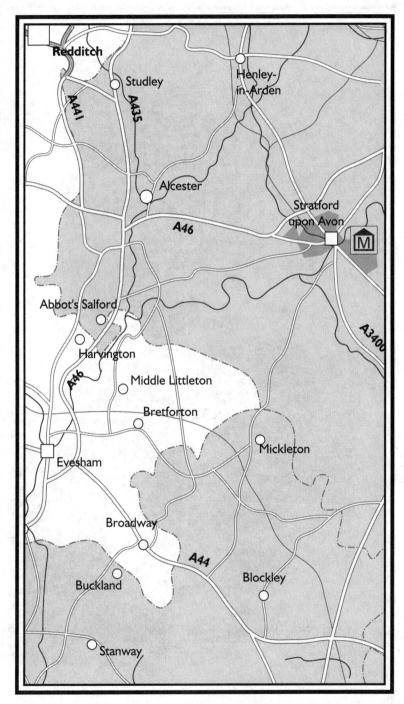

Evesham

CHAPTER FIVE

The Vale of Evesham

EVESHAM

The ancient market town of **Evesham** is an ideal base for exploring the area covered in this chapter. The town is easily located by following the A44 south-east from Worcester, and although the two towns are only about ten miles apart it is evident that this area is much more rural.

This part of the country, known as the Vale of Evesham, is renowned for its agricultural and horticultural expertise, particularly when it comes to growing high quality fruit and vegetables which are distributed the length and breadth of the country. As you travel along the pleasant country lanes, you are sure to come across roadside stalls displaying a wonderful array of colourful and 'organically' grown fruit and vegetables.

Evesham really is a delightful place. It is surrounded by a plethora of interesting small villages and hamlets in some of the gentlest and prettiest of English landscapes. The town lies on the River Avon and owes much to the Vale's fruit-growing industry.

It was here at the famous battle of Harvington Hill in 1265 that Simon de Montfort led the rebel barons against Prince Edward. Though they fought bravely, the rebel forces were defeated and Simon's mutilated body was buried before the altar in Evesham Abbey. Nevertheless, as history would later tell, the march of Parliamentary democracy went on and Simon de Montfort is remembered today as the Father of the English Parliament.

Relatively little of the once powerful **Evesham Abbey** which was founded in 714 AD, still stands. Its grounds now serve as a park, leading down to the River Avon. One entrance to the park takes you beneath the most impressive of the remains, the spectacular Bell Tower built by Abbot Lichfield and completed in 1539, the year in which the Abbey was dissolved. Standing some 110 feet high right in the centre of the town, this Perpendicular masterpiece forms a lasting impression in most visitor's minds.

It was during the time of this country's great Abbeys that Evesham first became famous for its fertile valley, producing some of the finest crops to be harvested from within the heart of England. Visitors to this part of the county will perhaps best appreciate the beauty of the surrounding countryside during the spring, when the profusion of fruit blossom can be best admired.

The Wychavon region, of which the Vale of Evesham forms an important part, contains many attractions for the short or long stay visitor. There are numerous places of interest to visit, and of course plenty of countryside walks and pick-your-own fruit farms.

If you plan to explore the area, finding suitable accommodation and a range of eating and drinking establishments will not be a problem. There is plenty of choice in the locality, ranging from reasonably priced first class hotels to comfortable bed and breakfast establishments and farmhouse accommodation.

SEDGEBERROW

A small, attractive village four miles south of Evesham and it is here that Alan and Daphne Stow laboured over many years to complete their award winning, imaginatively converted farm buildings. **Hall Farm Country Holidays** offers delightful Cottage accommodation in several beautiful cottages and spacious attractive en-suite apartments. Hall Farm consists of a large Georgian Farmhouse and cottages overlooking the green fields of the open countryside and set in over an acre of secluded, well-kept gardens with grass tennis court and orchard.

Hall Farm Country Holidays

Each property has been sympathetically modernised to meet today's high standards but retaining many original features. All are centrally heated and equipped to high standards. The elegant rooms in the main house with their high ceilings (now skilfully converted into four charming apartments), and the cottage atmosphere of the adjoining properties, give individuality to these delightful holiday homes. The proprietors live in the village and personally take the utmost care in ensuring the high standards are maintained. Other facilities include an outdoor heated swimming pool, free use of bicycles and fishing in the small river from the farm banks. Strolling around the fields and farm roads reveals an abundance of wildlife and for the more energetic, help is always welcomed at haymaking time! Regrettably pets cannot be accommodated. Awarded 4 key up to Highly Commended by the English Tourist Board. Well positioned for the Cotswolds and the Vale of Evesham.

Hall Farm Country Holidays, Sedgeberrow, Evesham, Worcs.
Tel: 01386 881298

One attraction not to be missed if you are in the area at the right time of year is the **Blossom Trail**. It is best enjoyed between late March and early May, depending on the climate. The spectacular blossom display can be seen by following the signposted route from Evesham's High Street. The trail takes you from the High Street to Greenhill, where the Battle of Evesham took place in 1265. Further details can be obtained from the Tourist Information Centre which is situated in the Almonry Museum.

The Almonry, Evesham

The Almonry Museum is housed in a fine example of a 14th century, black and white building and is set in typically English gardens. Be warned, the building is very old and none of the floors are even. The Almonry has formed an important part of Evesham's history and is the ideal setting for displays relating to the Battle of Evesham and to Evesham Abbey. Much care has been taken to label every item, so you can easily understand what you are seeing.

The peace of Evesham is frequently disturbed at night by the mysterious ringing of the security alarms at the Almonry. When the police look for the intruders, nothing has been disturbed and nothing has ever seen. The local belief is that The Almonry is haunted by the ghost of

The Round House, Evesham

a monk who has not found release since the Dissolution, and if he cannot be at peace, then why should anyone else.

It's always preferable to travel around the countryside surrounding Evesham by taking the back roads, this way you can discover some of the delightful hidden villages in the area.

Travelling north, on the west bank of the Avon you will come to **Norton**. This was once a pretty village, but now has to contend with the A435 Evesham to Redditch road which passes through it. There is a new road, the B439, soon to open, that will take away much of the traffic, and return it to quieter times.

HARVINGTON lies a little further on and is quite large by village standards. In contrast to the old cruck built cottages surrounding the church, Harvington is fast becoming better known as part of the executive commuter belt, with expensive detached houses much in demand.

What could be more pleasant on a summer's day than to gently drift along the River Avon in a narrowboat or small craft enjoying the delights of the river and its scenery. In just such a way you could arrive at **The Mill at Harvington,** tie up at the moorings and book into this fine Georgian Hotel. More conventionally, you would arrive by road, easily reached from the M40 at Warwick or 14 miles from the M5. Built in 1750 and originally a malting mill serving the local community, it was later used as a bread mill. The beautiful cast-iron bakery oven doors together with many of the original beams and features, can still be seen in current use today in this fine hotel. It is set in almost eight acres of wooded parkland with splendid willows shading its six hundred feet of river frontage.

The Mill at Harvington

Fishing is available directly from the grounds. For the sporting there is a hard tennis court and a heated outdoor swimming pool. The fifteen comfortable bedrooms all face the morning sun and overlook the garden and river. They have en-suite bathrooms and are thoughtfully equipped for guest comfort. For the physically handicapped, special provision has been made for wheelchair access in certain bedrooms and bathrooms.

The Restaurant offers interesting menus of carefully prepared dishes cooked and served by an enthusiastic young staff. Menus are changed frequently to take advantage of the fresh food available through the seasons. An interesting wine list offers good variety at sensible prices. The Mill at Harvington offers good old fashioned standards of service and hospitality. Ask about special breaks.

The Mill at Harvington, Anchor Lane, Harvington, Evesham, Worcs.
Telephone & Fax: 01386 870688.

THE LENCHES

A little to the west, beyond the A435, you will find a collection of villages called **The Lenches**, which lie in an area renowned for the richness of its soil. **Rous Lench** church was restored by the Reverend W.K.W. Chafy, the wealthy country squire and parson who came to live at Rous Lench Court in 1876. Formerly the seat of the Rous family from 1382, the Court is a splendid half-timbered mansion with an exquisite topiary garden and sculpture.

Chafy put up a number of interesting estate houses in these villages, all monuments to his particular architectural style. **Church Lench** is the largest of them, and from here you'll be rewarded with fine views over the Vale of Evesham, back to the Malvern Hills.

Crossing back over the Avon, and right on the county border is the village of **Cleeve Prior**. The houses here are, surprisingly, made of stone instead of the more familiar timber. On one side of the main road is the King's Arms pub, which was built in 1542 and boasts a large stone dovecote in its yard. Next to it is the Old Cider Mill with agricultural tools from bygone days adorning its walls, and opposite, behind the lovely Queen Anne Vicarage and hidden from view by a group of farm buildings, is St Andrew's church.

In the churchyard, it's amusing to see a headstone which declared that one Sara Charlett had passed away in 1693 at the ripe old age of 309. You wonder as to the type of life-style she must have adopted to have attained this most respectable age! It's more likely however, that her apparent 'longevity' was more probably due to an inattentive carver with other things on his mind!

The Littletons - North, Middle and South - lie close to the River Avon to the north-east of Evesham. North and Middle Littleton appear to merge together with hardly a noticeable break between them and visitors can be forgiven for thinking they are one and the same village. **Middle**

Littleton is well worth a visit for its truly outstanding Tithe Barn, dating back to 1260 and once the property of the Abbots of Evesham. It is now owned by the National Trust. Nearby, **Offenham** stands on the banks of the Avon and is surrounded by acres of greenhouses, a familiar sight which the tourist eventually tends to take for granted.

BRETFORTON

A little to the south is Bretforton, a lovely village of mellow Cotswold stone, and here you will find the delightfully quaint **Fleece Inn**, another National Trust property. It is one of the few inns owned by the Trust, who acquired it in 1978 when it was bequeathed to them by Miss Lola Tabling, whose family had owned it for generations.

This timber-framed 14th century building was originally a farmhouse until it was converted into a 'beerhouse' in 1848. In those days, the pub had its own brewery and all three parlours were served from one hatch in the hall. Ale was stored in casks away from the bars in order to keep it cool, and this is in fact the origin of the 'taprooms' to be found in many Victorian pubs.

Progress determined that this original system was to be replaced by hand pumps, but thankfully very little of the interior has changed since the old days. When the National Trust acquired the Inn, all of the furnishings came with it and this included a number of fine antiques - not least of which was a superb collection of forty eight pieces of Stuart pewter. A fascinating reminder of the Inn's medieval origins are the 'witch marks' that can still be made out on the stone floor inside, put there to ward off evil spirits.

Fleece Inn, Bretforton.

Broadway Tower

BROADWAY

The next port of call is the all-time favourite of many visitors to Worcestershire. **Broadway** is often referred to as 'a village for all seasons' and it is undoubtedly one of the most beautiful villages in England. American tourists in particular seem to adore it and flock here at all times of the year. Six miles south-east of Evesham, it is the quintessential Cotswold village, with a broad main street that gave it its name, lined with cottages and houses built of golden Cotswold stone. Even the most modern housing, tucked away out of sight behind the 'showpiece' buildings of the main street, is built of the same weathered stone to blend in with the surroundings. The most outstanding building in the main street is the **Lygon Arms Hotel**. Formerly a private house, it makes an interesting centrepiece for the village.

This area is steeped in history, Broadway having been settled by the ancient Beaker people around 1900 BC, and later the Romans came and occupied the hills above the village. Both peoples have left reminders of their time here. Broadway was probably re-established after the Battle of Dyrham in 557 AD by conquering Saxons advancing towards Worcester.

The Parish Records tell of hospitality being offered at a Broadway hostelry as far back as 1532. This was the time of the advent of horse-drawn carriages, when Broadway was an important staging post. A typical journey from London to Worcester took approximately 17 hours including stops and a change of horses, and at one time Broadway boasted an incredible 33 public houses!

Over the years, Broadway has established an international reputation for the high standards it sets in caring for visitors and travellers, and the leisure industry plays a vital role in its economy. The area is well-loved by fishermen, and its golf course, which enjoys breathtaking views of the Vale, is just one of over a dozen first class courses within a 25 mile radius.

During weekends and Bank Holidays, the streets are crowded with visitors who come to browse in the shops and galleries and to sample the fare of Broadway's fine restaurants, hotels and public houses.

Before leaving this delightful village, a visit to the **Teddy Bear Museum** is a must - for *all* ages! There's a great deal more to see than one might imagine.

Horse racing enthusiasts can visit nearby Cheltenham, home of the famous National Hunt Festival in mid March, and Stratford, Warwick, Worcester and Bath are also easily accessible via the M5 motorway.

In the centre of Broadway is a wide village green and from there the main street continues gently upwards for nearly a mile, with the surrounding hills constantly in view. The gradient increases at Fish Hill, then rises to more than 1000 feet above sea level at Broadway Beacon, the second-highest point in the Cotswolds.

At the top of the Beacon is **Broadway Tower**, standing in a delightful country park known as Broadway Tower Country Park. The tower was built by the 6th Earl of Coventry in 1800 as part of the great 18th century movement to picturesque and romantic landscapes. You can climb to the very top of this 65 foot tower and admire the spectacular views over 12 English counties. James Wyatt designed the tower and it now houses, among other displays, a William Morris exhibition.

Travelling west, and in the triangle formed by the A44 and the A435, to the south west of Evesham, is **Bredon Hill**. Bredon Hill has an interesting history and is the largest of the limestone outcrops that once formed part of the Cotswolds, prior to being separated from them by erosion during the Ice Age. The hill rises to over 900 feet and some say that you can see as many as 14 counties from its summit. The remains of prehistoric and Roman earthworks have been found here, and on its slopes stands an 18th century tower called Parson's Folly.

BREDON

The Fox and Hounds at Bredon has been in the Hardwick family for almost half a Century, starting first as a cider house with one small bar and a couple of spittoons. It was also one of the many locals for the late John Moore, author of The Blue Field, A Portrait of Elmbury and Brensham Village, novels which were set around the Tewkesbury area. Today after several alterations and extensions, it is a well established venue for dining out.

The Fox and Hounds

The extensive Bar and Dining Lounge menu offer home-cooked food at very reasonable prices with various Soups, Ploughman's, Hot open sandwiches, specialities like 'Crispy Prawns' and 'Cod Roe' and much more. For something more substantial or that special occasion, the A' la

Carte menu is available in the Brensham Restaurant and throughout the premises. There are dishes such as 'Half a Shoulder of Lamb with a Mint and Honey glaze', 'Half a Crispy Roast Duck with Orange and Grande Marnier' or for something a little more unusual you could try the speciality „Chicken, Banana and Stilton'. The Steaks prove very popular, served either plain or with one of the chef's excellent sauces and the blackboard 'Seasonal Specials' include a variety of fresh fish dishes.

Sunday is a favourite with a selection of at least four Roast Meats, Pies, Casseroles and specials from the blackboard, and all are served from midday until 2.30 p.m. and 6.30 p.m. until 9.00 p.m.. Bar meals are also available and children and vegetarians have their very own menu, all produced to suit everyone's palate and pocket, this is definitely one of the better pubs serving better food, seven days a week.

The Fox and Hounds, Church Street, Bredon, Tewkesbury,
Glos. GL20 7LA Tel: 01684 772377

ELMLEY CASTLE

Encircling the hill is a network of narrow lanes which link a number of attractive villages and hamlets, each worthy of a closer look. If you investigate Elmley Castle, for example, you'll soon discover that the castle no longer remains, just a memorandum of 1540 which states: 'the late Castle of Elmley standing on high and adjoining the Park, compassed in with wall and ditch is uncovered and in decay.' **Elmley Castle** is a beautiful village though. Its main street is very wide and lined with trees, with a little brook flowing to one side. Picturesque black and white cottages and thatched roofs lead you up to a well-preserved 15th century cross, then to St. Mary's church with its handsome tower and battlements. Inside are some of the finest monuments to be found anywhere in England, most notably the 17th century alabaster table tomb of William Savage, his son Giles, and Giles's wife and children.

PERSHORE

The small village of **Eckington** can be traced back to 172AD, when its name was spelt Eceynegtune. Originally it was a Roman settlement on land belonging to a British tribe known as the Dobuni, and later the village was mentioned in the Domesday Book. Turning north, you will come to **Pershore** on the A44, by-passed earlier, en-route to Evesham from Worcester. Pershore's most majestic feature is its magnificent Norman Abbey. The building which survives today may only be the choir of the original church, but it is still an architectural treasure. It has superb 13th century features which have been little worn by time,

Elmley Castle Village

making it the perfect venue for many concerts during the year, including the well attended Pershore Festival held each June.

Modern Pershore grew from the settlement that surrounded the Abbey, and it was the monks from the Abbey who built the 14th century bridge. It still shows the scars of the Civil War - the central span was destroyed by Charles I in 1644 as he retreated from the Parliamentarians, but has since been replaced. Life in the town has not always been as peaceful as it is today; in fact it is reputed that the deciding battle of every great civil war in England has taken place within ten miles of Pershore.

During the 18th century, improvements to roads and river navigation brought prosperity to the town, together with many fine Georgian buildings and residences for the wool merchants who built them. A superb example of 18th century architecture in Pershore is **Perrott House**, built by Judge George Perrott around 1770. The plaster work and ceiling decorations are exquisite and are often attributed to Robert Adam.

Oddly enough, the town all but turns its back on the River Avon; yet the superb riverside walks, fishing and picnic areas are ideal for those who seek peace and tranquillity and the quiet life. Look out for The Royal Arcade, on the corner of Bridge Street, which has royal associations. It was previously the Royal Three Tuns coaching inn, and Princess Victoria once stayed there on her way to Malvern.

The **Pershore College of Horticulture** is just one mile east of the town. Originally part of the Wyke Estate, the college has been developed around the mansion known as Avonbank, built in 1806 by Thomas Hubs of Wick House. Designated the Royal Horticultural Society's Centre for the West Midlands, the extensive ornamental and amenity grounds feature interesting and unusual trees and shrubs. The Glass Houses contain tropical, temperate and cool decorative plants. The commercial nursery produces and sells container grown plants, and admission is free to the grounds and gardens.

Pershore

Also just off the A44 is a well known landmark much favoured by young families, the **Pershore Bridge Picnic Area**. The bridge is surrounded by over an acre of grassland and is ideal for day trippers who wish to picnic there. It is also a canoe launching point for the River Avon, and there are lots of riverside footpaths.

WYRE PIDDLE

Just a mile or so north of Pershore Bridge Picnic Area, on the B4084 at **Wyre Piddle,** is the wonderful **Anchor Inn,** run by Mike and Scarlett Senior. Dating back to the 17th century it was formerly boatman's cottages, later becoming an ale house and today an inn of true character. A real picture awaits you to the rear of the Anchor Inn, the beautiful gardens gently slope down the River Avon, and the picturesque views beyond. The inn also has river moorings available. On a fine day it is ideal to sit outside and drink in the view of Bredon Hill.

The Anchor is renowned for its fine cuisine. Mike does the chefing himself and earned his reputation in some of London's top class hotels. It is a reputation that has earned The Anchor Egon Ronay's approval. Good beer isn't forgotten here either, with a well kept selection available.

The Anchor Inn and Restaurant, Wyre Piddle, Pershore , Worcs.
Tel: 01386 552799.

Please Don't Forget...
Tell people that you read about them in
The Hidden Places

PINVIN

From Wyre Piddle it is but a short distance to the village of **Pinvin** on the B4082 where Michael and Christine Harris are the hospitable owners and licensees of the **Coach and Horses**. Built in the 18th century, the inn offers a traditionally warm welcome with a good variety of beers and bar snacks. The interior is pleasing with tasteful decor and a cosy atmosphere. There are facilities suitable for children and disabled patrons - pets are welcome too. Although it's a little hidden away - the Coach and Horses is well worth a visit. Nice country location with easy parking.

Coach and Horses, Main Street, Pinvin, Nr. Pershore, Worcs.
Tel: 01386 552858.

FLADBURY

The impressive **Chequers Inn** is situated in a quiet position at the end of a lane in the lovely old Vale of Evesham village of Fladbury. It can be reached from the B4084 Pershore to Evesham road, and stands a short distance from the River Avon with its beautiful riverside walks and excellent angling. A handsome white-painted building with parts dating back to the 14th-century, the inn forms the hub of village life. It is owned and personally-managed by Daphne and Alun Corfield, friendly and experienced hosts who provide a warm welcome, charming hospitality and first-class food, drink and accommodation.

The Chequers is renowned for its fine cuisine and offers an extensive choice of dishes, either in the bar or in the more intimate atmosphere of the restaurant. The à la carte menu includes succulent steaks, fish, meat and vegetarian dishes, along with a wide range of starters, desserts and wines to accompany the meal; there is also a popular carvery at weekends.

A similarly wide-ranging selection of meals is available in the bar, along with a range of light meals and snacks. For those wishing to stay, the inn offers eight individually-decorated guest bedrooms which are all superbly-equipped with en suite facilities, televisions, radios and telephones; some also have balconies, and some views across beautiful open countryside.

The Chequers lies within easy reach of the many famous attractions of Stratford-upon-Avon, Worcester and Cheltenham, and is ideal for weekends away from it all, wedding receptions and small business gatherings.

Chequers Inn, Fladbury, Near Pershore, Worcestershire
Tel: 01386 860276 Fax: 01386 861286

UPTON SNODSBURY

Upton Snodsbury lies at the junction of the B4082 and the A422, and an ancient Saxon burial site was once excavated here. If you are looking for convivial company and wholesome food, a good place to head for is **The Royal Oak.** This is a traditional village pub with a really friendly atmosphere, and offers a good range of beer and bar meals.

The Royal Oak has a reputation for being one of England's haunted inns. The spirit in question is the ghost of a crying baby, who was apparently murdered by being thrown out of one of the pub windows. The murderer was hanged just across the road. It seems that the ghost refrains from materialising openly, but various types of childish poltergeist activity are known to occur now and again. Salt and pepper are poured onto the tables at night and doors close with no one there. Nothing too disturbing, but just enough to add to the character of the place!

KINGTON

To find an establishment that offers their guests old-fashioned hospitality is always a treat and **The Red Hart Inn** is no exception. This 400 year old coaching Inn offers a unique blend of personal service, traditional charm and a warm welcome, all under the personal supervision of the owner David Drinkwater. For a quiet drink or a special celebration, a business conference or family outing, the Red Hart's oak beams and log fires, lively bar and secluded corners invite exploration and relaxation.

Memorabilia abounds in this country Inn, signed photographs, original prints and a fascinating collection of artifacts that reveal a famous association with local, national and international cricket stars.

The friendly atmosphere pervades every room at the Red Hart, from the private dining room so suitable for that special occasion, to the newer Monarch Suite - ideal for celebrations and receptions, conferences, training courses and seminars. A delight to lovers of traditional and more adventurous cuisine, the Red Hart's award winning dishes are complemented by a cellar that's home to a collection of wines from traditional vineyards and newer producers alike. So whether your stopping for a simple ploughman's lunch or a dinner dance for 150 guests, the Red Hart is dedicated to offer the perfect meal for any occasion.

Red Hart Inn, Kington, Flyford, Flavell, Worcestershire WR7 4DD
Tel: 01386 792221 Fax: 01386 792745

INKBERROW

Further east on the A422, and you'll soon find yourselves in the village of **Inkberrow,** one of the prettiest and best kept villages in the county. The houses around the village green are a pleasant assortment of black-and-white half-timbered dwellings together with those of red brick. Inkberrow's most famous building is the 16th century timber-framed **Old Bull Inn** where William Shakespeare is said to have stayed in 1582, en-route from to Worcester to pick up his marriage certificate.

Old Bull Inn

The major claim to fame however, is that it is the original of the Bull Hotel at Ambridge, the setting of Radio 4's long-running series 'The Archers'. Photographs of the cast adorn the walls, and the Old Bull is a mecca for loyal fans of the programme.

Close to the inn is the **Old Vicarage**, a handsome 18th century building in the Tudor style, which played host to none other than King Charles I, who stayed there on his way to Naseby, leaving some rare maps behind - now safely stored away in the village church.

Abbots Morton, just south of Inkberrow, is another very attractive village and consists mainly of 17th century former yeomen's houses. The village was once the site of the Abbot of Evesham's summer residence, but all that now remains is a series of mounds and fishponds.

ASTWOOD BANK

Charnwood is a family house of good proportions set in beautiful countryside on the boundary between Warwickshire and Worcestershire. It's within easy distance of Shakespeare's Stratford, Worcester and the Malverns, the Vale of Evesham and the Cotswolds. The two beautifully furnished rooms consist of one family and one single room with en-suite bathrooms, colour television and tea/coffee facilities. Guests have a choice of light or full English breakfast, often served in the lovely conservatory area where the view of the garden makes an enjoyable backdrop. Local pubs offer a superb choice of traditional or contemporary food at reasonable prices. Spacious and spotless bed and breakfast at a very reasonable cost. Children and dogs welcome. No smokers please.

Charnwood, 35 Wood Lane, Astwood Bank, Nr. Cookhill.
Tel: 01527 893647.

From the delightful Vale of Evesham, we now move northwards, to Droitwich.

CHAPTER SIX

Droitwich to Kidderminster

Droitwich Heritage Centre

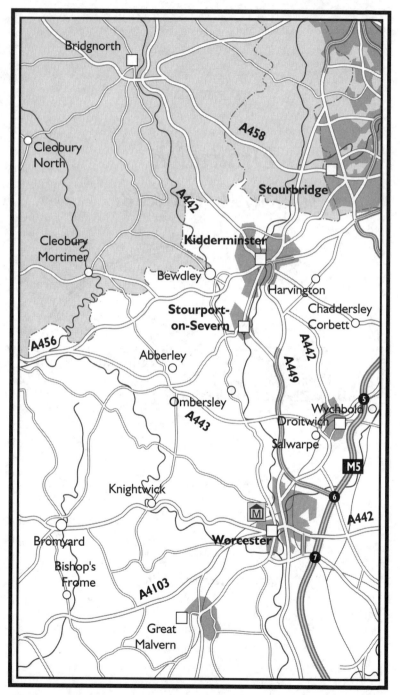

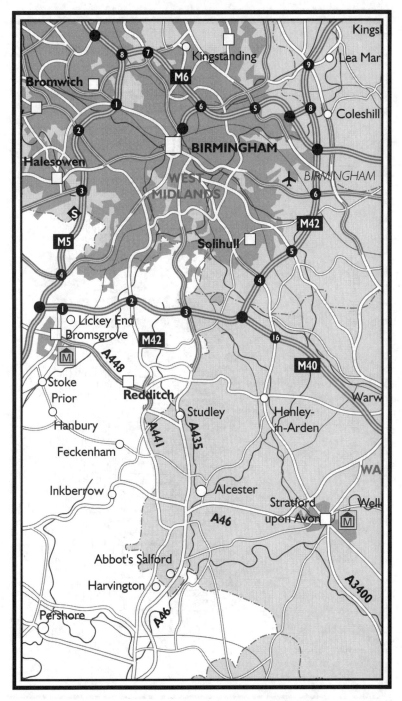

Droitwich Heritage & Information Centre

CHAPTER SIX

Droitwich to Kidderminster

The north eastern corner of the county is cut almost exactly in two by the M5. Although it is probably considered an eye-sore, it nevertheless offers a quick journey between the towns in the area. We begin this chapter by leaving the M5 at exit 5 and taking the A38 to Droitwich.

DROITWICH

The Roman name for Droitwich Spa was Salinae, or 'the place of salt', which gives an indication of the origins of the town. It is believed that there was once ancient, landlocked sea that covered much of this part of Worcestershire. Eventually the huge body of water dried up and left substantial salt deposits below the place where Droitwich now stands. The town has been the site of a settled community for over 2,000 years and has been important as a source of salt. Both the Romans, and later the Saxons, came here to produce this important commodity.

Droitwich, or Droitwich Spa as it is still sometimes called, is an inland town, unique among the Spa towns of Britain, as this ancient and historic place achieved fame and recognition as a Brine Spa. The natural Droitwich brine contains approximately two and a half pounds of salt per gallon - ten times stronger than that of normal sea water - and often likened to the salt content of the Dead Sea. Droitwich brine is pumped up from an underground lake which lies 200ft below the town. Visitors do not drink the waters at Droitwich as they do at other spas, but enjoy the therapeutic and remedial benefits by floating in the warm brine of the bathing pool.

The first Brine Baths were built during the 1830s and were soon renowned for bringing relief to many and effecting miraculous cures. By 1876, Droitwich had developed as a fashionable Spa through the efforts of a leading entrepreneur John Corbett, Member of Parliament and later crowned Droitwich 'Salt King'. This popular pastime has recently been revived and is considered one of the newest leisure activities.

The distinctive appearance of many of the town buildings is also directly related to the salt industry. Methods of extraction involved pumping huge amounts of water underground to dissolve the salts. This was done on such a large scale that subsidence resulted, causing many of the High Street buildings to lean at alarming angles. The reaction of present-day town planners has been to deliberately put up new buildings in the same haphazard style, with windows and walls leaning every which way.

Whilst on the High Street, call in at the **Mulberry Tree Coffee House.** Here, Honor Parkin has been running her business from this lovely old black and white beamed, 400 year old building for the past three years with the help of her daughters Victoria, Nicola and occasionally Justine.

This building has most of its original beams intact and much of the fayre on offer compliments these traditional surroundings - no chips on the menu here! With beautiful homemade soups, hotpots and casseroles, the Mulberry Tree is also renowned for its cakes (try Passion Cake) and in particular, its superb Bread and Butter Pudding. A tea garden has been a recent addition and it really is a gorgeous suntrap. Small gifts are on offer including delicate decoupage pictures by local artist Heather Francis and items made by Victoria and Justine, who even helps out with the unique hand-drawn menus.

All in all, a charming, relaxed atmosphere in which to while away a little time over the best cup of coffee in Droitwich Spa!

The Mulberry Tree Coffee House, 22 High Street, Droitwich Spa.
Tel: 01905 796115

If you would like to discover more about the history of this great Salt Town, and the secrets of salt water hydrotherapy, you should make your way to the **Heritage Centre,** housed in Richard's House, Victoria Square.

The Roman Catholic church of the Sacred Heart is also worth a visit, as its whole interior is covered with beautiful mosaics of Venetian Glass,

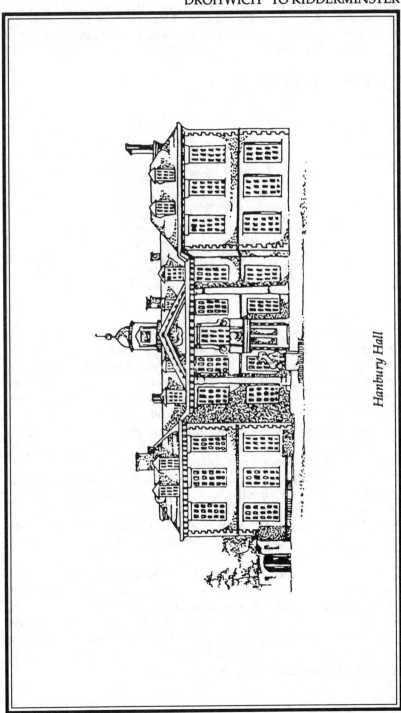

Hanbury Hall

illustrating the life of local saint, St. Richard De Wyche. They are considered to be the most outstanding mosaics in England outside of Westminster Cathedral.

AROUND DROITWITCH.

The Chateau Impney

As well as being renowned as one of Britain's Spa Heritage Towns, Droitwich also offers an excellent golf course, bowling greens and tennis courts. Horse riding is close to hand and coarse fishing is available on the nearby rivers Severn and Avon. **Westwood Park**, in the grounds of the magnificent Elizabethan Westwood House, has windsurfing and bird watching, together with swimming in the heated indoor swimming pool. In the summer months the open air lido is very popular, utilising the salt spa water, diluted to the strength of sea water. This allows visitors the luxury of 'seaside' bathing right in the heart of England.

While driving in and around Droitwich, it is likely that you will at some point notice through the trees an unusual building which looks very like Cinderella's Castle and more appropriate to a children's story book than the English countryside. It was originally designed by the French architect Auguste Tronquois as a home for John Corbett, the Salt King and his wife.

Now called the Chateau Impney Hotel, it has soaring turrets, a mansard roof and classical French Gardens. Situated on the town's eastern outskirts at **Dodderhill**, it was considered in its day to be the epitome of nouveau riche and flamboyant in the extreme. It would seem that Corbett's wife shared this view, for rumour has it that she refused to live there! Today it is a super hotel and conference centre, and can be enjoyed by its guests for the comforts it offers.

OMBERSLEY

Just a short distance from the centre of Droitwich to the west, and perhaps a quintessential 'English village'.

The main street is delightful - bordered by superb examples of half-timbered black-and-white dwellings, giving a true feeling that you have been transported back in time to Old Worcestershire. St Andrews church with its wooden galleries and box pews was built as recently as 1825, replacing the old church which now houses the mausoleum of the Sandys family in its ruins. For such a small place it has much to offer the casual visitor and you can escape the rat race and try one of the pubs.

The present Lord and Lady Sandys reside at the early-18th century **Ombersley Court**, a splendid Georgian mansion to the west of the church featuring a porch with Ionic columns, which is said to be quite beautiful inside.

Overlooking the Severn Valley towards Elgar's beloved Malvern Hills, what better place to unwind than **Tytchney Gables**, an unspoilt 16th century farmhouse offering a family room, a double and a single room. Relax in front of the inglenook fireplace as Margaret Peters entertains you with her soprano voice, if you can play the piano perhaps you can accompany her! A most friendly and open welcome is given to all, which guarantees guests return year after year from all over the globe.

It is a wonderful location for country walks and fishing in the River Severn. Smoking is allowed in the garden under the watchful eye of the horse. A typically English farmhouse atmosphere has everyone 'mucking in' to create a memorable and enjoyable stay. Situated between Worcester and Kidderminster (A449) near the Dunhampton junction, taking the Woodfield Lane turn off.

Tytchney Gables, Boreley, Ombersley, Nr. Droitwich, Worcestershire.
Tel: 01905 620185

SALWARPE

One of several villages in the area, which serves to remind us by its name that this was an area famous for its salt production. It is truly a hidden hamlet, located just south-west of Droitwich and approached by a road over a stone built bridge which spans James Brindley's famous Droitwich Canal. Originally opened in 1771, the Canal linked the town to the River Severn at Hawford. Salwarpe is an altogether charming village and is ideal to stroll around after lunch or dinner at one of the local historic inns.

Be sure to visit the **Salwarpe Valley Nature Reserve** while you are here, as it is one of the few British inland sites where salt water occurs. The natural brine nearby enables salt marsh and seawater plants to grow in profusion, creating a unique wild life feature for the area.

HAWFORD

In another small village near here, Hawford, you will find an unusual 16th century half-timbered dovecote. This small National Trust property is open daily between April and October.

Heading east now, back across the M5 to **Huddington, Tibberton** and **Oddingley**. This small group of villages are particularly well kept and contribute greatly to the beauty of the local countryside making driving or walking here a most pleasurable experience. Huddington is especially worthy of a visit due to **Huddington Court**.

Huddington Court has been described as the most picturesque house in Worcestershire and is certainly a house of immense beauty and grace. It is an excellent example of a 16th century timber-framed building, with elaborate chimneys and was once the home of the Wyntours, a staunchly Catholic family who were involved in the Gunpowder Plot. When the plot was exposed and the conspirators finally apprehended, both Thomas and Robert Wyntour confessed their guilt and were executed. Although Huddington Court is still a private residence, you can get a good view of it from the churchyard of St. James's church.

HANBURY

Just a couple of miles north of here is **Hanbury Hall**, an imposing red brick house in the style of Wren. It was built in 1701 and apart from some restoration work, little has altered since. As with many National Trust properties, the house has outstanding painted ceilings and a staircase by Sir James Thornhill, famous for his masterpiece, the painted Hall at Greenwich. Also to be found in the house is an impressive collection of porcelain and Dutch flower pictures.

The grounds are of particular interest as they house a handsome contemporary Orangery, and perhaps best of all, an 18th century ice house in an exceptional state of preservation.

Set in beautiful rural surroundings within easy reach of junction 5 on the M5, the award-winning **Jinney Ring Craft Centre** is situated on the B4091 to the northwest of the old Worcestershire village of **Hanbury**. A fascinating attraction for visitors of all ages, the centre is housed in a collection of old timbered barns which have been lovingly restored and converted by Richard and Jenny Greatwood. Over a dozen individual craftspeople can be seen at work in their own craft studios, including a violin maker, potter, jeweller, picture framer, milliner, leather worker, sign-maker, antiques restorer and rocking-horse maker.

Jinney Ring Craft Centre

There is also a craft gallery offering changing exhibitions of work by British craftspeople and artists, a clothing and knitwear department, and a needlework shop which stocks a wide range of materials for embroidery, cross-stitch and quilt-making. The delightfully-furnished farmhouse kitchen provides the ideal atmosphere to enjoy a delicious morning coffee, home-cooked lunch or afternoon tea.

Open daily except Mondays, all year round; admission free. The centre also offers one and two-day courses by professional tutors of calligraphy, stained glass, embroidery, decorative paint finishes and other specialist skills.

Jinney Ring Craft Centre, Hanbury, Nr Bromsgrove, Worcs
Tel: 01527 821272 Fax: 01527 821869

WYCHBOLD

North-east of Droitwich, just north of Junction 5 on the M5, is the delightful little village of **Wychbold**. Drive through the village, and you'll come across a thriving and very colourful garden centre. Whether you are interested in landscaping, nursery gardening, or just pottering around a tiny patio, you'll find that the whole complex incorporates everything the enthusiastic gardener could possibly wish for. In the garden you will also find **The Thatch**, a beautiful little thatched restaurant. It's quite unusual to find a Grade II listed building in a garden centre, particularly one that serves wholesome, home-cooked food.

STOKE PRIOR

In order to appreciate the many faceted achievements of the 'Salt King', John Corbett, visit the village of **Stoke Prior**, which can be found just north of Wychbold. Corbett was responsible for building many of the cottages in this village. Even the school dating back to 1871 bears testimony to him and his crest is proudly ensconced amongst the school buildings. His saltworks south of the village, where the Birmingham and Worcester Railway meets the canal, were a model factory designed to provide his workers with congenial working conditions and surroundings.

Just to the north of Stoke Prior is the **Avoncroft Museum of Buildings**, a unique museum that gives you the opportunity to stroll through seven centuries of English history. This collection of historic buildings started when the Bromsgrove house, a 15th century timber merchants house and Bromsgrove's oldest, was under threat of demolition in 1962. It was saved by being dismantled and re-erected on the museum's 15 acre site. Since then over 20 other historic buildings have been added to the collection. These include a 19th century Tollhouse from Malvern, the splendid 14th century roof from the monastic buildings of Worcester cathedral and a marvellous 16th century cruck-framed thatched barn from a farm in Herefordshire. There is a working windmill, an ice house, a post-war austerity Prefab and even a three seater earth closet! All these authentic buildings really capture the atmosphere of bygone days.

There are plenty of other activities to see, including regular demonstrations of blacksmithing, brickmaking and the like, as well as rallies and other events. You will also find a gift shop, refreshments, a picnic area and a variety of displays giving details of the collection. The museum can be found off the A38 Bromsgrove by-pass, three and half miles south of Junction 1 on the M42. Do make the effort to go see it as it really is a fascinating place.

The Avoncroft Museum of Buildings, Stoke Heath, Bromsgrove
Tel: 01527 831886/831363

STOKE POUND

Following the A38 route from Worcester to Bromsgrove, we turned off at the sign to **Stoke Pound** down Sugarbrook Lane aiming to find the

Avoncroft Museum of historic Buildings, Bromsgrove

renowned **Queens Head.** Arriving at Stoke Pound Bridge No.48, there it was on the banks of the Worcester - Birmingham Canal. Seen from the canal, the building almost looks to be floating on the still water.

Owned by John and Martine Wakefied for the past two years, the Queens Head had previously been in the Wakefield family until sold ten years ago. Under the careful management of Jim Goodwin, the Queens Head is rated as one of the best Carveries in the Midlands, boasting a 176 seat restaurant where there is always a selection of at least three meat roasts and fourteen choices of vegetables.

All the food on the extensive menu is homemade. As well as the usual refreshments, the bar has three or four traditional ales to offer the thirsty traveller. The Carvery is open seven days a week and because of its excellent reputation is always busy.

Queens Head

Parts of the building date back to the 1600's, and over the centuries it has been, amongst other things, an 'Off Licence' and a Blacksmiths before the Wakefield Family bought it and converted it to an Inn. It would have been used as a stop-off and watering point for the barge horses of the previous century. Today, The Queens Head has parking for 170 cars, a children's play area, a beautiful canal-side garden and terrace complete with barge moorings. If travelling on the canal, the Queens Head is the first refreshment point after negotiating the 30 Tardebigge Locks, so you will need some nourishment after all that exertion!

Queens Head, Stoke Pound, Bromsgrove. Tel: 01527 877777
Fax: 01527 575656.

BROMSGROVE
Although **Bromsgrove** is now a relatively modern industrial and

residential town, it boasts many buildings of architectural interest. One of the oldest of these is the Parish Church of St. John the Baptist, which has a 14th century tower with a tapering spire, and the tombs of the Stafford and Talbot families. It is known that there was a village and a church here as far back as the 5th century, but by Norman times the parish of Bromsgrove had expanded dramatically with the Domesday Survey showing it to have no less than 18 'berewicks' or villages within the manorial division. In the 16th century, the town's nail making industry grew rapidly. This lasted for 300 years but died out with the introduction of machine made nails.

The Bromsgrove Guild of applied arts was founded by Walter Gilbert in 1890 and survived until 1953, achieving international fame and recognition. Among the work of its craftsmen are the impressive bronze gates of Buckingham Palace.

An attractive feature of the town, and particularly notable in the High Street, are the Georgian timber-framed buildings and gabled houses. The shopping facilities are excellent, with a wide selection of shops, tea houses, restaurants and inns. One of the more interesting shops is Daub and Wattle's Pottery in Windsor Street.

The name of Alfred Edward Housman has become synonymous with the mention of Bromsgrove worldwide. Housman is reckoned to be one of the greatest classical scholars this country has ever produced, and while his output of verse was comparatively small, it contains some of the most perfect and best known and loved poems in the English Language. Born on 26th March 1859, Housman's academic career was to take him to the dizzy heights of Kennedy Professor of Latin at Cambridge.

His first and most famous book of poems was 'A Shropshire Lad', first published in 1896 and widely acclaimed. The formation in 1972 of a Housman Society has brought this distinguished gentleman to the forefront of public attention. A specially produced brochure will guide the poetry lover around the properties associated with Housman, including the 18th century Perry Hall (now a hotel) south of the church in Kidderminster Road, where he lived for much of his life. There is a pedestrian route covering approximately one and a quarter miles and a vehicle route of some six and a quarter miles, so the enthusiast will find plenty to see.

The people of Bromsgrove are particularly proud of their annual Music Festival, held during the month of May. It is a very well supported event, during which the town plays host to a wide range of musical entertainment from orchestral concerts to jazz, featuring international artists.

An excellent place to stay which is easily accessible from the A38, junction 1 on the M42 coming from Birmingham Airport and the NEC, and junctions 4 and 5 on the M5 is **The Conifers** in Bromsgrove. Situated in a quiet neighbourhood within the town, this pleasant establishment is run by resident proprietor Ingrid Rossall, a German-born former teacher. The family can converse in English, German, French and Spanish. The accommodation comprises a ground floor twin bedroom with en suite shower and separate toilet and own sitting room, and an upstairs single room with shared facilities; both rooms have their own TV and are very comfortable. Breakfast is enhanced by homemade bread and jams.

The Conifers Guest House, 137 Pennine Road, Bromsgrove, Worcestershire
Tel: 01527 832864 / 0973 489682

The nearest Saturday to Midsummer's Day sees the celebration of The Court Leet. This was an ancient form of local administration, and is brought to life each year through a colourful procession, with the bailiff and court in full regalia. An exciting event for visitors to the town.

Bromsgrove has a number of other interesting buildings and places of local interest, such as the grammar school which was built in 1553 and the Hop Pole Inn which was re-erected in New Road in 1867, having been originally built in the town centre some 300 years earlier. The Bromsgrove Museum in Birmingham Road has displays on bygone local industries and crafts such as glass, lead, salt, button and nail making, and covers the social history of the area.

The area surrounding Bromsgrove is largely undulating farmland, rising in the north to the Clent and Lickey Hills. Strange tales abound in the area - the Devil and his huntsman are said to hunt wild boars on the Lickey Hills by night, mounted on two white bulls. Notwithstanding such alarming nocturnal activities, it is an outstandingly attractive part of the county with fine views and lovely quiet walks.

Dormston Church Tower

LICKLEY

The Honeypot at Lickey could best be described as a B & B & B! Lying just a mile from junction 4 on the M5 and junction 1 on the M42, this delightful bed and breakfast establishment is run by Ena and Philip Stanworth, charming hosts who have been enthusiastic beekeepers for over forty years. Formerly a grocery store and then a beekeeping shop, the main room has now been converted into a sunny guest lounge which overlooks the large garden.

The Honeypot

The accommodation comprises one twin and one double room, both with colour TV and access to a shared shower room. Children are most welcome, and the home-cooked breakfasts provide the opportunity to sample the Stanworth's own delicious honey.

The Honeypot, 305 Old Birmingham Road, Lickey, Bromsgrove, Worcs.
Tel: 0121-445 2580

TARDEBIGGE

Leaving Bromsgrove on the A448 you should head east towards **Redditch**. On the way, it's worth stopping off at the village of **Tardebigge**, split in two by the main road passing through it.

The village features the enchanting Georgian church of St. Bartholomew, built by Francis Hiorn in 1777. The tower and spire are most impressive and there is also a splendid art nouveau lectern by the Bromsgrove Guild and a touching monument to Lady Mary Cooke, showing her in a loving embrace with her husband.

In Hewell Lane in Tardebigge, you will find a very friendly pub called, originally enough, The Tardebigge. A good place to stop off if you are in the area.

REDDITCH

Redditch has been a 'new' town for the past 30 years and it would be easy to dismiss the town as such, believing it to have little history and few places of interest. Visitors will soon discover there is much more to the town, particularly if they take the time to visit two of its hidden gems.

Forge Mill Museum, Needle Mill Lane, Redditch Tel: 01527 62509

The fascinating **Forge Mill Museum** lies down the aptly named Needle Mill Lane. Opened by Her Majesty the Queen in 1983, it is home to the National Needle Museum. Redditch and the surrounding area was formerly the world's centre for the manufacture of needles and fishing tackle, and home to such famous firms as Milwards and Allcocks. Forge Mill itself was converted to needle scouring (otherwise known as polishing) in 1730, and the machinery which was used continuously until 1958 has been restored to working order together with the water-wheel, providing a unique insight into technology and working conditions in the 18th and 19th centuries. There are life-like models and audio-visual aids which give a step by step guide to the complex processes of needle making, whether it be knitting, surgical, crochet, hooks, gramophone needles or hat pins. A selection of free children's activity sheets are available from the Museum shop, which fully explain how a simple sewing needle was made about 150 years ago. The manufacture of fish hooks, which are produced in a similar way to needles, started in about 1770 and, by the turn of the century, Redditch had also become world famous for the manufacture of all types of fishing tackle.

Next to the museum is **Bordesley Abbey**. Founded in 1138, it was the earliest Cistercian foundation in the West Midlands. The Abbey was destroyed by Henry VIII during the Dissolution of 1538 and the site lay dormant until the first archaeological excavations of 1864, which were carried out by local school teacher James Woodward. Mr Woodward believed he had found the bones of the Earl of Warwick, nicknamed the 'The Black Dog of Arden', for late one night he saw the ghostly apparition of a large black dog. More recent excavations on the Abbey Church have not unearthed any more ghosts but they have produced many spectacular finds.

Excavations of the monastic industrial site have uncovered the timber remains of a watermill, and the Gateway Chapel and graveyard have recently been uncovered and the site restored. Many of the finds from the site are on display in the Visitors Centre, next to Forge Mill Museum. A booklet is available to guide visitors around the 100 acre precinct, one of the largest monastic precincts in the country.

Bordesley Abbey, Needle Mill Lane, Redditch Tel: 01527 62509

Redditch has a number of well established footpaths and country walks, including **The Arrow Valley Country Park**, just a few minutes walk from the town centre. There are over 900 acres of parkland, nature trails, picnic areas and lovely walks to explore, and the Park is ideal for lovers of sporting activities.

The centrepiece of the Park is the Arrow Valley lake, which provides an ideal opportunity to try sailing, canoeing or windsurfing. Rowing boats and canoes are available for those who enjoy messing about on the river, and it is reported that some of the best fishing in the Midlands is to be found here as well.

The town as a whole provides a wealth of sporting facilities and boasts four superb sports centres and two swimming pools. The Kingfisher Centre has many super little shops, ideal for browsing around and purchasing a memento of your visit to the area.

Those of you who enjoy a visit to the theatre, will be sure to enjoy a visit to **The Palace** in Redditch. It is a fine example of an Edwardian theatre and has tremendous atmosphere.

Redditch has a wealth of good restaurants and pubs serving bar food, and these range from traditional English fare right across the board to Tandoori, Chinese, French and Italian.

FECKENHAM

Feckenham lies on the B4090, the old Roman road which was once used as one of the Droitwich Salt Ways and is only a few miles south of Redditch. This large and obviously well-to-do village was at one time surrounded by an important royal forest, but this was felled for fuelling the saltpans and there is no trace of it today. On both sides of the road are fine timber-framed cottages and handsome red-brick Georgian houses.

In the Church of St John the Baptist, a board displays the benefaction which Charles I bestowed upon the village in 1665, giving to 'ye ffree scoole of ffeckenham ye yearly Sume of £6 thirteen shillings and ffoure Pence Payable out of ye fforest land'. The school in question still exists as a private residence, but the money continues to be distributed by a trust to the present village school - a sure sign that royal decrees hold good throughout the passage of time!

Orchard House is a charming listed Georgian house which offers everything you could wish for to make your stay 'extra special'. It's the lovely home of Phyllipa Horsley with superb views of the area from its promontory position taking in its own lake and orchards.

Guests can enjoy horse riding, and croquet on the lawn. With two twin rooms and one double room and a candlelit 16th century dining hall, This is no ordinary bed and breakfast establishment. Phyllipa keeps the atmosphere of her home very informal and relaxed; guests may entertain their friends here and on occasions, they have been allowed the use of the 1935 family Bentley! Much of the food is home produced and breakfast is very 'hearty' indeed. If you wish to enjoy the trappings of an elegant Georgian house in a very agreeable setting with just the right ambience, then this is for you. Highly Commended by the English Tourist Board.

Orchard House, Berrowhill Lane, Feckenham, Nr. Redditch.
Tel: 01527 821497

An area known as **Wylde Moor** can be found south of the village. Over the centuries, the accumulation of debris from the ancient forest has formed this area of undrained marshland, where the Worcestershire Conservation Trust has now created a major bird reserve, complete with nature trails and hides.

Moving north again and heading beyond Bromsgrove towards Kidderminster, try investigating the village of **Chaddesley Corbett.**

Chaddesley Corbett is a fairly large village, dominated mainly by the 14th century church of St. Cassion which stands at its southern end. It is the only church in England to be dedicated to this particular saint, who was apparently a Christian schoolmaster at Imola, condemned to death by his own pupils. The main street is a glorious combination of architectural styles, where black-and-white timbered buildings and handsome Georgian houses of mellow brick vie for your attention. The best of these are the Georgian Lychgate House with its attractive doorway, the Old Schoolhouse of 1809, the Charity House which stands opposite the church, and of course the 17th century Talbot Inn.

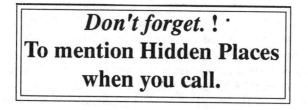

Don't forget. ! ·
To mention Hidden Places when you call.

KIDDERMINSTER

And so to Kidderminster, a name long associated with the carpet industry but also famous for its award-winning 'old' railway station, which recreates the railway architecture of yesteryear.

The carpet industry began here early in the 18th century as a cottage industry. It was the introduction of the power loom that brought wealth to the area and instigated the building of carpet mills. Subsequently, Kidderminster became known as the leading carpet manufacturing centre in the world.

Standing on the River Stour, Kidderminster has a variety of mills, their enormous chimneys dominating the skyline and serving as architectural monuments to the industrial heritage of the town.

Monuments also exist in the form of statues to Sir Rowland Hill and Richard Baxter. Hill founded the modern day postal system in 1840 with his invention of the adhesive postage stamp, and Baxter was a 17th century Nonconformist preacher and writer.

One of the oldest buildings in Kidderminster is the **Caldwall Hall Tower**, and in stark contrast to this is one of its newest additions, the **Wyre Forest Glades Leisure Centre**. An ideal venue for family outings, it provides entertainment in the form of a huge Mediterranean pool. The rest of the complex includes a wealth of water sports, a multi-gym, sunbeds and a restaurant.

South of Kidderminster, **Hartlebury Castle** houses the **Hereford and Worcester County Museum** in its north wing, and here you'll find a unique collection of costumes and horse drawn vehicles - in fact, everything, it seems, to do with the history of the county.

Several of the rooms have been set up so you can really experience what it must have been like to live in a fine manor house in the 17th century. There is also a superb collection of books in the Hurd Library, and portraits of some of the Castle's former residents. The Bishop of Worcester still uses the house as a residence, but visitors can view the State rooms during the summer months.

Built from pink sandstone and surrounded by a moat, the Castle stands on the edge of Hartlebury Common, a large sandy heathland that is the home of many species of birds and wildlife. The gardens of the Castle are in themselves worthy of a visit.

To order other books in the series see the order form at the back of the book

From here we move on to Bewdley, a small town adjacent to Kidderminster, to begin the next chapter.

CHAPTER SEVEN

Bewdley to Leominster

Berrington Hall

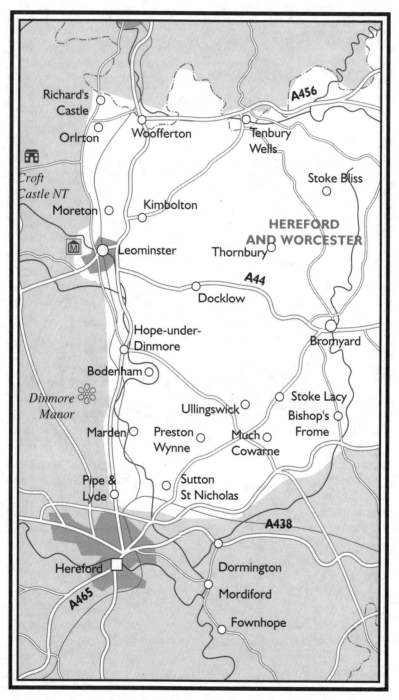

Richard's
Castle

Orlton

Woofferton

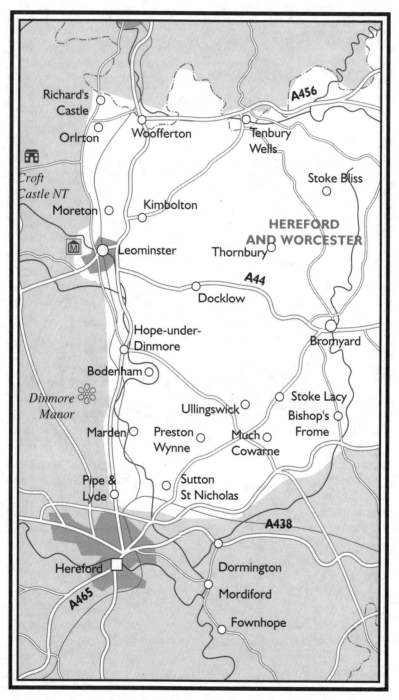A456

Tenbury
Wells

Stoke Bliss

*Croft
Castle NT*

Moreton

Kimbolton

Leominster

**HEREFORD
AND WORCESTER**

Thornbury

Docklow

A44

Hope-under-
Dinmore

Bromyard

Bodenham

*Dinmore
Manor*

Ullingswick

Stoke Lacy

Bishop's
Frome

Marden

Preston
Wynne

Much
Cowarne

Pipe &
Lyde

Sutton
St Nicholas

Hereford

Dormington

A438

A465

Mordiford

Fownhope

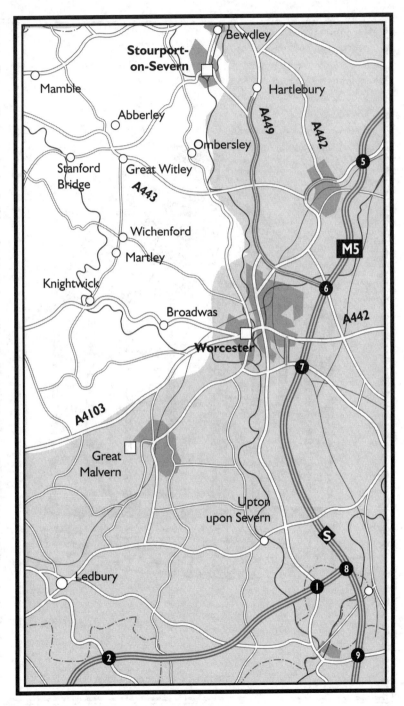

Wichenford Dovecote

CHAPTER SEVEN

Bewdley to Leominster

BEWDLEY

The town of Bewdley is a very attractive place, with a number of winding alleyways adding to its quaint appearance. It is situated on the banks of the great Severn river and so a port was once established here which naturally brought wealth to the town. However, when the Staffordshire and Worcestershire Canal was built, the town lost its status somewhat as a place for dispersing manufactured goods far and wide. As a consequence, the town appears to be set in a virtual time warp with its handsome houses and genteel air - a virtue for the hidden places seeker.

Although Bewdley is now by-passed, it was once a major town and some fine examples of Georgian architecture bear witness to this fact. It is also well situated, with a station on the picturesque Severn Valley Railway.

You can't fail to appreciate the impressive size of the **Wyre Forest**, which covers some 6000 acres and straddles the county border with Shropshire. It is the sort of idyllic place in which you will always find plenty to see and do, no matter what the weather. There is something rather comforting about being under a canopy of trees with the rain pattering down all around you! There are lots of woodland trails for you to follow, keeping an eye out for the plentiful wildlife, and the facilities for visitors at Callow Hill are good and thankfully unobtrusive.

The woodland is quite dense in places, and this ancient place is home to many deer. At one time, the wood was inhabited by a shifting settlement of people who would up and disappear at the slightest provocation. They made their living from the woods surrounding them, weaving baskets and brooms, charcoal burning and even making little wooden 'whisks' which were used to comb the pile out of the textiles and carpets woven in Kidderminster.

MAMBLE

Set beside the A456 Bewdley to Tenbury Wells road in the beautiful pre-Norman village of Mamble, the **Mamble Craft Centre** is a fascinating place to visit at any time of the year. This unique concern is housed in a collection of Grade II listed 17th-century barns which once formed part of the Shakenhurst Estate farm. Founded in 1995, the centre was originally conceived as a retail outlet; however, it has since grown to incorporate a gallery, craft workshops, gift shop and tearoom.

It also organises an impressive programme of craft courses throughout the year encompassing such diverse interests as spinning, lace making, quilting, rug making, toy making and soft furnishings. The courses vary to suit differing levels of ability and cover a broad spectrum of rural, traditional and contemporary crafts. Regular demonstrations are also held at the centre, with visitors sometimes being encouraged to join in with the experts.

The gallery shows regularly changing exhibitions by artists and craftspeople from the local area and beyond, and the tearoom is renowned for serving the best cream teas in the area. Open 10.30am to 5pm on Tuesdays to Saturdays, and 11.30am to 5.30pm on Sundays and Bank Holidays, all year round.

Mamble Craft Centre, Church Lane, Mamble, Near Bewdley, Worcestershire Tel: 01299 832834 Fax: 01299 832132

STOURPORT-ON-SEVERN

At the centre of the Worcestershire waterways is the unique Georgian canal town of Stourport-on-Severn, famous for its intricate network of canal basins. While you are walking around the town, look out for the churchyard where you can see a cast-iron monument to the Baldwin family - they were local ironmasters. This is common practice among the great iron families, but it is an impressive sight.

Unlike nearby Bewdley, the Staffordshire and Worcestershire Canal brought great prosperity to Stourport. Despite being located on the river, there was not much trade here before the canal construction got under way. Some 220 years later, the Canal still brings wealth and life to this town. Where once barges laden with coal, timber, iron and grain were moored at the wharfs, pleasure craft now reign supreme. Many old narrowboats are being refurbished to take visitors on guided trips or to be let out for hire.

Heading south-west along the A451 brings you to **Abberley** village, a delightful place surrounded by hills. Here you will find **Abberley Hall** - a handsome 17th century red-brick house with its landmark tower which is well worth a visit. Centuries ago, from the outcrops of the nearby Abberley Hill, you could have witnessed the bloody skirmishes between Owain Glyndwr and Henry IV.

GREAT WITLEY

Our journey heads to nearby Great Witley, where there is a most impressive parish church. If you never visit another, may we recommend that you go and look at this one, for there are few more glorious. Dating back to 1735 when it was built for Lord Thomas Foley, it looks from the outside like an attractive, but not particularly unusual church. Once inside, it is a blaze of rich colours and Baroque flamboyance which must be credited to his successor, the 2nd Lord Foley.

The interior was actually removed from the Chapel of Canons in Edgware, which accounts for the glorious and priceless treasures on show. These include Venetian paintings depicting biblical scenes and ten beautiful stained glass windows by Joshua Price, and as the church is open daily, visitors are welcome at any time.

Adjacent to the church is **Witley Court**, a hauntingly beautiful house now, sadly in ruins. If at first it seems astounding that a building of this importance and beauty should be left to fall into disrepair, there is a good reason for it. In 1935, this glorious mansion, where royal heads of state would once have dined, and described by many as one of the grandest in Europe, was destroyed by fire. Beautiful statues, like that of Poseidon which apparently used to send a jet of water 100ft into the air, stand sad and forlorn. It only needs to have a 100 ft hedge of thistles surrounding it to make this a fairy-tale castle with a sleeping beauty hiding within.

The house and church are now in the capable hands of English Heritage, the church has been greatly restored, but the house still requires a large input of money and a lot of hard work. In the meantime, there is much to enjoy by exploring the ruins, and each entrance fee goes a small way towards renovating this and many other important properties.

There are so many historic houses and castles in this area that it tends to be a form of pot luck when deciding which one to visit next. **Holt Castle** is well preserved and, if for no other reason, is worth a visit due to the fact that one of its former residents was a member of the Bromley family. Sir Henry Bromley was instrumental in discovering the four plotters who wanted to overthrow Parliament in the infamous Gunpowder Plot. A commemorative tablet to Sir Henry can be seen in the church at Holt, and would he ever have believed that so many years on, one of the men he exposed would continue to roast throughout the land on the 5th of November!

Wichenford Court lies to the south of Great Witley following the B4197, and here you'll find a delightful timber-framed dovecote. Overlooking a pond, this quaint building is owned by the National Trust and is open to visitors throughout the summer. Although it has to be admitted that it is not the stuff of legends, it does make a nice photograph!

LEIGH

Continuing south, you reach **Knightwick**. Following the River Teme, which is abundant with fish, to the south-east you will pass through **Broadwas** and on to the little hamlet of **Leigh**. Here you'll come across St. Eadburga's Church which is famous for a rather strange legend.

A man called Edmund Colles is said to have robbed one of his colleague's who was returning from Worcester and known to be carrying a full purse. It was a dark gloomy night, and as Colles reached out to grab the man's horse, holding on to the bridle, his friend struck at him with a sword.

When he visited Edmund the next day, the appalling wound testified to the man's guilt. Although forgiven by his intended victim, Colles died shortly after and his ghost once haunted the area. A phantom coach pulled by four fire-breathing steeds would appear and race down the hill to the church by Leigh Court, where the coach and team would leap over the tithe barn and disappear beneath the waters of the River Teme.

It was only following a midnight service attended by twelve clergymen that his spirit was exorcised. Leaping over the tithe barn would have been no mean feat, even for a supernatural horseman. It is an impressive building, some 150ft long, and is built of cruck trusses with a tile roof.

Leigh brook is a tributary of the Teme and wends its way through a spectacular 60 acre valley which is cared for by the Worcestershire Nature Conservation Trust. If you are a hardy walker, you could carry on and climb the 670 foot peak known locally as The Beck. The countryside here is lovely, with footpaths that are said to hark back many centuries.

Up on **Old Storridge Common**, birch, ash, oak and bracken have taken a firm hold, and there is a weird, rather unearthly feel about the place. At the top of The Beck, where Augustine is said to have held conference with Welsh clergymen, the views across to Wales are breathtaking. Another place, particularly favoured by Edward Elgar the composer, is the little hamlet of **Birch Wood**, where in 1900 he composed his work 'The Dream of Gerontius'. This was Elgar's vision of this glorious landscape, and you cannot fault his inspiration.

BISHOP'S FROME

Taking the A4103 west and then turning north onto the B4214, you will come to **Bishop's Frome**. This valley has for many years been famous for growing hops, and it is sometimes possible to visit the premises of a grower. Why not try **The Hop Pocket Craft Centre**, where there is much more than the name implies. You can visit the kilns and machinery or try the restaurant, as well as buy gifts in the craft shop.

Continuing in the traditions of its past, **The Five Bridges**, on the A4103 (Hereford to Worcester road) welcomes travellers for good fayre and fine ales as it has done for centuries. The original building dated back to 1580 but was virtually destroyed in 1645 during the Cromwellian period.

The Five Bridges

It was rebuilt in 1780 and used as a coaching inn and resting place for weary travellers. Mark and Bea Chatterton are the present day resident proprietors of The Five Bridges and "desire that this historic dwelling place provides the very best for all who enter".

The mainly home produced food gives them a good start in their aim of satisfaction. The traditional food is of extremely good quality and well known in the region. Typically, main courses would include; Trout, Steaks, Carbonara, good Vegetarian and children's dishes. But there's a great deal more than that on offer and you could start by popping in for coffee and some specially prepared sandwiches to get the rest of the story. Two lounge bars provide plenty of seating area, and once settled in the large comfortable sofas in front of the lovely old open fire, it's hard to move!

The Five Bridges, Nr. Bishops Frome, Worcs. Tel: 01531 640340.

STOKE LACY

It would be impossible to write a book on this part of England without spending some time on the subject of cider. Everywhere you look there seem to be apple orchards, a sign that this is most definitely cider country.

Symonds Cider Mill

There is a fascinating brochure produced by Symonds Cider of **Stoke Lacy** near Bromyard, who have been masters of their trade since 1727. In those far off days, cider making was a little hit and miss, and the resulting brews somewhat variable in quality. Nowadays, with high technology and a demanding market, there is no such room for error, and the modern surroundings and the spotlessly clean conditions would be a totally alien environment for the cider makers of yesteryear. What has not changed however, is the basic ingredient of the best English cider apples which are grown in small orchards within a 30 mile radius of the mill.

At the end of the day, it is the taste of the product which counts, and Symonds have recently had an outstanding success with their Scrumpy Jack brand of draught cider. This product can now be seen in the best of circles and Symonds Cider promote Scrumpy Jack with sponsorship of the England Rugby Union team.

The mill is a great place to visit and makes a welcome change for a day out. There is a shop which sells souvenirs clothing and gifts, as well as the full range of Symonds products. For larger parties of 20 or more a private mill tour can be arranged. Please phone for details. The mill is open all year, and is situated on the A465 between Hereford and Bromyard.

Symonds Cider Mill, Stoke Lacy, Bromyard Tel/Fax: 01885 490411

If you like cider, and are tempted to purchase some samples from the

228

cider mill, why not try using it to make a traditional Old English Cider Cake.

The recipe is very simple - sift together 8oz of plain flour, half a teaspoonful of ginger, half a teaspoonful of bicarbonate of soda, and add a pinch of nutmeg. Cream 4oz of butter with 4oz caster sugar until fluffy, beat in the eggs and then fold in half of the dry ingredients. Whisk a quarter of a pint of cider until it has a good froth on it and add to the mixture. Fold in the rest of the ingredients and give it a good beating. Try to avoid drinking too much of the amber brew during preparation, or you might find your co-ordination going a bit haywire at this point! Turn into a greased tin 8" x 6" and bake at gas mark 4 or 350 degrees Fahrenheit for about 45 minutes. In the recipe we read, it suggested leaving the finished product to settle for a day - if you can resist the temptation of tucking into it beforehand, of course!

To the east lies the village of **Ullingswick**, and in the parish church here is a monument to John Hill who died in 1591. Although the figure depicted has him wearing fur-trimmed robes, it is likely that his origins were more humble, and that his family could not afford a stone tribute. The monument is no more than a painting rendered on stone, but it is visually every bit as fine as a sculpture and rather more interesting for this reason.

Take the Preston Wynne turning off the A417 Leominster to Ledbury road and you pass the small hamlet of **Felton**. Mentioned in the Domesday Book, Felton only has a population of 85, though up until the 1960's that number would swell to over a 1000 during the hop and fruit picking season.

PRESTON WYNNE

Those looking for exceptional bed and breakfast or self-catering accommodation set deep in the heart of Herefordshire's apple country should make a point of finding **New House Farm** in the lovely old village of **Preston Wynne**.

New House Farm

Resident proprietor Julie Rogers and her daughter Rachael offer comfortable accommodation at their extensive farmhouse which is situated to the north of the A465 Bromyard road, five miles northeast of Hereford. They also have two beautifully-appointed self-catering cottages which have been converted from an Elizabethan barn. ETB 4 keys highly-commended and superbly-equipped throughout, one sleeps six and the other four. Residents also have access to a children's pets corner, games room, sauna, solarium and small swimming pool.

New House Farm, Preston Wynne, Hereford Tel/Fax: 01432 820621
Mobile 0589 107696

SUTTON ST. NICHOLAS

Heading south brings you to **Sutton St. Nicholas**, where just outside the village there is a group of stones known collectively (if somewhat ungrammatically!) as the **Wergin Stone**. In the hollow base of one of the stones, rents or tithes were laid to be collected later by the local squire. There is a story that in 1652, the Devil picked up the stone and removed it to a spot a little further away. It took a team of nine oxen to return the stone to its original place, and the temptation is to wonder why the locals didn't simply leave it where it was! If God moves in mysterious ways, it appears that Old Nick has some odd quirks as well. It is thought that whenever a large lump of rock is found where it doesn't belong, the Devil has put it there. It may be that his reputation for more serious evils is vastly overrated - given the work hours devoted to his rock redistribution activities, how he could ever find the time!

MARDEN

On the edge of the village of **Marden**, on the Sutton St. Nicholas to Bodenham road, is a nice pub called **The New Inn**. It is set in an agricultural area of undulating farmland, with a backdrop of hills in the distance in nearly every direction you look. If you like a real pub where the locals are of prime importance, where the ale is well kept and the publicans are welcoming, then make sure you call in.

Legend has it, that the River Lugg has a resident mermaid. One story says that a bell fell into the river and the mermaid refused to hand it back. Despite several attempts to find it, it was never retrieved. The bell remains beneath the waters, and on occasions it can apparently be heard ringing.

Saint Ethelbert was buried for a time in the churchyard here at Marden, but when his body was excavated to be taken to Hereford Cathedral, a rush of water broke from the grave which became known as St Ethelbert's Well. The present church was later built enclosing the well. The church rather charmingly doubles up as a conservation area, and it's worth taking along a spotter's guide to note the variety of wild flowers to be found there.

To the south of the village is the Iron Age hill fort known as **Sutton Walls**. It has a rather grisly tale associated with it, again concerning Saint Ethelbert. On this occasion, in 794 AD, Offa, the King of Mercia, promised the hand of his daughter Alfrida to Ethelbert, who was at that time King of East Anglia. Ethelbert journeyed to Offa's palace at Sutton Walls, and the trip was full of ill omens. The earth shook, there was an eclipse of the sun, and he had a vision that his mother was weeping bloody tears. He really should have heeded the warnings, for after he had arrived at the palace and before the wedding ceremony could take place, Offa beheaded him. Some believe that Offa's wife, Queen Quendra, had something to do with this rather drastic reversal of attitude towards their intended son-in-law.

Although there is not much to see at the camp, as a lot of the land has been worked on, skeletons have been excavated here, showing evidence of much fighting. Some had been decapitated and others bore hideous injuries.

LEOMINSTER

The largest town in this part of the county and is where many of the farming community gather to shop and exchange their news, particularly in the market place which lies to the west of the town.

Much of Leominster's wealth was generated from the wool industry, and it remains a prosperous market town today. There is a weekly market, regular antique auctions, and a great variety of antique and bric-a-brac shops, which can keep the curious collector busy browsing for hours.

The town attracts a wide international following of those who come seeking a bargain, and when you consider the number of quaint villages tucked away in the surrounding countryside, you can well imagine that they must be a rich source of collectable antiques for the local dealers.

Standing on the site of the old Waterway Galleries, **Highbury House** is a splendid building from which is run the thriving family business of Antiques and Restoration. Headed by Robert Fosbrook and assisted by his daughter Deborah, the corner stone of this interesting establishment is furniture restoration, conservation and hand French polishing. However, many other goods and specialist services are offered from Highbury House including upholstery, cabinet making, gilding and gesso work, mirror bevelling and re-silvering, antiquarian bookbinding, metalwork and metal polishing. In these days of mass production and our throw away society, it is getting harder to find crafts people able to provide such specialised services. The in-house French Polisher is Bob

Jones, acknowledged to be one of the best at his craft. Robert also sells Fine antique and reproduction furniture. He offers a highly personal service and will make, repair or alter any item of furniture to customers' specifications.

Highbury House, 25 Broad Street, Leominster, Herefordshire.
Tel: 01568 610620.

With its unusual name you could be forgiven for wondering if the town was in some way connected to the brave Richard the Lionheart. It is little known that there was in fact an earlier king who earned this title. In the 7th century, Merewald, King of Mercia, was renowned for his great courage and ferocity and was known to his subjects as the 'Lion'. He is said to have had a dream concerning a message from a Christian missionary, while at the same time, a religious hermit by the name of Ealfrid had a vision of a lion coming to him and eating from his hand. They later met up at Leominster almost by accident, and when the King heard of the hermit's strangely coincidental dream, he was persuaded to convert to Christianity. Later, the King requested that a convent and church should be built in the town, and indeed the stone lintel on the west door of the church depicts their fortuitous meeting.

This is one theory behind the origin of the name, although less romantic explanations point to both Welsh and medieval Latin words meaning 'streams' and 'marshes', from which it was more probably derived. Of course, any associations with lions are immediately lost when you hear the name spoken, as it is pronounced 'Lemster'.

The Priory Church of St. Peter and St. Paul, which started out as the convent built by King Merewald, became a monastery in the 11th century. The fact that this fine church once enjoyed some religious importance is evident from the three naves that were built in the 12th, 13th and 14th centuries. It also boasts a ducking stool which was the last one to be used in England, and strikes a rather incongruous note in such ecclesiastical surroundings.

And if you walk a little way to **Priory Park**, you will find yourself at **Grange Court**, a magnificent timber building which once stood in the market place but was re-sited here. It was built in 1633 by John Abel, who had a great love for the flamboyant. Much of his work features a richly decorative style of birds and beasts, some recognisable, some obviously based on mythology.

Leaving Leominster, and travelling north just a little way along the A49, keep an eye out for signposts to **Berrington Hall**, a National Trust property. The somewhat austere exterior of Berrington Hall belies the lavish interiors. The strikingly harmonious colour schemes, until recently assumed to be the original, date mainly from around 1900. The house was designed by Henry Holland and built in the late 18th century and the surrounding parkland was laid out by Capability Brown.

Throughout the house there are fine examples of attention to detail, and the drawing room ceiling is thought to be one of the best examples of Henry Holland's work. The central medallion of Jupiter, Cupid and Venus is a composite scene taken from 'The Council' and 'The Banquet of the Gods' by Francesco Penni and Raffaellin del Colle in the Villa Farnesina in Rome.

It's thoroughly enjoyable wandering around the house and grounds, and definitely worthy of a visit.

TENBURY WELLS
Situated on the river Teme and on the county border, is where some of the keenest fishermen get together. It could have been so different! Mineral waters were discovered here in 1839, and efforts were made to build suitable bathhouses to thrust the town into the fashionable world of a spa town. It never happened, and today Tenbury is nevertheless a good place to stop and browse round the shops.

The delightful **Burford House** is tucked away down a lane in the village of **Burford** to the west of Tenbury, although at first you may think you are on the wrong track! Sitting on the banks of the River Teme, the house itself is fairly impressive but is particularly well known for its gardens, which include a delicate 18th century summerhouse. It was owned by a succession of great families: the Cornwalls, the Bowles and the Rushouts; and in the church, several of the Cornwall family have monuments. A massive wooden triptych is displayed which, when opened up, reveals life-size effigies of Edmund Cornwall and his parents. Amazingly Edmund was a towering seven feet three inches tall.

The churchyard at **Thornbury**, just north of Bromyard, is a good place to catch a glimpse of the Iron Age hill fort up on the hillside of Wall Hills. It's quite a climb up there, some 740 feet, although most will admit to being content to view it from the comfort of the churchyard.

BROMYARD

Bromyard is a fine little market town standing on the River Frome, reassuringly sheltered by the hills which surround it. There are some fine buildings here, typically representative of its prosperity, and the Market Place is most attractive. Bromyard was recorded in the Domesday Book and was once a town of major importance, but time has mellowed it. The atmosphere today is lively but unhurried, and all in all it is a peaceful place where you can escape the crowds. The pace quickens in July however, when the Bromyard Gala is held, while autumn sees devotees of folk music flocking from all parts of the country to the annual Folk Festival.

Along the A44 just east of the town, you will find fresh air in abundance up on Bromyard Downs. This heather clad expanse is truly beautiful, especially with a light summer breeze to blow your cares away. From here you can see the distant hills of Wales and the peaks of the Malverns to the south-east.

Driving a little further up and over the Downs into the valley, you'll discover the most beautiful medieval manor house, **Lower Brockhampton**. Owned by the National Trust, this timber-framed house is a treat to look at in the spring when the daffodils really set it off. For the photographers among you, the sight of the house reflected in the moat in front of it, is quite breathtaking.

Although modern farm buildings seem to be advancing on it, the interior is very much as it would have been when it was built in around 1380. Visitors can only enter the hall and parlour, but these, together with the timbered gatehouse, are well worth seeing. There is a very pleasant approach to the house through the Brockhampton estate with its fine stands of oak and beech. Lower Brockhampton is open all year round and is a delightful place, whatever the season.

Lower Brockhampton House

CHAPTER EIGHT

Eardisland and the Marches

Eardisland

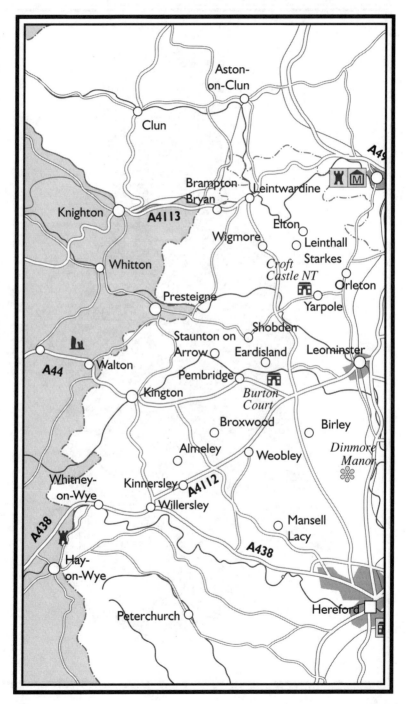

Eardisland

CHAPTER EIGHT

Eardisland and the Marches

THE MARCHES

The evocative name, 'The Marches', refers to the border country region between England and Wales. It is a strangely isolated region, where for many centuries the Lords of the Marches held sway, meteing out their own brand of justice as they saw fit and only paying a token tribute to the monarch hundreds of miles away.

The task of defending the border and erecting the numerous castles that stand along it fell to Edward I who, around 1276, decided that the Welsh princes were becoming too powerful. Before then, border warfare consisted of the occasional Welsh raiding party - nothing on a scale that could inflict real damage. During the next 25 years, castles that were already linked strategically along the border were revamped, and some were specifically built as part of the new initiative. Many still remain, in various states of disrepair and as you travel along the border you are sure to notice them. However, we begin this chapter in Eardisland, situated 5 miles west of Leominster, off the B4457.

EARDISLAND

Glorious Eardisland must be one of the most beautiful villages in Herefordshire, no mean feat as there are so many that deserve the title. Many of the cottages in the village are timber framed, making this one of the most attractive and best loved Tudor villages in the region. The River Arrow flows through heart of the village, with expanses of green sweeping down to its banks. This naturally makes an excellent focal point for the visitor, especially as flocks of ducks and swans regularly gather for a photo-call!

To help you plan your stay, opposite the church you'll find a very helpful information centre which incorporates a heritage centre, book shop and tea rooms. Don't forget there is a full list of all the Tourist Information Centres in the region at the back of the book.

Just south of the village is **Burton Court**, an enchanting manor house, with a soft fruit farm attached, which stands between the A44 and the village of Eardisland. Open to visitors between the spring Bank Holiday and the end of September, it offers a variety of attractions, including displays of historic European and Oriental costumes, model ships, natural history specimens, and a superb working model fairground. The oldest part of the house is the impressive 14th-century great hall which contains a fine Cromwellian overmantel. Open from 2.30pm to 6pm on Wednesdays, Thursdays, Saturdays, Sundays and Bank Holiday Mondays from Spring Bank Holiday to end-September. Visitors are also invited to pick their own fruit in season.

Burton Court, Eardisland, Near Leominster, Herefordshire
Tel: 01544 388231

PEMBRIDGE

Pembridge can be found a little way along the A44, six miles west of Leominster. Half-timbered cottages, inns and almshouses all lend an air of Old English charm to the village, but the jewel has to be the delightful market hall, which dates from the early 16th century. It lies in the tiny market square (well, more of a triangle really), a small, solid building standing firmly on its eight oak pillars.

From the market place, old stone steps lead you up to the Church of St Mary. The church dates back to around 1320, and has one of the best examples of a detached bell tower, a trait that seems to be common across the region. The church has a slight oriental feel, looking a little like a pagoda, and slits in the walls through which bowmen could fire their arrows indicate that the tower doubled up as a stronghold during the time of the border skirmishes.

The impressive **Old Chapel Gallery** is housed in a converted Victorian chapel in East Street, Pembridge. Since moving here in 1988, proprietor Yasmin Strube has turned this into a gallery which not only shows works of fine art, but also offers a superb selection of hand-crafted jewellery, ceramics, woodcraft, ironwork, furniture and designer-made textiles. Local craftspeople are well represented, and visitors will be hard pressed not to find that special gift or item for themselves. Well worth a visit, the Old Chapel has been named a Selected Gallery by the Crafts Council and is open seven days a week throughout the year.

Old Chapel Gallery, East Street, Pembridge, Herefordshire
Tel: 01544 388842

From the village, it is possible to stroll along the peaceful banks of the River Arrow to the ancient earthwork of Rowe Ditch. Little is known of its origins except that it probably predates Offa's Dyke, which could put it at about the 8th century.

STAUNTON ON ARROW

Crossing over the river, and only a mile to the north, is Staunton on Arrow. Staunton is a most attractive village, not least because of the lovely views that one can enjoy from it. The Arrow is a deceptively quiet little river that can rise in the flood months to do an astonishing amount of damage.

When looking for the hidden places for these books, it is always a pleasure to find somewhere a little out of the ordinary. Tucked away here in Staunton on Arrow, is a real gem - **Horseway Herbs** run by Judy and Roger Davies. At Horseway Herbs, the ancient art of cultivating herbs is carried on in grounds absolutely full of herbs and flowers. You can buy all sorts of fresh cut herbs, herb plants, and herbal medicines, while enjoying the magical surroundings. You can also buy bedding plants and hanging baskets. There is a tea room housed in an old barn and we could not think of a more delightful way of spending some time, than just

241

relaxing and walking around the gardens enjoying the smells, with a cup of tea and a light snack before heading off again, A perfect spot.

Horseway Herbs, Staunton on Arrow, Hereford. Tel: 01544 388212.

In the heart of Herefordshire's black and white villages stands **Staunton Park Gardens** set in 14 acres of grounds. Until 1988 this was a private garden owned by Mr. E.J.L. Savage and his family, who have now opened it to the public.

The peaceful ambience of the gardens with its' specimen trees, colourful herbaceous borders, herb and lakeside garden, encourages the visitor to sit and enjoy the beautiful views. The woodland walk around the lake is a delight and when ready for refreshment, the tea-room beckons with its home made teas, where you may also browse through the paintings and country crafts for sale.

Staunton Park Gardens and Lodge

In this lovely pastoral setting, **Staunton Park Lodge** offers self-catering accommodation in a fully modernised cottage, a self contained first floor flat is also available in the main house. They are fully equipped and everything is provided for your comfort. The location offers delightful views from all aspects and the area provides excellent walking country. Three miles from Pembridge on the Titley Road.

Staunton Park Gardens and Lodge, Staunton Park, Staunton-on-Arrow, Leominster. Tel: 01544 388474.

SHOBDON

Turning north again, then taking the B4362 east, and you will shortly come to **Shobdon**. It is worth paying a visit to the parish church, which is most rewarding.

The Church of St. John the Evangelist with its rather plain exterior stands in the grounds of **Shobdon Court**, and although the house is closed to the public, there is a right of way to the church. There was once a 12th century priory here, but this was demolished by Viscount Batement and replaced by a chancel arch with two doorways and three pointed arches. He then went on to rebuild the church in a style that was influenced greatly by the fanciful Strawberry Hill, the house of his friend, Horace Walpole.

The interior of the church is breathtaking. It has been likened to standing inside a giant wedding cake, and the description is accurate. It looks as if someone has taken a great platter of white and pale blue icing into the church and liberally decorated it! Beautiful stained glass windows add to the overall effect and cast a multi-coloured shimmering light about the nave.

Just north of Shobdon Court are the remains of some sand-stone sculptures which have sadly suffered from exposure to the elements over the years. Known collectively as the 'Shobdon Arches', many of the features can now only just be made out. This was Norman sculpture at its finest, possibly the best in England at the time, with the fine details showing zodiacal symbols and dragon heads, both fanciful and exotic. Further sculptures are on show at Kilpeck (5 miles south west of Hereford), where the local 12th century masons can be seen to have been strongly influenced by the skills and styles imported from the Continent. These craftsmen formed the basis of the highly renowned Hereford School of sculpture.

MORTIMER'S CROSS

From Shobdon, it is only a short drive to the site of one of England's greatest battles, the Battle of Mortimer's Cross, at the intersection of the A4110 and the B4362. Here, on the 3rd of February 1461, the final bloody episode in the War of the Roses was enacted. Although hundreds died that day, Edward Mortimer, the Duke of York's eldest son, survived and was crowned Edward IV in the following month of March. All that remains in tribute to the fallen is a commemorative stone erected in 1799, which stands in front of the Monument Inn.

Visitors to this area would do well to find the **Mortimer's Cross Inn** which stands in a prominent position at the junction of the A4110 Watling Street and B4362 six miles northwest of Leominster. Here on the 3rd of February 1461, the final bloody episode in the War of the Roses was enacted. Although hundreds dies that day, Edward Mortimer, the Duke of York's eldest son, survived and was crowned Edward 1V in the following month of March. All that remains in tribute to the fallen is a comemorative stone errected in 1799.

The Eponymous Mortimer's Cross Inn stands in a prominent position at the junction of the A4110 Watling Street and B4362 Ludlow to Presteigne road.

This impressive pub, restaurant and place to stay lies within easy reach of the site of the Battle of Mortimer's Cross.

Popular with walkers, the inn lies approximately halfway along the Mortimer's Trail, the heritage footpath which runs from Ludlow to Kington. As well as good food and fine ales, the inn offers comfortable accommodation in six well-appointed guest rooms, some of which have en suite facilities. There is also a small camping and caravan site to the rear.

Mortimer's Cross Inn, Mortimer's Cross, Near Kingsland, Herefordshire
Tel: 01568 708741

There are some lovely walks around the nearby village of **Aymestrey**. You could take a leisurely stroll through some spectacular countryside above the River Lugg before descending through the gorge that provided

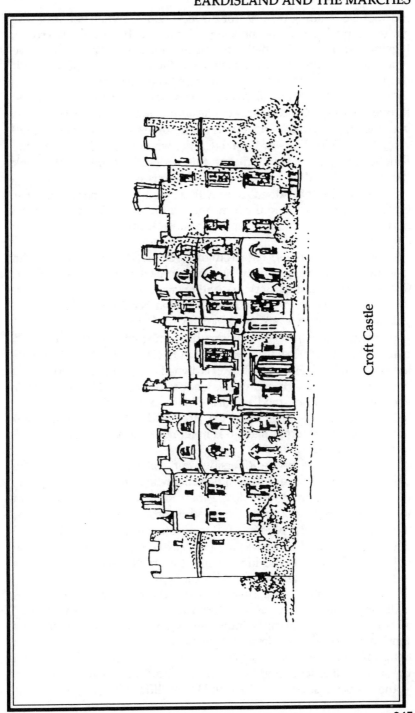

Croft Castle

much of the building material for the local houses. When you leave the gorge, keep a look out for the many wildflowers that colour the rocks, together with several varieties of unusual fungi that appear to thrive here. There is a fine church in the village, the nave having been rebuilt during the 16th century using stone from Wigmore Abbey.

Croft Castle, a National Trust property, is approached from the east through a 350-year old avenue of chestnut, oak and beech trees. It has been the property of the Croft family since Domesday, with a break of 170 years from 1750. The story of the Castle, when it was lived in by the Knights and Johnes family during this period, is related in the book 'Peacocks in Paradise' by Miss Elizabeth Inglis-Jones.

The Castle estate extends over 1,400 acres, and incorporates Bircher Common to the east, and the Iron Age hill fort at Croft Ambrey in the north. The fort dates back to the 4th century BC, and can be reached by a footpath.

The walls and towers date from the 14th and 15th centuries, but the interior is later, being mainly 18th century, when the fine Georgian-Gothic staircase and plasterwork ceilings were added.

The impressive **Riverside Inn** is situated beside the A4110 in the village of Aymestrey, six miles northwest of the old wool town of Leominster. This superb 16th-century half-timbered restaurant, pub and place to stay is an ideal base from which to explore the beautiful rural landscape of north Herefordshire. It is owned and personally-run by Val and Steve Bowen, very friendly hosts who provide outstanding hospitality and some of the finest food and drink in the area. The lounge bar, with its low beamed ceiling, open log fires, old settles and congenial atmosphere, is the perfect place to sample one of the many fine traditional ales or local ciders on offer.

Diners come to the Riverside from miles around to enjoy the cuisine prepared by Steve Reynolds, a chef who trained at La Gavroche, the London restaurant owned by Albert Roux. The menu features an imaginative choice of freshly-prepared dishes, such as Welsh lamb or wild venison, and there is also a full selection of starters, specially-made desserts, and a well-chosen cellar of wines to accompany the meal. The adjacent Old Barn is the ideal venue for small weddings, business meetings, and private lunches and dinner parties.

The Riverside also has four exceptionally comfortable guest bedrooms either with en-suite facilities or a convenient bathroom opposite; all have tea/coffee making facilities and TV, if required. In addition to the rooms within the inn, the former stable block has been converted into two delightful suites, each sleeping up to four people. Dogs are welcome, and the surrounding lanes and woodland are ideal for walking. (For those without a pet, resident dogs Sam and Heathcliffe will be happy to act as a guide.) The inn is situated a mile from the site of the Battle of Mortimer's Cross, the final bloody encounter of the War of the Roses.

The Riverside stands approximately halfway along Mortimer's Trail, a 25-mile signposted walk between Ludlow and Kington that takes in some of the loveliest countryside in the Welsh Marches. For anglers, the adjacent River Lugg offers excellent fly fishing, and there are many other facilities in the locality, including those for canoeing, climbing, pony trekking and cycling. The Bowens also have a well-appointed self-catering cottage available in the nearby hamlet of Bircher. Forge Cottage sleeps up to six and stands on edge of Bircher Common, the site of the National Trust-owned Croft Castle.

Riverside Inn and Restaurant, Aymestrey, Near Leominster, Herefordshire
Tel: 01568 708440

YARPOLE

Back on the B4362, and you will come to Yarpole, where there is another fine example of a detached bell tower. The belfry tower of St. Leonard's, which is believed to date back to the 14th century, is quite separate from the church. A small stream runs through the village, which is a delightful place with its jumble of cottages and their blooming gardens, making it a riot of colour in the spring.

If you take the Ashton road at Luston, towards Berrington Hall, you will come to the village of **Eye**. **Eye Manor** is open to the public and next door in the rather gloomy Church of St. Peter and St. Paul, a former Lord Mayor of London, Thomas Harley, is buried. The unusual pulpit redeems the church, as it is liberally carved with Red Indians and you can clearly make out the feathered head-dresses.

ORLETON

Orleton lies just off the B4361, and for some unfathomable reason, the churchyard here is traditionally thought to be the likely setting for the Resurrection when the Day of Judgement finally arrives. In the past, people from all over the country have specifically requested to be buried here, in the hope that they would be among the first to be brought back to life.

Up on Orleton Hill is a six foot hole, near a break in the rocks, known as Palmer's Churn. A 12ft long narrow passageway connects the hole with the surface, and many foolhardy youths have attempted to crawl through it. Local folklore claims that those boys who get stuck in the passageway will forever remain bachelors.

Heading north from Orleton, takes you to the village of **Richards Castle** on the Shropshire border. The Norman castle, which lies in ruins on the hillside above the church was built, as so many of them were, as a defence against the Welsh. St. Bartholomew's church was also used as a stronghold during the skirmishes, and in the 14th century it was refurbished for use as a chapel by the Knights Hospitallers.

WIGMORE

Wigmore is noted for its ruined castle and Abbey. The Forestry Commission have set about creating a trail here so that visitors can get the most out of this geologically rich area.

With its impressive vantage point, the hillside at Wigmore was a natural site on which to build a castle. Although there was an earlier castle on the site, the main defensive structure was built by William FitzOsbern as one in a chain of fortifications erected along the Welsh border.

By the time of his death in 1071, FitzOsbern had built Chepstow, Berkeley, Monmouth, 'Guenta' (either Norwich or Winchester), Clifford and Wigmore, and had rebuilt Ewyas Harold. Wigmore then passed to the Clifford family, then the Mortimers - and indeed it was from this very castle that Edward Mortimer would have strapped on his armour and ridden to victory with his troops at the Battle of Mortimer's Cross. Although now in ruins, it is plain to see that the castle was once a massive structure, and the village of Wigmore nestled contentedly under its protection for many centuries, until the Civil War.

Two miles north of the village there are signs to Wigmore Abbey, which is situated on the bleak windswept moorland. Hugh Mortimer built the Abbey in 1179 for the Augustinian Order, and it is now a private house. Continuing north, turn right onto the A4113 and make a short detour to **Leintwardine**. The village is made up of colourful cottages built from a variety of stone and the rivers Teme and Clun merge just outside the village by the stone bridge.

BRAMPTON BRYAN

Many of the thatched cottages here, and indeed the castle itself, had to be rebuilt following a seige during the Civil War in 1643. Near the churchyard of St. Barnabus is a delightful 18th century house whose gardens are open to the public, and within the walls is the ruined gatehouse of the castle, which dates back to the 14th century.

Sir Robert Harley (a relation of Thomas Harley of Berrington Hall) owned the castle, and it was due to his allegiance to Cromwell that the castle and village were besieged, not once but twice, by the Royalist army. The Royalists later captured the castle in 1644 and destroyed it. Following this, Harley fell out with Cromwell, and their quarrel had still not been patched up by the time Cromwell died. On that fateful day, 3rd September 1658, it is said that a violent storm swept through Brampton Bryan Park, destroying a great number of trees. Harley was convinced that it was the Devil dragging Cromwell through the Park down into Hell that brought so many trees down.

The lanes from here lead you south past **Letton**, where there is the small Bridge End Gallery, to **Lingen** a simple but charming village. It is here that you will find the ruined Limebrook Priory sheltering in the valley. In this remote and unspoiled landscape, a small Augustinian community thrived up until the Dissolution.

KINGTON

Located at Kington on the Welsh Border, **The Working Horse Centre** has a wide variety of different breeds including the large and powerful Shire horses. Watch the Clydesdale and Suffolk Punch as they demonstrate their might and pay a visit to the pets corner where you will find a variety of smaller animals. The Working Horse Centre is the perfect place to take the children for an experience that is both entertaining and fun, whatever the weather.

The Working Horse Centre, Kington.

Kington

From here, the new **Mortimer Trail** follows a succession of ridges in a north east to south westerly direction covering a 30 mile route to Ludlow. It offers ideal walking for a two to three day period.

To the west of the market town of **Kington** is **Hergest Croft Gardens,** nestling in a delightful valley setting. Here has been created what appears to be a Himalayan scene, with huge banks of native rhododendrons, some as high as 30ft, blooming in great profusion. Maples and birch, magnolia and azalea all live harmoniously together, while if you visit the gardens in spring, the sight of the apple avenue with its carpet of daffodils and primroses is a vision you will never forget.

From the church, you can walk up onto the impressive **Hergest Ridge,** which, rising to around 1,400ft, inspired the musician Mike Oldfield to write the piece of the same name, following his more familiar and enormously successful 'Tubular Bells'. If you carry on along the track for a couple of miles, you will reach Hergest Court, which lies on the southern side of the ridge. This used to be owned by the Vaughans, who at one time owned vast tracts of land in the area.

Two members of the family who gained infamy were Thomas or 'Black' Vaughan and his wife, who was known as 'Gethen the Terrible'. She is said to have taken revenge on a man who had killed her brother by taking part in an archery competition disguised as a man. When her turn came to compete, she shot him dead at point blank range and escaped detection in the mêlée.

Thomas, who was reputed to be an evil tyrant, died during the War of the Roses in 1469, at the Battle of Banbury. His spirit continued to 'ravage' the countryside wreaking havoc, and he is said to have haunted the church in the guise of a bull, upset farm wagons, and even managed to turn himself into a horsefly to annoy the local nags! How on earth anyone knew it was him in this latter role defies imagination, but after terrorising the populace for some time, he was finally overcome while in the guise of a bull. Apparently, one of the 12 parsons sent to exorcise him managed to shrink his bull-like form and cram it into a snuff box, which was then quickly disposed of in Hergest Pool. However, the effigies of Thomas and Gethen in the church show a rather gentle looking couple, who you couldn't imagine harming a fly!

Church House in Kington is a delightful, elegant Georgian house where Andrew and Liz provide bed and breakfast. Particularly popular with walkers (the house is on Offa's Dyke footpath) and welcoming to children. Walkers will appreciate the drying rack above the Aga and guests can enjoy a good old-fashioned bathtime in the large cast-iron bath which has been preserved. The spacious rooms offer fine views from all windows and in the evening you climb into bed between fine pure cotton sheets. After a peaceful night, The final treat is the morning view and aroma of breakfast drifting up the stairs. Mountain bikes are available for hire to work off the wonderful breakfast. No smoking please.

Church House,Church Road, Kington, Herefordshire Tel: 01544 230534
Fax: 01544 231100

Kington can also boast the highest golf course in Britain, possibly even in Europe, on top of **Bradnor Hill** at 1,284ft. The land is held by the National Trust and although a border castle once stood guard over the town, little remains to be seen of it now.

The Talbot Hotel is a popular pub and eating place which occupies a prominent corner position on one of the approaches into the old market town. A handsome Grade II listed property reputed to date from 1603, it contains a fine Jacobean staircase thought to be over 350 years old. It is also rumoured to be the home of a friendly ghost which is said to hide when children are present, much to the chagrin of the proprietors' 11-year-old son, Andrew. Since taking over in 1996, parents Pam and Alan Morris have built up a reputation for providing a warm welcome and some of the finest food and drink in the district.

Talbot Hotel, 52 Bridge Street, Kington, Herefordshire Tel: 01544 231744

Besides its 'lofty' golf course, Kington is well served for sporting and recreational activities of all kinds, mainly centred around the Recreation Ground on the riverside. A cultural import from over the border is the Kington Eisteddfod which is held in June, while the major event of the year is the annual agricultural show, held on the second Saturday in September, and drawing crowds from far and wide. In the autumn stock sales, the stars of the show are the Clun Forest and Kerry Hill breeds of sheep, both ideally suited to life on these border hills.

Chris and John are your hosts at the **Royal Oak Inn** - 'the first and last' in England. Situated in the centre of Kington this is a family run inn offering bed and breakfast, friendly service and very good food. A beer garden provides for 'al fresco' eating in the summer and dogs under control are welcome in this area. In the kitchen is an old post reputed to be where people were tied up to have their teeth pulled out! This 16th century black and white inn is on the Offa's Dyke Path and provides the last mounting block in Kington. Food is served at normal opening hours and is freshly prepared. In addition to the normal menu, 'Specials' are usually available and all offer good value. Popular real ales are served here and what nicer place to enjoy a pint accompanied by freshly prepared tasty food.

Royal Oak Inn, Church Street, Kington, Herefordshire.
Tel: 01544 230484.

During much of your travels in this western part of the county, you may have several times caught sight of signs for **Offa's Dyke**, the impressive ditch that extends around 150 miles along the border between England and Wales; from the Severn estuary at Sedbury Cliffs near

Chepstow, across the massive Black Mountain ridge, through the Wye Valley and Herefordshire, and north to Prestatyn on the North Wales coast. A well preserved stretch of the Dyke can be found on Rushock Hill to the north of Kington, and it's an ideal opportunity to take a closer look at it. This is quite a demanding walk, not a canvas shoe stroll, so be warned. You will need stout walking shoes and protection against the rain, as there is very little cover.

Offa was a Mercian king, who took the precaution during the 8th century of building the ditch to keep the Welsh firmly in their place. He ruled the land south of the River Humber from 757 to 796 AD, and though he was an influential and powerful ruler, his most lasting monument is the Dyke. Although the Dyke was originally thought to be intended as a mainly psychological barrier, excavations in recent years show that it probably had more of a defensive role than was previously reckoned. Remnants of wooden stakes and stone breastwork discovered here and there would seem to support this theory. It was a massive construction, almost 60ft in width, and although the Dyke 'disappears' in places, much of it can still be seen and walked today - particularly in the Wye Valley. For those of you who wish to take advantage of the spectacular Offa's Dyke Long Distance Footpath, the Wye Valley AONB have produced an excellent guide which can be obtained from Tourist Information Offices.

LYONSHALL

The village lies three miles east of Kington and the 'Offa's Dyke Path', in a tranquil setting in the heart of the famous 'Black and White Villages'. It is here you find **The Woodlands**, where Margaret and John Parker will greet you with a warm welcome.

The Woodlands

Built at the turn of the 16th century, this half-timbered 'Gentleman's

Residence' with orchard and gardens, provides comfortable accommodation which captures a true period atmosphere. The Woodlands has twin and double centrally heated bedrooms with washbasin or own bathroom, each having tea and coffee making facilities. There is a separate TV lounge for guests with open log fires in the colder months. Margaret prepares either English or Continental breakfast which may be taken in the dining room, conservatory or the garden when weather permits.

The Woodlands, Lyonshall, Kington, Herefordshire HR5 3LJ
Tel: 01544 340394

In Domesday it was Lenehall. There is a plated salver inscribed "Lionshall 1783" in the church (constructed in 1250), but it is Lyonshall since the last decade of the 18th century. The area was visited during mesolithic and neolithic periods. A rare socketed dagger from the village is in Hereford City Museum Bronze Age collection. During King Offa's reign (756-795 A.D.) his famous dyke marking the border with Wales was constructed and one and three quarter miles of this dyke runs through the village and is one of the most impressive sections in it's southern lenght, it being twenty one feet in height (300yds. from "The Woodlands").

In the 10th century Lyonshall was joined to the lands of Leominster Priory. The castle was built in 1090 occupied by a branch of the Devereux family. It was in a state of defence in 1473 due to Owain Glyndwr's revolt. The ruins still survive within the area of the wet moat from the 13th century. In the 15th century the lands came into the hands of Sir John Merlaury, a personal attendant of King Henry V who left him £100.

16th century buildings include the Royal George Inn, the former Maidenhead Inn, the Old Post Office, Upper House Cottage, Ivy House, the Old Forge, Lower Holm Farm, Elsdon House, the Wharf and the Woodlands.

The Kington and Eardisley Tramway, a continuation of the line from Brecon, ran through the village in the 19th century. The raised trackway is visable in front of the church. This orse tramway received Royal Assent on 23rd May 1818. In 1874 the Aerdisley Railway followed the route of the tramway.

There are two 12th century water corn mills in the parish, one, Bullock's Mill being one of the best documented mills in the country from 1580 to 1928.

ALMELEY

Located in the pretty village of Almeley near to Kington, **The Old**

Granary is an ideal centre for exploring the Welsh border country, including the black Mountains, Brecon Beacons, Offa's Dyke and the Wye Valley. Offering self-catering accommodation throughout the year, this half timbered, Grade 2, beautifully converted detached barn has a large and comfortable living room complete with attractive exposed timbers. There are two bedrooms, one twin downstairs and one double upstairs and a fully equipped kitchen and bathroom with separate toilet. The Old Granary has been lovingly restored by owners Peter and Buzz Cripwell and Architect Peter spends much of his spare time painting watercolours, many of which adorn the white walls of the barn. Situated just across the drive is a delightful, tiny, 300 year old black and white, Grade 2 cottage set amidst the cider orchards. Here you'll find a sitting room, dining/kitchen, bathroom, sun room and two bedrooms, one of which is a twin, the other a double. Both properties are completely private and have full heating, with fuel and power included in the rent, also provided is all bed linen and a colour television. In the substantial gardens there is a barbecue area for those long summer months and pets are always welcome.

The Old Granary, Lower Upcott, Almeley, Hereford HR3 6LA.
Tel: 01544 327351

EARDISLEY

Heading further south on the A4111 brings you to **Eardisley**. This is a village of black-and-white half-timbered cottages lining the one street, with the handsome church of St. Mary Magdalene taking pride of place. The Domesday Book records the village name as Herdeslege - meaning 'Herde's clearing in the wood'. In those days, an enormous forest surrounded the village, and half a mile to the east on Hurstway Common

256

there stands the Great Oak, the last survivor of the forest, which has a girth of 30ft.

KINNERSLEY

Hidden behind the church in the village of Kinnersley, the tower of **Kinnersley Castle** can just be seen from the main road. Originally a Norman border castle, major alterations around 1580 have left it looking more like a fortified manor house.

Kinnersley Castle

Many famous families have lived here over the centuries, including the Dela Beres, the Morgans (brother of buccaneer Sir Henry Morgan) and the Vaughans. Black Vaughan's huge dog is believed to have been the inspiration for Conan Doyle's Hound Of The Baskervilles, and the animal's head can been seen depicted on a frieze in the fine Elizabethan gilded plasterwork ceiling in the solar. The eight acres of grounds contain some fine specimen trees, including one of largest ginkgo trees in the country. As guardian of the property, Katherina Henning is currently undertaking a major programme of restoration using a range of organic and environmentally sensitive techniques. She is an experienced homeopath and is happy to talk about the healing properties of many of the plants to be found here. Kinnersley Castle is primarily a family home, but on certain days it is open for guided tours. It also hosts a number of public events throughout the year, including an open air Shakespeare performance, and musical weekends specialising in traditional-style French music and dancing. The castle is also made available to residential groups from time to time. All enquiries to the address below.

Kinnersley Castle, Kinnersley, Near Hereford, HR3 6QF Tel: 01544 327407
Fax: 01544 327663

BROXWOOD

Travelling further along the A4112, and turning left into the village will bring you to **Broxwood Court,** an English country home which offers stylish accommodation. Occupying a commanding position, with superb views of the Black Mountains and surrounding countryside, the main house was totally rebuilt in 1954, using the stone from the old manor house and retaining the original courtyard and clock tower. Designed by Nesfield in the last century, the garden, with its 1kilometre avenue of established Wellingtonias and Scots pines, sweeping lawns, magnificent trees and lake, covers almost thirty acres and offers a unique atmosphere of peace and tranquillity. Ferdie the dachshund greets guests in a lively manner and the pure white and coloured peacocks, who roam the grounds, are a particularly popular feature. For the more energetic, there is an all weather tennis court, archery, clay pigeon shooting, fishing or punting on the lake and numerous walks around this twelve hundred acre estate which has been in the family for over 300 years.

The accommodation has been totally refurbished over the last four years, guest have exclusive use of the drawing room, dining room and library. There are three bedrooms which have either en-suite or private bathrooms. Ann is an excellent cook who trained at the 'Cordon Bleu' in Paris - her delicious dinners include vegetables and fruit from the extensive organic kitchen garden. Guests can choose from the house cellar, or if they prefer, bring their own wine. Candlelit dinners are served in the elegant dining room, closely watched over by a variety of family ancestors!

Broxwood Court, Broxwood, Leominster, Herefordshire. Tel: 01544 340245 Fax: 340573.

WEOBLEY

One of the stops on the 'Black and White Trail' through Herefordshire, the delightful half-timbered village of Weobley is the location of one of the finest bed and breakfast establishments in the area. **Mellington House**

Weobley

is an imposing 16th-century residence with a Queen Anne façade which stands in an elegant row of houses near the parish church.

The centrally-heated guest bedrooms are all comfortably furnished and equipped with excellent facilities, including tea/coffee making facilities. There is also an attractive lounge with colour TV and a magnificent garden to the rear incorporating a lawn for croquet; in fine weather, guests can enjoy breakfast here al fresco. Resident proprietors Ann and Mervyn Saunders organise enjoyable themed breaks throughout the year, including bridge, croquet and rambling. An experienced walker herself, Ann is a mine of information on the best footpaths in the district.

The Saunders' also have two centrally-heated self-catering apartments available which combine 16th-century character with 20th-century comfort. The Hayloft comprises one twin and one double bedroom, plus lounge, kitchen/dining area, bathroom and separate toilet, and the Annexe comprises a twin bedroom, sitting room, dining area, kitchen and shower room with toilet.

Mellington House, Broad Street, Weobley, Herefordshire
Tel: 01544 318537

After trying 'Wabeley', 'Wee-oh-bly' and even 'Wobbly', it turns out that the name of this delightful black-and-white village is pronounced 'Webley', and that it comes from Wibba's ley, or meadow.

The Castle, which dates from the 13th century, is surrounded by ditches and walls and must have been a fine defensive position, while the church with its towering 14th century spire makes a fine landmark for this charming village.

In the church is a marble effigy of Colonel John Birch who died in 1691. He originally hailed from Bristol, but due to his successes with Cromwell's army he was made Governor of Hereford and later became

MP for Weobley. Rather like Robert Harley mentioned earlier, he too fell out of favour with Cromwell and turned his support to the Stuarts - a rather timely decision as it turned out! After the Restoration, he claimed that he had been imprisoned by Cromwell no less than 21 times. Obviously a man of vision, he apparently put forward a plan for the rebuilding of London after the Great Fire, but this came to nothing.

One of the most colourful and interesting attractions in this part of Herefordshire is **Faraway Flowers,** specialists in the growing of flowers for drying which can be found to the north of the A4112 Brecon to Leominster road near the village of Weobley.

Faraway Flowers

Since founding the business in 1990, proprietor Jill Okell has established a reputation as a floral designer. The walls and rafters of her barn workshop are hung with a breathtaking array of flowers and grasses, creating a wonderful Aladdin's cave atmosphere. She offers a vast selection of floral arrangements, including baskets, garlands, wreaths and bouquets of every shape and size, along with expert advice. She also supplies both fresh and dried accessories for weddings, either to hire to buy. Among Jill's most popular designs are her arrangements on bark, all-natural products which provide a colourful and unusual backdrop in churches, hotels and restaurants. She also stocks a delightful range of handmade crafts and gifts, including pottery and pressed flowers, and offers half-day courses in dried flower arranging. A fascinating place to visit, especially between July and September when the fields are ready for harvesting, Faraway Flowers is open daily between June and Christmas.

Faraway Flowers, The Hurst, Whitehill, Weobley, Herefordshire Tel: 01544 318194 Mobile 0860 648776

STAUNTON ON WYE

Turning south again, and just off the A438, is Staunton on Wye. Although it suffers from some fairly heavy modern development, the views from the village across the orchard meadows are lovely, especially at blossom time when you can catch glimpses of the River Wye through the branches of the trees. The church of St. Mary also has a treasure of its own - some fascinating carvings which date from the reign of Henry VIII. These are more like caricatures than anything else, as they are singularly unflattering: the women have Neanderthal foreheads, the men sport beards that jut out like spades, and both sexes wear weird, flamboyant headdresses. They do not seem to be depicting anything of a religious nature, so where the carvings come from, why they are here and what they are meant to represent is anybody's guess.

Heading north-east from here, the next port of call is **Canon Pyon** on the A4110, which was in fact an old Roman Road. In the village is the quaint church of St. Lawrence, which appears at first sight to be on the verge of total collapse. The nave protrudes at an alarming angle and the pillars all seem to be defying gravity, but apparently the building has been in this somewhat eccentric state since at least the 15th century. There are, in fact, massive supporting buttresses inside that help shore up the church, but it is not clear what caused the edifice to lean so dangerously in the first place. There are some usual carvings inside too, which bring to mind Aesop's fables. A fox, a goose, a pelican and an angel are depicted, all said to have been transposed from the fallen abbey at Wormsley.

HOPE UNDER DINMORE

Hope under Dinmore lies on the A49 Leominster to Hereford road, and offers the opportunity to visit **Queenswood Country Park**, a 170 acre site with massive oak stands. The area has been designated a Site of Special Scientific Interest, not least because of the wonderful variety of trees - over 400 species have been established in the arboretum. The Park attracts around 400,000 visitors each year, but even with this number of people visiting the Park, it is quite possible to get away from the masses by following the trails or veering off them to explore on your own.

The forest itself once stretched to Wales and is a marvellous place to stop for a while, instead of driving past without realising what the park has to offer. It is beautiful at any time of the year.

Adjoining Queenswood Park is **Dinmore Manor and Gardens** where the Knights Hospitallers had their local headquarters. The gardens are sheltered, but as they rise some 550 ft above sea level, you can see for miles across to the Malvern Hills - a truly magnificent sight. The gardens attract many visitors and it is easy to see why, for they are beautiful. The

Dinmore Manor Chapel

12th century Chapel is situated near to the rock garden and pools, while the 'grand old man' of Dinmore must be the ancient yew tree which is about 1,200 years old. Many varieties of plants, shrubs, alpines and herbs can be purchased from the Plant Centre, and other attractions to enjoy are the medieval sundials, an Aeolian Pipe organ, the views from the Rook Walk, and the Grotto. The Music Room in the Great Hall is occasionally used for recitals and the acoustics of the room must be splendid.

The Murray family have owned the Manor now for over 60 years, and you may be surprised to learn that we all owe a great deal to the present owner's grandfather - especially those of us who drive a great deal! It was Richard Hollins Murray invented the reflecting lenses which were later used by Percy Shaw to develop the familiar 'cat's eyes' that we see every day on our roads. He bought the estate in 1927, and restored and developed many of the buildings and gardens that can be enjoyed at Dinmore today.

CHAPTER NINE

Hay-on-Wye to Hereford via the Golden Valley

Abbey Dore Court

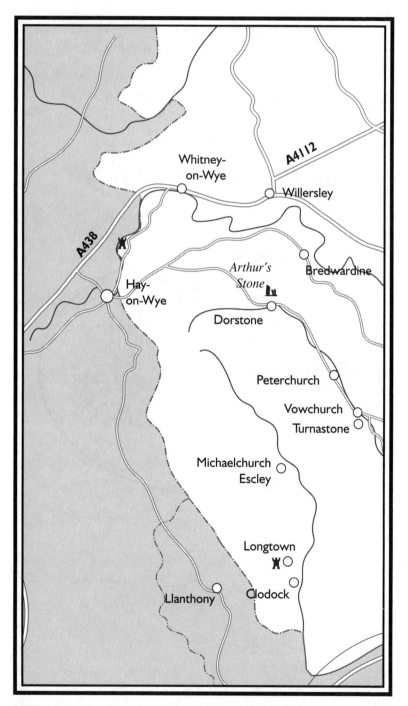

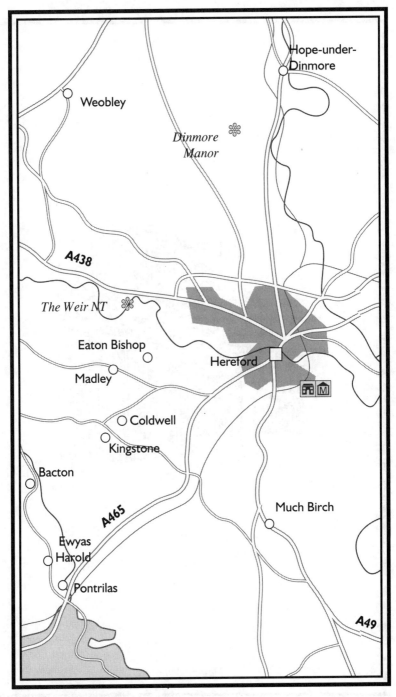

Hay-on-Wye

Hay-on-Wye to Hereford via the Golden Valley

HAY-ON-WYE

The small market town of **Hay-on-Wye** is strictly in the county of Powys, in Wales, but on many maps can be seen to straddle the county border. It originated as a fenced-in hunting ground, which is also the literal translation of its welsh name, Y Gelli Gandryll. Extensive hunting forests existed in the 11th century, and stretched from the Herefordshire borders to Talgarth in the west.

Unlike the River Severn, the Wye is a more easy-going river. While the Severn has borne the brunt of industrial development, the Wye has escaped much of the overspill of industry, leaving us today with a waterway that is unsurpassed in beauty and relatively unspoiled. In these peaceful, clean waters, some of England's finest salmon fishing takes place. Above the land, Offa's Dyke guards the waters of the Wye, and the earthwork, which rises in places to 30ft, still offers a good vantage point over the border river.

Before the building of the Elan Valley reservoirs with their elaborate water control system, this area was particularly prone to flash flooding by the River Wye. The ferry and ford were badly affected until a bridge was built in 1763, although this, and its successor were swept away. A high-level bridge is now in place.

Claiming the best situation (and probably the biggest cat) in this popular and historic town, **Kilvert's Hotel** remains privately owned and continues to provide a personal level of service. Kilvert's is ideal as a base for those wanting to explore the numerous bookshops for which the town is famous. Equally, it offers a warm and comfortable haven after a day's walking in the beautiful surrounding countryside. All eleven centrally heated bedrooms are en-suite, with hospitality tray, radio, colour television, hairdryer, trouser press and direct dial telephone. One of the most popular rooms has oak-beamed eaves, a half-tester bed and a delightful view over the hotel gardens to the hills beyond.

Colin's Restaurant, which forms part of the hotel, has been in existence for ten years at various premises in Hay, moving to this location when its owner, Colin Thomson took over the ownership of Kilvert's four years ago. Colin's offers an interesting menu with a robust cooking style often with subtle influences from other cuisines around the world. Whenever possible, a good selection of fresh fish is available and there is always a choice of vegetarian food included.

The bar of the hotel has become very popular with the locals and tourists alike, not least because of the real ales and the bar food, which comes in generous portions. During the summer, the hotel is very lively, as is the town; in good weather it is a pleasure to take advantage of the garden, play croquet or relax by the fishpond and fountain. This is also the venue for Hay Jazz, which is a small celebration of jazz music held over the last weekend of July, with appearances by both local and international jazz musicians. W.T.B. 4-Crowns.

Kilvert's Hotel, The Bullring, Hay-on-Wye, Hereford.
Tel: 01497 821042 Fax: 01497 821580.

Book addicts will fall in love with the town of Hay because of the number of second-hand bookshops for which it has become internationally known. The man responsible for this was Richard Booth, who bought the Castle and set up his first second-hand bookshop in it.

Since then, both new and second-hand bookshops have sprung up all over the town, transforming Hay into a veritable Mecca for bibliophiles. There's nothing more pleasant than spending an hour or two leafing through old books, and although admittedly some are musty and worn, there is always a chance that you may spot a special edition. Whether you are here to add to your own collection or simply to browse, you have to be pretty hard-hearted to walk out without one or two worn copies tucked under your arm!

Those looking for first-rate bed and breakfast accommodation in the heart of the town should make a point of finding **Skynlas House** in Church Street. This imposing stone-built residence stands adjacent to the Hayes Cinema Bookshop, the world-renowned specialist bookshop which occupies a former picture house in the centre of town. Resident proprietors Anne and Mike Day offer a warm welcome and first-class hospitality.

Their house is furnished and decorated in charming traditional style, and is the ideal place in which to relax and enjoy the unique atmosphere of Hay-on-Wye. The three spacious and comfortably-appointed guest bedrooms are equipped with colour televisions and tea/coffee making facilities, and two have the added benefit of en suite facilities.

Anne and Mike are renowned for their wonderful breakfasts. Hearty and delicious, they are prepared from fresh local ingredients and are sure to provide a nourishing start to the day. Skynlas House enjoys far-reaching views over the town to the Radnor hills, and is the ideal holiday base from which to tour the Black Mountains, the Brecon Beacons and the many superb attractions of the Welsh Marches.

Skynlas House, Church Street, Hay-on-Wye, Herefordshire
Tel: 01497 820368

There are traces of a Normon motte here, believed to have been started by Revell, the first Norman in the area, soon after Henry I came to the throne. After King John had captured and burnt the original castle, a second castle was built on the site, and the remains can still be seen today.

The building was apparently carried out under the direction and supervision of one of the most reviled and treacherous Marcher Lords, William de Braose and there is a local story that his formidable wife, Matilda, built it with her bare hands. Gerald of Wales wrote of Matilda as an excellent woman, prudent, chaste and a marvellous housekeeper. This was a most flattering description of a woman whose reputation as

Lady Chapel, Hereford Cathedral

a baby-eating, demon-conjuring witch persisted in the Brecons seven centuries after she died.

Just outside the town is the mysterious Twyn-y-Beddau, roughly translated into English as the Mound of the Graves. They say that here, the Welsh met with the army of Edward I, and during the three day skirmish, the little river Dulas ran with the blood of the fallen. Legend has it that the mound contains the skeletons of all who died during this bloody battle, but historians in fact believe the grave to be several thousand years older.

The Seven Stars

The creeper-clad old stone frontage of **The Seven Stars** in Hay-on-Wye is deceiving indeed, It's charming exterior looks for all the world a double fronted house, yet it offers bed and breakfast accommodation in ten guest bedrooms, most with en-suite facilities and exposed beams. Television and tea/coffee making facilities are provided in every room. With twenty six years experience as Hoteliers, Mary and Dai Ratcliffe recently acquired this lovely 16th century house which is full of character and charm. A licensed resident's bar, full central heating and an open fire in the resident's lounge makes for a very comfortable and relaxing atmosphere. However, a little further exploration reveals, very surprisingly, a heated indoor swimming pool and Sauna - What luxury! The only such facility in Hay - a wonderful addition. Home cooked meals are another special feature of The Seven Stars, Mary provides a formidable breakfast menu with many options. A packed lunch is a further service available, and after your day of exploring, what could be better than returning to the comfort of The Seven Stars, a swim or Sauna, an apéritif overlook the river and some home cooking? Excellent!

The Seven Stars, Broad Street, Hay-on-Wye, Powys.
Tel: 01497 820886.

South-east of Hay-on-Wye is **Michaelchurch Escley**. Although Michaelchurch is little more than a hamlet, it is virtually the only place of habitation in the little valley of Escley Brook. In the church, on the northern wall, is an unusual picture of Christ, where he is depicted with a workingman's tools, which is worthy of closer inspection. The short drive down the Escley Brook Valley takes you into **Longtown** where the Escley, the Ochlon and the Monnow rivers converge. To the west, the Black Mountains rise and the village seems to straggle up the hillside to the ruins of Longtown Castle.

Dating back to the 12th century, the Castle was built on the site of a much earlier Roman fort and must have made a spectacular vantage point from which to keep an eye on the forbidding mountain range. It is easy to forget that these mountains must not be taken for granted, and the village Mountain Rescue Post is a visible reminder to take care at all times.

The temptation is to wander off the beaten track, as there are some splendid walks around here. The Offa's Dyke Path extends westwards, while for less hardy souls there are considerably easier walks around the Olchan Valley, following the brook upstream.

Less than a mile further south is **Clodock**, named after the 6th century local lord, Clodack. It is said that when his burial procession arrived at the River Monnow, the team of oxen pulling the cart steadfastly refused to move. The ropes containing his coffin broke, and this was accepted as a celestial sign for a church to be built on the spot.

Clodack was buried by the river and the church was built on top of his remains. There are similar tales found around the country.

WALTERSTONE

Walterstone is to be the southernmost point of this particular chapter. It stands on a hillside in this remote corner of the county of Hereford and Worcester, and offers breathtaking views of the mountains. In the past, this area was a hot bed of rebellion and political manoeuvring and a glance across the valleys will soon bring to mind the bloody battles that were once fought for this border country.

Midway between Abergavenny and Hereford, situated on the wooded banks of the River Monnow in rural tranquillity, is **Allt-yr-Ynys Country House Hotel and Restaurant** - a perfect setting for such a fine hotel. The gracious former home of Robert Cecil who came to this picturesque spot in 1091, after the conquest of Glamorgan. He was knighted by Henry 11 following the wars against the Welsh. The house stands in an acre off well-established gardens where flowers, shrubs and roses abound. Beyond the gardens, a further 16 acres of fields and woodland provide pleasurable rambling and the setting for certain hotel amenities.

Allt—yr-Ynys as it is today was built about 1550. It retains much fine craftsmanship of the period which can be seen throughout the house. Individuality and tradition are much in evidence in the bedrooms, each of which are furnished differently; one with a particularly fine Jacobean fourposter. Concessions to modernity include en-suite bathroom, telephone, colour television and radio. Providing additional accommodation are the luxury suites adjoining the main house. Once part of the ancient outbuildings, the have been sympathetically transformed and blend perfectly with the surrounding architecture.

Particular attention is paid to the quality and presentation of the food, using only the finest cuts of meat and the freshest of vegetables and other ingredients and the cuisine will be found imaginative and of high quality. The chef is very happy to prepare special dishes for any special occasions. At Allt-yr-Ynys much importance is attached to personal service. The owners, John and Janet Manifold and their excellent staff, do go out of their way to meet individual requirements.

Allt-yr-Ynys Hotel, Walterstone, Herefordshire. Tel: 01873 890307
Fax: 01873 890539

From Walterstone, head north passing through the village of **Rowlstone** which sits almost 1,000ft up on the hillside. The church has some marvellous sculptures by the Hereford carvers, including many of birds.

EWYAS HAROLD

Set in the centre of the village of Ewyas Harold on the edge of the Golden Valley of Herefordshire is the centuries old **Temple Bar Inn and Restaurant.** Even though the inn was built in the 17th century its character still remains - with an open fire, stone walls and flagstone flooring in its character bar. There are many myths as to how the Temple

Bar Inn acquired its name, one being the possible use of the inn as a small court, used by circuit judges coming from the Temple Bar in London.

The popular public house is owned by licensee Clark Castle, his wife Lorraine and Clark's parents Carol and Dennis. The family owned Free House offers a warm and friendly atmosphere with home-cooked food, bar snacks an a 'la carte restaurant menu, Sunday lunches and take-away meals seven days and nights a week. The pub provides regular entertainment with music, darts, pool, Quoits and family fun quiz nights.

The Temple Bar Inn

Annually, the Temple Bar hosts its own three day Beer Festival which is held in its Stable Barn offering a range of the most popular to the most unusual real ales. The Inn is also the starting point for one of the many fine walks of the Golden Valley. The quality and comprehensive facilities combined with the tranquil yet easily accessible location, make the Temple Bar inn one of the fine stops in the beautiful Golden Valley.

The Temple Bar Inn, Ewyas Harold, Golden Valley, Hereford.
Tel: 01981 240423.

West of the village lies the ancient Welsh kingdom of Ewias, and 'Harold' derives from the English king who was overthrown by William the Conqueror. As far back as 1051, Osbern Pentecost, had built one of the first castles to use the motte and bailey concept, here. Harold, some 14 years before his demise in the Battle of Hastings, had Pentecost killed in a furious attempt to rid the country of the accursed Norman settlers.

The castle rose again during William the Conqueror's reign and survived into the 15th century following the defeat of the Welsh hero Owain Glyndwr. Today, only the distinctive mound remains in memory of this once important border castle.

Abbey Dore is where a Cistercian order was founded in the 12th century. At one time, the Abbey was important enough to boast a 250ft long church, but the Dissolution brought about its downfall like so many others. However, in 1630, Lord Scudamore appointed John Abel to instigate a restoration project on the building, and he was responsible for installing the magnificent oak screen. From the abbey ruins, he built a new church which seems somewhat unsure of its status today - is it an ancient monument or simply a parish church?

Well worth a visit too is the garden at **Abbey Dore Court**, opposite the church. The River Dore flows through the garden, and visitors can enjoy the pond, rockery and walled garden with their colourful array of hardy perennials and shrubs.

Abbey Dore Chancel

BICTON

Set among one and a half acres of nursery and gardens, Wendy and Fred offer you a very warm welcome to **Pentwyn Cottage Garden**. Situated in the very heart of the picturesque Golden Valley, one mile from Dore Abbey and central to Hay-on-Wye, Hereford, Ross-on-Wye, Abergavenny and the Black Mountains, you will known when you have found the cottage when you see the bedecked floral mini at the entrance. The Bed and Breakfast accommodation comprises of one double/family/twin, en-suite bedroom and second double room with separate bathroom facilities. Each light and airy guest room comes complete with a colour TV, full central heating and a complimentary tea and coffee tray. Throughout the day Morning Coffee, Light Lunches and Afternoon Teas are served in the peaceful and colourful garden setting.

Offering a large selection of Home-Made preserves to accompany your cream tea, Wendy makes sure that all the home-baking is prepared using only the freshest ingredients. In the gardens you will find a whole host of bedding plants, perennials and alpines, with a separate sales area for the unusual selection of attractive Hand-Made Garden Furniture. So if you are travelling through the Bacton area, be sure to pay a visit to Pentwyn Cottage Garden and browse freely through the secluded greenery.

Pentwyn Cottage Garden, Bacton, Hereford HR2 0AP
Tel/Fax: 01981 240508

Just a little north, situated in open country in the very heart of the beautiful Wye Valley, is **Webton Court,** a late 17th century Georgian black and white farmhouse offering bed and breakfast accommodation throughout the year. Your hosts are Robert and Gill Andrews who have owned and personally this attractive farmhouse for over 30 years and it is down to their warm and friendly welcome that guests keep returning year after year. The guest accommodation comprises of a sitting room with colour television, a family bedroom that sleeps up to four people, a double bedroom, two single bedrooms and large bathroom.

Packed lunches can be provided on request and three course evening meals are available by arrangement and can include such home-cooked delights as Local Trout, Beef Casserole and a selection of Roast Meats. Gill breeds and races thoroughbred mares on the premises and there are also plenty of cows, sheep and lambs for the children to watch and learn from. Gill also has a new hobby, taking out her new Driving Cart and showing her guests some of the 200 spectacular acres that make up this fully working farm.

So for holiday accommodation that is both pleasurable and educational,

HAY-ON-WYE TO HEREFORD VIA THE GOLDEN VALLEY

Webton Court Farmhouse is a must for those who wish to experience the taste of real country living.

Webton Court Farmhouse, Kingstone, Hereford HR2 9NF
Tel: 01981 250220

Returning to the B4347 which follows the natural route of the Golden Valley northwards, you will come to the villages of **TURNASTONE** and **VOWCHURCH**. Thw villages are linked by a stone bridge over the river, and even though they are set so close together they each have their own church. The reason for the close proximity of the churches (and the origin of the villages' names) can possibly be explained in a rather quaint, if fanciful, local tale. It is a tale of two sisters who both declared that they could build a church before the other. "I vow my Church will be completed before you turn a stone of yours", one of the sisters apparently challenged the other!

Whatever the reason, the church at Vowchurch has an unusual carved depiction of the story of Adam and Eve dating back to 1614, where a pear is featured rather than the more familiar apple.

PETERCHURCH suffers a little more than the other villages in the valley as most of it is right on the road, yet it is the self-styled capital of the Golden Valley and has a fine parish church. In 786AD, it was King Offa who brought monks to the village to found the original church. Introducing the Christian faith to all parts of his kingdom appeared to be high on Offa's list of priorities. It was a sign of his great power and influence that a bishop from Rome was included in the missionary party established here.

St Peter's Church

DORSTONE

Dorstone lies just off the B4348, and not only is it a very attractive village with neat sandstone cottages centred around the green, but it lies at the head of the Golden Valley on the River Dore. The name of the valley is thought to be due to a misunderstanding by the Normans, who took the Welsh word dwr, meaning water, and translated it as the French word d'or, meaning golden. Whatever the source of the name though, the Golden Valley is without doubt a beautiful part of the county and is an extremely popular area with visitors.

St. Faith's Church in Dorstone has a connection with far off Canterbury, as Richard de Brito, one of the four knights who murdered Thomas à Becket, established a chapel here after serving 15 year's penance in the Holy Land for his crime.

Rather like Robin Hood, it seems that you can be in almost any county in England and find some reference to King Arthur, and on nearby Merbach Hill above Dorstone, you'll come across **Arthur's Stone**. Conflicting reports state that beneath this arrangement of massive stones is the grave of a king who provoked Arthur into a fight, a giant who was killed by him, or even the body of Arthur himself! No matter what the legends say however, it is a megalithic tomb and dates way back to between 3,000 and 2,000 BC, which makes it one of the earliest signs of civilisation in the region.

At 1044ft, there are spectacular views from here over the **Golden Valley** to the Black Mountains beyond, and some say that on a clear day you can see as many as 11 counties from this vantage point. A little way from Merbach Hill is a field, beneath which a lost town is supposed to lie, buried by an earthquake hundreds of years ago. It is said that if you gaze into the depths of the pond that lies in the field, you may just catch a glimpse of a steeple far below.

Here in Bredwardine churchyard lies the Reverend Francis Kilvert, whose diaries concerning local parish life in the mid-Victorian era were republished in 1969. The 11th century church also features a pair of grotesque carvings on the northern lintel and some effigies of medieval knights. You can pick up a leaflet in the church which offers a guided walk around some of the hills surrounding the village, taking in special features like the medieval fishponds.

BREDWARDINE

Brobury House can be found by following the brown tourist signs, and it is very close to the Red Lion at Bredwardine. You will probably recognise the house if you were watching the television drama 'Dandelion Dead', based on the true story of a solicitor who poisoned his wife, when it was used as the residence of a Major Armstrong.

The gardens are delightful, and if you sit for a while to take in the stunning view, you can see across the river Francis Kilvert's vicarage. This local diarist was an important figure, active in the 1870s and his diaries still widely read. The gardens are also the best vantage point from which to obtain a view of the Bredwardine bridge built in 1776, and reputedly the oldest brick built bridge in the country still in public use.

The house itself is set in 8 acres of semi-formal gardens and at first glance looks somewhat like a Scottish hunting lodge with a conical tower. This feature was added by a Scots owner to the rather square original of 1880.

Brobury House

Today, the house has the added benefit of being able to offer 4 guest rooms which carry a 2 Crown rating, for anyone who finds it difficult to tear themselves away from this peaceful haven. Each room is individually named, and has either en-suite facilities or shares with one other room. This grand house has a large lounge in which to relax, and a terrace on which you may have breakfast on fine days.

Brobury House, Gardens, Gallery,. Tel: 01981 500229 (Gardens & Gallery)
Tel: 01981 500595 (Accommodation)

Guests are able to take full advantage of the grounds, and with the river literally at the bottom of the garden, Brobury House is ideal for fishing enthusiasts. For those who prefer to look after themselves, the owners will shortly be opening 2 self catering cottages. Phone for details. As if this were not enough, there is a quite outstanding and very interesting gallery situated in the former coach house and surrounding buildings.

Here, Mr Okarma houses his collection of over 100,000 antique prints of every conceivable subject and place. Why not pick up a small print for your home, which can be authenticated on the spot and even framed while you wait. There is also a collection of watercolours dating from 1820 to the present day.

There are courses at Brobury on crafts and watercolouring. But whether you are artistic or not, want to enjoy the fishing, or just find a place to visit for a couple of hours or a few days, this is one of those interesting gems of a place which this book is all about. Well recommended.

MOCCAS
Just south of here on the B4352 is the village of Moccas, where the beautiful 12th century church of St. Michaels was built from the unusual local stone known as tufa. The composition of this rosey-pink stone is formed when a limestone deposit drops onto vegetable debris, thus giving it a slightly spongy appearance. The church has been competently restored and is a fine building in the Norman tradition. Nearby **Moccas Court** was built in 1775 for Sir George Cornewall, and when you first catch sight of it the overwhelming impression is of a giant's doll's house. The extensive grounds were landscaped by Capability Brown, and in the Park the terraces slope down to the banks of the Wye and deer roam free. The house and grounds are open to the public from April to September.

MADLEY
Madley lies six miles west of the city of Hereford, with a rather splendid church boasting some fine stained glass and an immense stone font which is said to be the second largest in his country. There is also a well preserved 14th century cross in the churchyard. This is a very old place indeed: St. Dyfrig, the man who is said to have crowned King Arthur, was born here in the 5th century.

EATON BISHOP

Entering Eaton Bishop brings you even closer to the city. The village retains a lovely country air about it, despite the fact that it is barely four miles from here to the outskirts of Hereford. The church at Eaton Bishop is famous for its east window, containing 14th century stained glass which is said by many to be unsurpassed anywhere in England. Even to the untrained eye, the clarity and detail of The Crucifixion, Madonna and Child and the Archangel Gabriel in greens, yellows and browns immediately strikes you as something special.

HEREFORD

Founded around 700 AD, this cathedral city which sits on the banks of the River Wye was in Saxon times the capital of West Mercia. Hereford is full of legends, and perhaps the best one concerns **Hereford Cathedral**, which is, externally at least, a relatively plain and stalwart building in contrast to the soaring edifices to be found in some cities.

Ethelbert is the Cathedral's patron saint and it was built on his shrine. Ethelbert was supposed to wed Offa's daughter, and arrived at court only to be decapitated. In the tale, the king had great trouble disposing of Ethelbert's remains, as whenever they were interred, a strange light shone above the spot. So great was Offa's guilt over the terrible deed that he set off to Rome to confess and hopefully be forgiven. In the previous chapter it's described how Ethelbert was dug up from the graveyard at Marden and brought to Hereford, and apparently, when his head rested on the ground here, a gush of water appeared which became known as St. Ethelbert's Well.

Another saint enshrined at the Cathedral is Thomas de Cantilupe, who went to Rome to seek the Pope's backing in a disagreement he had with the Archbishop of Canterbury. He died while returning to Britain and was brought to Hereford for burial.

Hereford Cathedral is home to the world famous Mappa Mundi. This beautiful world map dating back to 1290 may not be geographically accurate, with Jerusalem being quite explicitly central, but as an historical and religious artifact it is quite unsurpassed. Drawn on vellum, it measures 65in by 53in and was the work of Richard of Haldingham. It is interesting to note that East is at the top, obviously indicating that all things good and with religious significance were thought to come from that part of the world. Richard was Treasurer of Lincoln Cathedral for a time, and if you look closely at the map, you may notice that Lincoln appears more prominent than Hereford.

In the Chained Library there are a staggering 1,400 chained books and around 225 medieval manuscripts, dating from the 8th to the 15th century. Two of Thomas Caxton's books are here and the library houses

Hereford

the largest collection of printed and handwritten books in the world. The Mappa Mundi, the Treasury and Library can be visited on weekdays between Easter and October.

The Cathedral also houses the interesting Hereford Brass Rubbing Centre, which always appeals as it is so nice to go somewhere steeped in history and take away a little part of it - legally! The brasses, which hark back to medieval and Tudor times, depict all classes of medieval society: the knights and their ladies, the priests and scholars, and the merchants. You can have a look round for free, and any costs are purely for the paper and wax crayon and the time required to accomplish your masterpiece.

Striking out from the Cathedral, turn into Capuchin Lane which used to go by the decidedly less romantic name of Cabbage Lane. Halfway down the street is Capuchin Yard, where many craft workshops are situated. Capuchin Street leads to Church Street, part of the pedestrianised area, having a marvellous selection of individually owned businesses so often lacking in towns and cities of a much greater size than this. **Hereford Castle** has a romantic legend associated with it, concerning the Governor's daughter, Isobel Chandos. She apparently fell in love with Hugh Despenser, Edward II's favourite. He did not however, reveal his royal connections, but warned her of an impending attack upon the Castle. Presumably he was hoping that she would flee with him, but loyal to her family, she hastened to her father to warn him.

Despenser led the attack himself and when the battle turned against him, he was captured and hanged. The tragedy continued, for when poor Isobel saw her beloved hanging high, her sanity was destroyed. They say that she only found brief solace after this by taking short river trips alone towards Ross-on-Wye, but on one such occasion the boat overturned and she drowned. Isobel's spirit is said to still haunt that stretch of the Wye today, wailing for Hugh. Furthermore, a sighting of her is said to bring extremely bad fortune!

The Cider Museum and King Offa Distillery in Pomona Place off Whitecross Road is well worth a visit. What an atmospheric place it turns out to be, with one of the finest collections of cider making memorabilia we had ever seen. The Museum is housed in a former cider works, and along with exhibitions showing how cider has been processed throughout the centuries, visitors are able to see a travelling cider brandy maker's still.

There is an enormous 17th century French beam press, a cooper's shop and massive oak vats dating back to the Napoleonic era. Apparently, the cider brandy distillery was the first to be licensed in Britain for over 250 years.

This historic city is full of museums, these are just a few that can be recommended. The **St. John Medieval Museum at Coningsby**, can be found in Widemarsh Street. The building itself dates back to the 13th century and today has been restored to show its use in the 17th century. There is plenty of information on the Ancient Order of the Knights of St John of Jerusalem, with displays including armour, emblazons and information about its wars during the 300 years of the Crusades. Here too you can find out about Charles II's mistress, Nell Gwynne, who was born in Pipewell Street. There is a costumed model of her and of the Coningsby pensioners who used the hospital. The museum also has its very own resident skeleton, thought to be a 15th century Abbot.

Churchill Garden Museum and Hatton Gallery has a fine display of furniture and costume collections of the late 18th and 19th centuries. Rooms have been laid out as they would have been in Victorian times, and feature a nursery, parlour, kitchen and butlers pantry. There is a Costume exhibition gallery and a special barometer exhibition. The Hatton Gallery is devoted to the works of local painter Brian Hatton, who perished during the First World War. His sketches of the conflict are particularly poignant. Open Tuesday to Saturday from 2pm until 5pm and Sundays in summer from 2pm to 5pm. Also open Bank Holiday Sundays and Mondays.

Hereford Library, which stands on Broad Street, is a solid and imposing four story stone building. Within it you will find the City **Museum and Art Gallery**. There are fascinating displays on the area's natural history, archeology and local history. In the art gallery there are occasionally displays of work from the permanent collection by local artists. Exhibitions change monthly. Open every day except Mondays and Bank Holiday Sundays and Mondays, and Sundays May to October.

Hereford City Museum and Art Gallery, Broad Street, Hereford
Tel: 01432 268121 ext 207

The Old House Museum, Hereford

The Old House stands right in the centre of High Town, which is very much the hub of Hereford. This wonderful timber-framed building dates back to 1621 and is a fine specimen of Jacobean domestic architecture. Today it houses a museum furnished in 17th century style on three floors, including the kitchen, hall and bedrooms. Open every day except Monday afternoons and also open Bank Holiday Sundays and Mondays, and Sundays May to October.

The Old House Museum, High Town, Hereford
Tel: 01432 268121 Ext 225

This is a lively city, still clinging to its farming traditions, with the cattle market coming to town on Wednesday. The cosy communal feel is intensified by the fact that through-traffic is barred, making it a much more enjoyable place to wander around. If you are looking for somewhere to stay for a few nights while you enjoy all that the city has to offer, then here are a couple of suggestions.

If you like travelling on makeshift boats, you could well have floated downriver from Hay-on-Wye to Hereford rather than taken the shorter route by car! The three-day River Wye Raft Race sets off from Hay in early May, and after an arduous journey, competitors arrive several days later in Chepstow on the River Severn. May is a great time to visit, for several other major events that take place in the city at that time are the Regatta, the May Fair and the Music Festival.

Whatever your reasons for coming to Hereford you are sure to enjoy this city, which although impressive, is small enough and cosy enough to allow you to get to know it in a very short space of time.

CHAPTER TEN

Ross-on-Wye and the Wye Valley

Ross-on-Wye

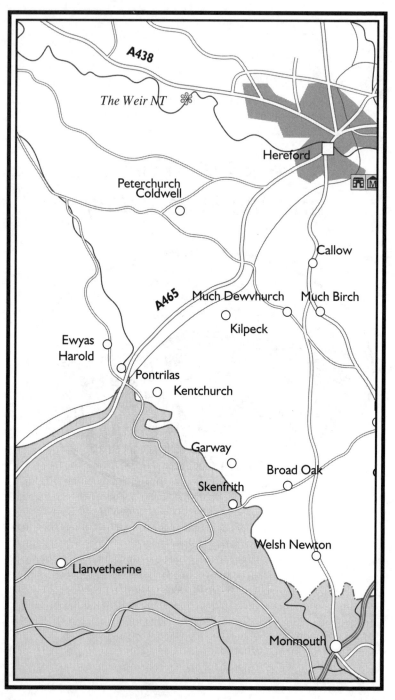

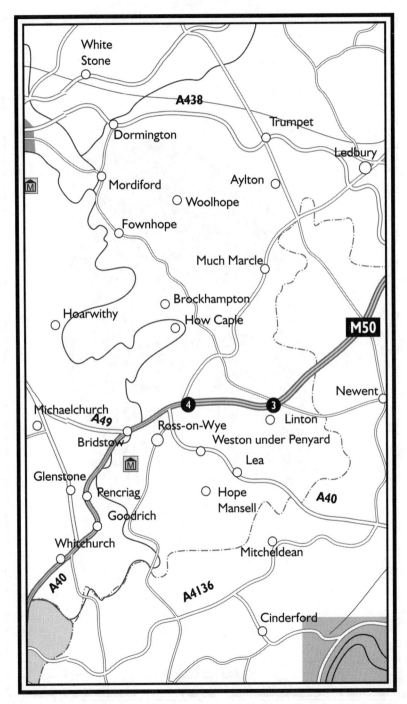

Kilpeck Church

Ross-on-Wye and the Wye Valley

MORDIFORD

Nestling at the base of a wooded hillside is the village of Mordiford, which can best be approached along the B4224. The village stands on the River Lugg, just above the place where it joins the Wye, and the River Frome flows into the Lugg just north of the village. It comes as no surprise, therefore, that the landscape around Mordiford is one of lush water meadows where flooding is an ever present danger. However, in 1811 when a storm hit the vicinity with some ferocity, it was the placid Pentaloe Brook that runs through the centre of the village that caused most of the devastation. Buildings were washed away in the rising floodwaters, which swelled to 20 feet deep and 180 feet wide, and several villagers were drowned.

The medieval bridge with its elegant span of nine arches was once the source of regular revenue for the ancient kings of this land. Apparently every time the monarch crossed the bridge, the local lords had to provide him with a pair of silver spurs as a levy on the manor.

Mordiford also has a legend concerning a dragon, and if you had visited the village church in the 1800s you would have seen a painting of a dragon on the west wall. The painting has long since gone, but the story lingers on. Apparently the dragon had been found by a local lass while it was still small. She nurtured it lovingly, and although at first it was content to feed on milk, and later chickens and ducks, it eventually developed a taste for cows, and finally people.

The beast terrorised the locals and indeed one of the paths leading from the woods is still known as Serpents Lane. It was here that he would slink along to the river to drink, and it is said that no grass ever grows there! No one put themselves forward as brave enough to combat the beast, but at last a man called Garson who was awaiting execution decided that he had nothing to lose. He hid in a barrel by the riverbank and when the dragon appeared, he took aim and shot the creature in the heart. The dragon fell but alas, poor Garson perished in the fiery breath of the dragon's last throes.

This story seems rather reminiscent of J.R.R. Tolkien's book, 'The 'Hobbit', where Bilbo and his comrades hid in barrels and floated down the river. When Bilbo confronts Smaug in a test of riddles, the hobbit admits to being a 'Barrel-rider', and we wondered if the great author had taken inspiration from this local legend!

Three weekends of the year are very special in **Marcle Ridge** Country, the area just to the south of the Ledbury to Hereford road, for here they celebrate the festival of The Big Apple - a unique opportunity to experience the season of mellow fruitfulness in countryside that is nothing short of fabulous. To find out exactly which dates the festival will take place, ring the Hereford Tourist Information Centre. You will find the telephone number at the back of this book. The slopes of the Marcle Ridge also have wonderful views across to the Malvern Hills to the east, while **Woolhope**, to the west, is within the Wye Valley Area of Outstanding Natural Beauty.

AYLTON

Set amidst two acres of south facing gardens in the peaceful hamlet of Aylton, **The White House** is a 16th century listed former farmhouse with a converted Oast House in a courtyard setting. This heavily timbered country retreat is situated only four miles outside the town of Ledbury, opposite Ayltons tiny Norman church, as is personally owned and run by David and Elisabeth Jones.

Offering excellent bed and breakfast facilities, complete with luxury bath and shower room and comfortable lounge area with colour television, David and Elisabeth also have four holiday cottages available to rent throughout the year. These pretty character cottages have been created by converting a selection of listed barns and an old red brick Oast house that all stand within the two acres of grounds. The Welsh cottage sleeps two people in a traditional beamed en-suite double bedroom with a cosy open-plan living/dining room with gas stove and compact kitchen area. There is also a pretty patio area complete with garden furniture for those summer months.

The Oast house has been skillfully converted into the very attractive Kiln cottage, again sleeping two people in a ground floor en-suite bedroom, the first floor offers open-plan living complete with night storage heaters and a compact kitchen. The spacious and comfortable Hop Pickers cottage sleeps up to four people in one double en-suite bedroom and one twin bedded room which boasts glorious views over the nearby Malvern Hills.

The living/dining room has a warming gas coal effect stove, modern kitchen area and a patio with garden furniture. Finally the Long Barn offers its guests spacious ground floor accommodation for up to four adults. There are two large and airy bedrooms, a living/dining area and a charming small woodland garden, where you can enjoy a meal al-fresco on those warm summer evenings.

The White House, Aylton, Ledbury, Herefordshire HR8 2RQ.
Tel: 015131 670349

It is well worth coming and staying here to discover for yourselves why this particular festival has won awards. There are a number of activities organised by the seven parishes of **Aylton, Little Marcle, Much Marcle, Munsley, Pixley, Putley** and **Woolhope**, and visitors are invited into farms and orchards, cider mills, churches, village halls and pubs. The aim of the festival is to help the general public to enjoy and understand their rural tradition, and secondly to ensure that there is a greater awareness of the need to preserve the apple.

The local growers have inherited the history of several thousand kinds of apple that have been considered worthy of a name. Victorian connoisseurs gave as much consideration to apples as they did to their claret and port! The flavour of each variety, the point of perfection in its season and its merits as a cooking apple were known, argued over and savoured.

Over one hundred years ago, one of these parishes had a very special link with the Victorian passion for varieties. The Woolhope Naturalists Field Club contributed outstandingly to the collection and classification of apple varieties, and to the improvement of British orchards. Within these parishes remain many fruit farms, and a far greater number of cider orchards.

As to what happens on the festival weekends - it is difficult to say. Events vary from year to year, but could include: a display of apple varieties; Apple Question Time - a variation on Gardeners Question Time; pruning demonstrations; and 'Apple' teas.

The seven parish churches are all tiny and full of character; each is decked out for harvest time over one of the weekends and the pubs produce special cider and apple dishes. Short walking routes have been specially identified, passing through orchards where possible, with leaflets available at venues throughout the area. You can even go on a special guided cycle ride. There might be a Barn Dance, an exhibition of Apple Paintings, or a visit to Hellens, a superb historic Herefordshire home.

WOOLHOPE

It is worth popping into the church at **Woolhope** for a quick glimpse at one of England's best known and bravest ladies, Godiva. Woolhope Manor was owned by her and her sister Wulviva, although later they gave the property to Hereford Cathedral. The church features a modern stained glass window depicting Godiva's nude jaunt through the streets of Coventry, her natural charms chastely concealed beneath impossibly long flowing locks!

MUCH MARCLE

In the church at **Much Marcle** there is a rare, painted wooden effigy, carved from solid oak and thought to be the likeness of a 14th century landowner called Walter de Helyon. It is a beautiful piece of work, rather pure in execution and showing the subject to have been 6ft 4in tall. Up until the 1970s he was painted a rather sombre stone colour, but was then loaned out to London Museum for an exhibition on 'Chaucer's London' and was repainted in his original colours. The great Marcle Yew is still standing, its massive trunk hollowed out allowing eight people to sit in comfort on the bench inside.

The village is quite large compared to others in the region and has several fine houses reflecting its past glory. It is the hub of the Hereford cider industry and has been so since the 17th century. Although the industry slackened a little in the 19th century, much was done to restore it by the local MP for Hereford, C.W. Ratcliffe Cooke. He avowed that cider should be adopted as the national beverage, and this earned him the title 'The Member for Cider'. Great names in cider making like Henry Weston thrived, and the cider works still operate today.

A fascinating place to spend an hour or two is **Weston's Cider Mill**, the home of traditional Herefordshire cider-making for over a century. Situated just off the A449 midway between Ledbury and junction 4 on the M50, it lies surrounded by cider-apple and perry-pear orchards in the wonderfully-named village of Much Marcle. The business was founded by Henry Weston, a tenant farmer who took over The Bounds in the 1870s. Looking for a means of supplementing his income from the farm, he made the decision to set up a commercial cider-making operation in 1880 which has grown steadily ever since. Fortunately, the original stone mill and screw press that were used in the early years have been retained, and they can now be seen in the beautiful grounds of the farmhouse. Still an independent family-owned business, Weston's is now an impressive cider-making operation which was the first of its kind in the country to receive the prestigious British Standard award for quality assurance.

Visitors can sample ciders with names like Stowford Press and Old Rosie, some of which are produced to recipes dating back well over a century. Tours of the cider mill lasting around two hours can be booked by writing or telephoning in advance; these incorporate a product tasting and take in the visitors centre and shop. At certain times, rides are also available on a wagon drawn by Weston's superb pair of Shire horses. Open Mondays to Fridays 9.30am to 4.30pm and Saturdays 10am to 1pm, all year round.

Weston's Cider Mill, Much Marcle, Ledbury, Herefordshire
Tel: 01531 660233 Fax: 01531 660619

Life in Much Marcle has not always been so peaceful and restrained as it is today. In 1575, between 17th and 19th February, a strange convulsion shook Marcle Hill and caused it to move about 400 yards; killing cattle and sheep, uprooting trees and hedges and demolishing a chapel in the upheaval. The cause of this violent tremor remains a mystery to this day.

HOW CAPLE

Just off the B4224 is **How Caple Court**, at How Caple, with its magnificent ornamental terraced gardens and woodland grounds. Set high above the River Wye with views towards the Forest of Dean and the Welsh mountains, you can discover a unique atmosphere of peace and tranquillity wandering through the eleven acres of delightful gardens. Originally laid out in Edwardian times, the gardens are currently undergoing a long-term extensive restoration programme.

The formal terraces with yew hedges, pools, statues and traditional rose garden contrast with less formal planting of mature trees, shrubs and shrub roses. Other notable features include a cascading waterfall and the sunken Florentine Water Gardens, which are currently undergoing reconstruction. New walks are planned among established woodlands. An additional attraction in summer months are Operas and Concerts held in the grounds. The Nursery holds many delights for the traditional gardener, selling many varieties of old English roses and interesting herbaceous plants, while those who enjoy the pleasure of making their own clothes will discover some lovely fabrics in the Stable Shop, as well as gifts and a selection of excellent-value clothes. -Teas and light snacks are available in the Tea rooms and parties are welcome.

The gardens and nursery are open all year round, but note the fabric shop is closed on Sundays during the winter. How Caple Church is noted for its stained glass windows, 16th century diptych, and carved wood. Keen Golfers might like to note, that How Caple's owners also run the South Hereford Golf Course at nearby Upton Bishop. The house itself is not open to the public.

How Caple Court Gardens, How Caple, Hereford. Tel: 01989 740626.
Fax: 740611.

If you carry on down the road you will find the church of St. Andrew and St. Mary, which is locked at all times to protect the priceless German Diptych inside - a sad indication of the days we live in. The marvellous eight-panelled painting depicts the martyrdom of St. Clare and St.

Francis, Mary Magdalene washing the feet of Christ, and various other events. It is well worth making an effort to view this masterpiece, tucked away in this remote little church. Visitors may obtain the key from the information desk up at How Caple Court.

A glance at a road map will immediately show the distinctive undulating loops of the Wye as it threads its way through this gentle valley country. This is lovely countryside, indeed the whole of the Wye Valley is recognised as an Area of Outstanding Natural Beauty. So clean is the Wye that it has also been designated a Site of Scientific Interest, and visitors can walk the stretch from Bishops Meadows just south of Hereford and carry on to Ross-on-Wye, a distance of around 17 miles. Eventually, if you are prepared for some strenuous walking, you could continue on to Chepstow where the Wye meets the Severn. Whether you choose to walk the entire route or just saunter along the peaceful tracks and paths through the meadows, it is a delightful opportunity to enjoy the Herefordshire countryside.

BROCKHAMPTON

Opposite the west entrance to Brockhampton Court Hotel lies the Church of All Saints, one of only two thatched churches in the country and built in 1902 by Alice Foster, as a memorial to her parents. The architect was William Lethaby, surveyor and architect of the Fabric of Westminster Abbey from 1906 to 1918.

It is without doubt an original piece of architecture. Apart from the Norfolk reed thatch, it has stained glass made in the Christopher Whall studios, and tapestries from the William Morris workshop from designs by Burne-Jones. Without intention, Lethaby produced a church which is totally in keeping with the medieval period.

It is rather sad to see that the original Brockhampton parish church, Holy Trinity, which stands in the grounds of the Court, has been allowed to go to ruin since the consecration of All Saints. It was built in the early 15th century and consisted of only a Chancel and Nave, with the Tower being added in the 16th century.

The lanes lead you back to **Fownhope**, where every year on Oak Apple Day in May, the Green Man Inn celebrates the restoration of Charles II with the Heart of Oak Club Walk. Members of the Club carrying sticks decorated with flowers process through the village and make their way to the Inn. The lovely old black-and-white building dates back to 1485 and is full of character. One of its earliest landlords was Tom Spring (whose real name was Thomas Winter), the bare-knuckle prize fighter who died in 1851. A one-time champion of All England, one of his most famous fights lasted nearly two and a half hours.

HOLME LACY

Holme Lacy was originally the estate of the de Lacey family in the 14th century, before passing to the Scudamores. It was the Scudmores who have lived on in local folklore, for following the first Viscount Scudmore's release from prison during the Civil War, he devoted his time to agricultural concerns. The cider makers of Hereford must pay tribute to him, for he was the first person to classify the various varieties of cider apple and introduced the well known Red Streak Pippin strain. The fine Palladian mansion you can see today dates back to 1672. Grinling Gibbons once designed the woodwork that graced the house, but today his notable work has travelled across the oceans, for although some of his pieces are now in Kentchurch, others have crossed the Atlantic and reside in the Metropolitan Museum of New York!

Near the village of Holme Lacy is **Dinedor Court**, a splendid 16th century listed farmhouse in a peaceful setting by the Wye. The magnificent oak panelled dining hall, brass beds and log fires are just some of the special features that would make a stay here most enjoyable.

Below **Grafton**, where signs of an Iron Age settlement have been found, drive up over Ridge Hill towards **Callow**, where there's a rather unpleasant tale connected with the coaching inn near to Callow Hill. Overnight travellers at the inn seemed to disappear without trace, but some time later their corpses were found in a house up on the hillside. The murderers were later convicted and hanged, and eventually the house fell into ruin.

However, in this particular ghostly story it is not the dead who haunt the spot but, most unusually, a phantom house, which has been seen upon the site of the old one. One woman in particular is said to have seen it on a number of occasions and was overwhelmed with the sense of evil that seemed to emanate from the apparition!

ACONBURY

There must be something about this quiet landscape which appeals to the paranormal, for there are a number of different legends associated with the area. Several of these centre around Aconbury, just east of Callow. It is said that on Twelfth Night, St. Anne's Well erupts in a fit of bubbling and the waters emit a strange blue mist or smoke. It was thought that these waters could cure any eye infection, but only the water drawn up in the first bucketful would be beneficial. The church has long been shut up, but it is a relief to know that the physical Aconbury is no less fascinating than its 'other-worldly' aspect. Here, many centuries ago, a priory for Augustinian nuns was established and this may account for the rare herbs that grow specifically in the region. Danewort and elecampane, both brought over from Europe, were probably introduced into the priory garden to aid in medicinal matters.

KILPECK

While in this corner of the county, you shouldn't miss the chance of visiting Kilpeck, famous for its Norman church of St. Mary and St. David. Visitors flock here to see the carvings, and not just one or two sculptures, but a plethora of images and motifs, including a splendidly vulgar sheelna-gig on the corbels. Happily displaying her private parts for all the world to see (and presumably put there to discourage lustful behaviour) one can only imagine what the various generations of churchgoers must have made of her and her decadent fellows. We have come across one of these particular figures before in earlier chapters, and as there are only a few of them in the country it is worth making her acquaintance.

The motifs around the south doorway are reminiscent of Viking decorative styles with dragons and other characters, the like of which would sit happily on the prow of any longship. This fascinating little church has been the subject of many theories and books, but whatever the reasoning behind the carvings, they are undoubtedly a source of amusement, pleasure and fascination for all who come to see them.

HOARWITHY

The unspoilt village of Hoarwithy stands on the banks of the Wye just two miles from the A49 and here the banks of the river are lined with willows. The name of the village even means 'white willow'. At one time, oak trees were in abundance too, and provided the area with an important industry. Bark from the oaks was transported to Hereford to be used in the tanneries.

The jewel of Hoarwithy is undoubtedly St. Catherine's Church, a splendid 'folly' which stands on a hillside overlooking the Wye. When the Reverend William Poole arrived in Hoarwithy in 1854, he was most dissatisfied with the style of the chapel he found there. Being a wealthy man, he had the means to do something about it, and over the next 30 years or so he brought in an architect and a team of craftsmen to build a new church around the chapel. The result was a complete transformation - a striking campanile, and arcades which could have been transported from a hillside church in southern Italy. A host of wonderful features inside include beautiful tiled floors and a white marble altar with a lapis lazuli inlay.

<CFrom the village it is possible to walk down to Sellack and view the suspension bridge that spans the Wye between **Sellack** and **Kings Caple**. However, to get to the next port of call, follow the road back to the A49. **St. Weonards**, which lies in picturesque hill country on the A466 Hereford

to Monmouth road, is named after an obscure Celtic saint of unknown origins. Figures depicted in a now vanished window of the church suggested that he may have been either a woodcutter or a hermit, or both. Near the church is a mound in which St. Weonard was once said to lie buried in a golden coffin. Excavations in the 1850s put an end to this idea, however, when nothing more significant was found than two bodies which had been cremated and buried during the Bronze Age.

KENTCHURCH
Further west, Kentchurch lies right on the border with Gwent, and here you will find **Kentchurch Court**, an impressive former border castle which is well worth making an appointment to visit for its fine decoration. John Nash of Regent's Park fame rebuilt the house around the 1800s, giving it a more informal appearance, and splendid wood carvings by Grinling Gibbons have been retained in all their glory. They were originally intended for the Scudamore's main seat at Holme Lacy and it is wonderful to see that they have survived. The Scudamore family have owned the Court since the 14th century.

GARWAY
A short distance away at Garway, there is a marvellous medieval dovecote. What makes this so strange is that the dovecote could accommodate nesting for exactly 666 birds, the Devil's number! This charming village is hidden away in the Monmow Valley, and one who fled here to find sanctuary in the church tower during Henry VIII's purges was the Abbot of Monmouth. The Knights Templar built the church and the influences from the Holy Sepulchre in Jerusalem are most apparent. The farm next to the church continued to be used as a Commandery for the Knights Hospitallers after the order of Templars was disbanded.

Heading south towards **Welsh Newton** you may catch a glimpse of **Pembridge Castle**, now a private house, although the grounds are open on Thursdays throughout the summer. In the churchyard of St. Mary the Virgin at Welsh Newton lies the body of John Kemble, a Roman Catholic who was executed in 1679 for daring to hold a mass in the Castle.

Travelling south to Monmouth and beyond the county border, there is a very pleasant waymarked trail which can be joined from the A4136 Monmouth to Staunton road. It will take you northwards through Highmeadow Woods to the River Wye. One of the largest boulders in the country lies off the path, the weirdly named Suck Stone, which at 60 feet long and nearly 40 feet wide, is an impressive monument to the forces of nature.

The path leading west will take you past the Seven Sisters Rocks up to King Arthur's Cave on **Great Doward Hill** where in 1870, the remains of hippopotamus and elephant, bear and bison were discovered, together with several flint tools. This cave had probably sheltered Stone Age man some 60,000 years before the legends of Arthur ever began.

If you follow the path to the east, one of the most breathtaking views over the Wye will be your reward, and the promontory of **Symonds Yat** rock near **Whitchurch** is a spectacular landmark, standing at the neck of a great four mile loop in the river around Huntsham Hill and rising 504ft above sea level. Near here too, is one of several places along the Welsh Marches where Caractacus is said to have made a last stand against the Roman invaders, led by Ostorius Scapula.

SYMONDS YAT

Leaving the A40(M) at Whitchurch we followed the winding B4164 for a mile and a half to arrive at Symonds Yat and the totally unexpected beauty of this hidden area. Here we delighted in finding the Victorian **Riversdale Lodge Hotel** which stands by the site of a long-vanished Roman trading post and iron works. To its west rears the ancient forest mass of dolomite rock - Great Doward. It is a naturalist's delight for people of all ages many of whom come regularly to enjoy the peaceful surrounds, the truly lovely views and tremendous hospitality of Riversdale Lodge.

Those making the hotel their new discovery may well enjoy a lunch or cream tea on the terrace, entranced by the racing rapids of the River Wye or the climbers clinging-on hundreds of feet above. But for those already in the know, The Riversidale Lodge is a totally relaxing experience for a week or two where Brian Morgan who runs the hotel, has found just the right blend of efficiency and homeliness with a touch of good humour to attract guests to return time and time again. For the warm balmy summer days there is a superb outdoor swimming pool landscaped into the terrace and gardens, ideal for sun and atmospheric bathing.

For those striding out in all weathers, there's cosy log fires to return to. Using the Lodge as your base, there's lots to do in the area; canoes can be hired, horse riding, rock climbing, bird watching and nature trails to follow. A leisurely game of golf or perhaps a few hours on a mountain bike to get your circulation going! Whatever your challenge or relaxing pursuit, The Riversdale offers many attractions. Make your reservations early though or you may be disappointed. Brian will be more than pleased to fax. a brochure to you.

Riversdale Lodge Hotel, Symonds Yat West, Hereford.
Tel. & Fax: 01600 890445

A fun way to while away an afternoon is to explore the **Jubilee Maze** in Symonds Yat West. The maze was devised by brothers Lindsay and Edward Heyes to celebrate Queen Elizabeth's 1977 Jubilee. There is also a museum of mazes which is 'amazing', and a puzzle shop with books and games. During the evening, the maze is illuminated to give it a real air of fantasy, and you can explore the twists and turns until late in the evening. To find the maze (if not your way out!) look out for signposts when you enter Symonds Yat West.

A visit to **Symonds Yat Garden Centre** at any time of the year is well worthwhile. Keen gardeners can browse over the extensive range of plants, shrubs and trees many from the Centre's own nursery, while helpful and informed staff are on hand to give advice on how best to care for them. All tastes are catered for in the retail area of the garden centre which stocks a huge range of top quality garden products. There is also an interesting selection of specialist goods to help you with your flower arranging and an attractive range of gifts are featured for all ages. Other displays feature garden furniture, greenhouses, tools and accessories.

Symonds Yat Garden Centre, Jubilee Park, Symonds Yat West,
Herefordshire. Tel: 01600 890580.

It would be wrong to get the impression, by the way, that visiting Symonds Yat East and West is something that can be accomplished on foot. Although the two halves of the village are only 100 yards apart, the

River Wye divides them, with no bridge between. The distance from East to West is therefore some four and a half miles by car, unless you use the ferry.

WHITCHURCH

Whitchurch village, which lies in the shadow of Symonds Yat Rock seems quite a hub of entertainment and here you will find a fun fair and a Bird Park. At The World of Butterflies you can enjoy the warmth of the tropical hothouse, while the butterflies fly around your head. There are some rare specimens to admire and informative displays make your visit all the more interesting. A small, well-stocked gift shop, means you can buy a memento of your visit.

From Whitchuch we took the turning up the hill passing the Crown Hotel. Turning right just before the school in Llangrove, we continued for about three quarters of a mile and turned left up the drive to **Thatch Close,** a secluded Georgian farmhouse providing bed and breakfast on a small mixed animal farm with large colourful gardens and magnificent views.

The bedrooms have either en-suite or private bathrooms and give further panoramic vistas of the countryside. Guests have their own lounge and dining room with wood-burning stoves which can be used at any time of the year. Depending on the season, guests are welcome to feed the lambs or pigs, and sometimes bucket feed a calf. Whenever possible, home produced meat and vegetables, bacon and sausages are used. Evening meals can be provided and by request, diabetic and vegetarian diets can be catered for. A hidden place ideal for walking and taking in fine country air. E.T.B. 2 Crowns Commended.

Thatch Close, Llangrove, Ross-on-Wye, Herefordshire. Tel: 01989 770300.

One ancient building that everyone flocks to see in this area is **Goodrich Castle**, ruined but magnificent in its red sandstone splendour. It is said to be haunted by two lovers, Alice Birch and Charles Gifford, who sought sanctuary in the Royalist Stronghold during the Civil War. When the Roundheads arrived, led by Alice's uncle, Colonel Birch, the two fled on horseback and drowned while attempting to swim the Wye.

So strong were the Castle's defences that it was the last bastion to fall in that war. The massive attack launched upon it was greatly assisted by 'Roaring Meg', a siege gun cast in Whitchurch and capable of hurling a 200 pound ball, which caused great destruction. The defenders eventually surrendered and the four and a half month siege was over. It has remained a ruin ever since and is now maintained by English Heritage.

GOODRICH

Goodrich itself lies in the shadow of the Castle, a predominantly sandstone village with a number of Gothic exceptions. The most flamboyant of these, Goodrich Court, no longer stands, but was famous for having incurred the distaste of William Wordsworth, who thought it vulgar. The hotel called Ye Hostelrie was built here in 1830 and is said to have drawn direct inspiration from Goodrich Court. Although its shameless array of turrets and pinnacles are rather fun, you can imagine that Wordsworth would have been no more impressed with this particular building.

Before moving on, we will make a brief mention of the **Forest of Dean**, the huge mass of woodland which lies due south of Ross-on-Wye. Symonds Yat is probably the closest we will come in this book to the Forest, but it would be a shame to miss this ancient woodland. It stretches from Brierley and Woodside in the north to Whitecroft and Bream in the south, an area of some 120,000 acres. Of these, admittedly only 27,000 acres are now true forest as Dean has undergone much agricultural development over the years. Nevertheless, it is an impressive and hauntingly beautiful forest and the ancient oak stands still thrive with a suggestion of druidic mystery.

Tudor Almshouses, Ross-on-Wye

Iron Age man first settled here, and for very good reason, as beneath the forest floor great bands of iron ore were discovered, vital for their civilisation and growth. It became a Royal hunting ground under the reign of the Normans and was a place where charcoal burners could process the wood, an industry which dates back to before the Roman invasion. It was also a place for the common man to graze his flocks. The history of the Forest is long and diverse and its appeal is universal. Although much felling occurred during the First World War, the Forestry Commission took a hand in reinstating the trees. By the Second World War, it became the first National Forest Park and continues to support local crafts and provide a wonderful green haven for deer and visitors to this part of the country.

ROSS-ON-WYE

Ashe Leigh is a first class find; its a large country home set in 3/4 acre of garden with fine views over open countryside and includes an almost full size croquet lawn. Being only a few minutes drive from the market place of Ross-on-Wye, it is well situated for this attractive market town and has easy access to major cities via the motorway link. Lorraine and Peter Shepherd are truly welcoming hosts and guests will immediately feel relaxed in their lovely home. Two of the three bedrooms have en-suite facilities, one being a family room. Dinner is by prior arrangement which will be accompanied by home-grown vegetables when in season. Ashe Leigh has golf, fishing and lovely Wye Valley walks nearby with castles and gardens to visit. ETB - 2 Crowns Commended.

Ashe Leigh, Bridstow, Ross-on-Wye. Tel: 01989 565020

As you approach the lovely old market town of **Ross-on-Wye**, your eyes are immediately drawn to the towering spire of St. Mary's church and the houses clustered around it, high up on the sandstone cliffs. Indeed, the whole town seems to have a rosy hue about it and the best place we believe to appreciate this beautiful building material is the row of Tudor almshouses opposite the church. They are simply exquisite, and though repaired in 1575, they still have a crumbling, ancient look about them.

An excellent place to stay or enjoy a pleasant drink or meal can be found in the very heart of Ross-on-Wye, a few steps from the Market Place. **The Rosswyn Hotel** is a handsome former town house which dates back to the 15th-century. Full of historic character, the stone fireplace in the bar was discovered behind a wall and seven other fireplaces during renovations in the 1970s. Owned and personally-run by Rose Livesey, the eight well-appointed guest bedrooms mostly have private bathrooms; some also have the added luxury of a four-poster bed. The Rosswyn is also renowned for its cuisine, which can be enjoyed in the bar or in the more intimate atmosphere of the restaurant.

Rosswyn Hotel, High Street, Ross-on-Wye, Herefordshire
Tel/Fax: 01989 562733

The Black Death visited this town with a vengeance in 1637, and over 300 victims lie buried near the churchyard. Only a simple stone cross stands to commemorate these poor souls, who were committed to their unmarked grave during dead of night to avoid alerting the townsfolk to the severity of the situation.

Right in the heart of town stands the 17th century **Market House**, an impressive building taking pride of place in the Market Square. The ground floor is completely open and the upper floor, supported by stone pillars and arches, now houses the town library. Around the building, the busy street market is held.

The buildings around the Market Square, and indeed many throughout the town, serve as a reminder of Ross's greatest benefactor, John Kyrle. A wealthy barrister who had studied Law at the Middle Temple, Kyrle settled in Ross around 1660 and devoted the rest of his life to philanthropic works; keeping for himself just enough for his basic needs and using the remainder of his large income to the benefit of the town. His many generous benefactions included donating the town's main public garden, The Prospect, repairing the spire of St. Mary's church, and restoring the causeway to Wilton Bridge. More importantly, he provided the town with its water supply and set up funds for needy local children to attend school.

Kyrle was one of nature's true philanthropists and was immortalised in verse by Alexander Pope as 'The Man of Ross'. He was born in 1637, and over 100 years later, Pope wrote the lines:

'Rise, honest Muse, and sing the Man of Ross,
Health to the sick and solace to the swain,
Whose causeway parts the vale in shady rows,
Whose seats the weary traveller repose,
Who taught that heav'n directed spire to rise?
"The Man of Ross" each lisping babe replies.'

Though undoubtedly over-lyrical, these thoughts conjure up the image of a man who was highly regarded by the townspeople. When he died at the respectable age of 87, the whole town came to pay its respects to the man who had made their lives so much more civilised.

There's a local tale concerning the occasion when he attended a play put on by a travelling theatre group: the ticket seller took one look at the cut and quality of his clothes and proffered a ticket priced at half a crown. John Kyrle refused to pay the fee and returned a little later dressed in everyday working clothes. This time he was charged 'only sixpence for a farmer', with which he was quite content! Kyrle lived in a half-timbered Elizabethan building opposite the Market Square, which still stands but has now been converted into shops.

The Lost Street museum

Just behind the main street, tucked away in Palma Court, is a fascinating place called **The Lost Street Museum**, a time capsule of original shops and a pub dating from 1885 to 1935, re-assembled in a purpose-built setting.

Discover how we shopped before supermarkets, in the grocers. Explore the tobacconists, crammed full of cigarette and chocolate machines, sweet jars and a collection of matchboxes. Admire the breathtaking array of items in the Art Nouveau shop. Marvel at the mysterious coloured bottles in the chemists. Other shops sell old fashioned radios, motorcycles and toys and all sorts of musical boxes and automata while the 'street' outside is covered in many authentic enamelled signs, to help conjure up this lost era that spans 50 years.

Of course no High Street would be complete without a pub, and the 'Lillie Langtry', which originally stood in London's East End, is a fine example of a late Victorian public house, which features a mahogany bar as well as some splendid etched mirrors.

The stock is constantly being added to, so there is always something new to look at in this unusual museum, where you can step back in time to days gone by.

The Lost Street Museum, Palma Court, Brookend Street, Ross-on-Wye
Tel: 01989 562752

The Chasedale Hotel is an impressive family-run establishment standing in a secluded position, only half-a-mile from the centre of Ross-on-Wye. A handsome Victorian building constructed around 1870 as a private residence, it stands within a mature garden beneath a wooded hill which serves as an attractive backdrop. The hotel is perhaps best known for its fine cuisine which is prepared under the personal supervision of the chef/proprietor using ingredients from the hotel's own walled kitchen garden wherever possible. Centrally-heated and very comfortable throughout, the ten spacious guest bedrooms are equipped with private bathrooms, direct-dial telephones, remote control TVs, radios and tea/coffee making facilities.

The Chasedale Hotel, Walford Road, Ross-on-Wye, Herefordshire
Tel: 01989 562423 Fax: 01989 567900

Another unique attraction in Ross is the **Button Museum** in Kyrle Street. Here in this unusual collection - the first museum to be devoted entirely to the humble button - you can see 8,000 examples of man's and woman's attempts to hold their clothes together! It really is a fascinating collection, with some exquisite enamelled buttons; bone and wood, civil and military, spanning the past 200 years.

The Button Museum, Ross-on-Wye

AROUND ROSS-ON-WYE
Just on the outskirts of the town, you will find **The Ashe** offers something rather special, a 15th century farmhouse situated on a 200 acre

311

mixed farm just two miles north west of Ross-on-Wye. Positioned in the picturesque Wye Valley, fully equipped, self-catering accommodation is available in attractive barn and cottage conversions which can accommodate up to a total of 20 people. Ideal for large groups of families seeking a weekend or longer break. Guests have access to - walks on the farm, an 18 hole par 3 golf course, fishing lakes, barbecue area, a large garden and tennis court. Close to the Forest of Dean and facilities for canoeing, cycling and walking. this is a splendid place to take a holiday or weekend break.   Commended. ΨΨΨΨ

The Ashe, Bridstow, Ross-on-Wye, Herefordshire. Tel: 01989 563336.

WESTON-UNDER-PENYARD

Escape to the delights of the Wye Valley where a warm welcome awaits you in the graceful and tranquil ambience of **Wharton Lodge Cottages.** Wharton Lodge is a charming Georgian country house, set in twelve acres of beautiful parkland. The three self-contained cottages are annexed to the lodge and enjoy fine views, overlooking open parkland and the Italianate walled gardens. Recently restored and converted, the cottages, named Elgar, Grosvenor and Harewood, are luxuriously furnished with high quality antique and reproduction furniture. Wharton Lodge Cottages have gained the top quality award in the English Tourist Boards National Classification and Grading Scheme. To mark the achievement, Sir William Lawrence, Chairman of the Heart of England Tourist Board, presented the De Luxe Grading to the proprietors, Linda and Ivor Evans. The De Luxe Grading is extremely prestigious and the proprietors have joined an elite group, there being only three other self-catering establishments within the Heart of England region with this status. De Luxe in every respect!

Wharton Lodge Cottages, Weston-under-Penyard, Ross-on-Wye, Herefordshire. Tel: 01989 750140.

HOPE MANSELL

The Hope Mansell valley is tucked away in the hills between the River Wye and the Forest of Dean and is locally known as one of the most fertile and loveliest of the many valleys in this area. The name 'Hope' occurs frequently in south Herefordshire, and denotes a small enclosed valley. There are a number of farms along the valley with the tiny village of Hope Mansell at the far end. A Norman doorway shows that the church and surrounding settlement are of early medieval origin. The surrounding hills are crowned by woods, and many paths and tracks cross the fields and rise into the woods to connect the village and church with the outlying farms and cottages tucked away among the trees. Signs of even more ancient sunken lanes, or holloways, can be seen disappearing into the trees as you walk through the woods, evoking a long past way of life. From the surrounding hills there are spectacular views of the valley with its village and farms, and beyond to the distant Malvern Hills to the east, and Black Mountains of Wales to the west.

Those looking for comfortable bed and breakfast accommodation in an idyllic rural setting should make a point of finding the **Old Rectory** in the hamlet of Hope Mansell. This handsome Georgian house is set in beautiful secluded surroundings to the south of the A40 Gloucester to Monmouth road, four miles southeast of Ross-on-Wye. With its stone-flagged entrance hall and guest lounge containing a small library and zogoroscope (a rare Victorian 3D print viewer), the interior has a truly charming atmosphere. The centrally-heated guest bedrooms are fitted with attractive period furniture, colour TVs and tea/coffee making facilities, and two also have their own washbasins and shaver points.

The Old Rectory, Hope Mansell, Ross-on-Wye, Herefordshire
Tel/Fax: 01989 750382

GLEWSTONE

Standing in an idyllic rural setting approximately three miles southwest of Ross-on-Wye, **Glewstone Court** is an impressive country house hotel and restaurant with a delightful informal atmosphere. The largely Georgian house is set within three acres of grounds containing fruit orchards and one of the oldest cedars in the west of England.

Glewstone Court
Inside, the public rooms are spacious and elegantly appointed with deep sofas, open log fires, antique photographs and French windows

opening onto the garden. The guest bedrooms are furnished to an equally high standard.

Comfortable and spacious, they have wonderful views over the surrounding landscape and are superbly equipped with private bathrooms, colour TVs, telephones, radios and hospitality trays. The hotel is owned and personally-run by Christine and William Reeve-Tucker, friendly and experienced hosts who successfully manage to achieve the balance between high standards and relaxed informality.

The Georgian restaurant is renowned for its imaginative cuisine and is open to non-residents, with advance booking recommended. On the evening we visited, main courses included loin steak of wild boar, and crispy vegetable Wellington au gratin, along with a full range of starters, desserts and wines to accompany the meal. Good value meals are also available in the bar every lunchtime and evening.

Glewstone Court, Glewstone, Near Ross-on-Wye, Herefordshire
Tel: 01989 770367 Fax: 01989 770282

Pencraig Court is a fine Georgian **Country House Hotel** set in three and a half acres of its own gardens and secluded woodland, standing high above the banks of the river Wye. The hotel has a feeling of graceful days being both quiet and restful, blended with every comfort of present day living. All the bedrooms have private bathrooms, comfortable beds and a sitting area with easy chairs. For a wonderful dining experience, Pencraig serves local Welsh lamb, fresh Wye salmon and succulent Herefordshire beef, complimented by a truly excellent selection of wines from their impressive cellar; the elegant surroundings complete the experience.

Pencraig Court, Pencraig, Nr. Ross-on-Wye, Herefordshire. Tel: 01989
770306 Fax: 01989 770040.

MONMOUTH

As this is Border country you will soon find yourself crossing over into Monmouth. A fitting place to round off the chapter and this book.

A stone's throw from the historic Monnow Bridge and with views of the famous Kymin, **The Riverside Hotel** is the ideal base for travellers to Wales and the borders. All 17 bedrooms are en-suite including the family room which can accommodate three children and a baby. Delicately decorated, the rooms have been renovated and include tea and coffee making facilities. Rodney and Judith Dodd work hard at providing personal service for their guests but if they own the bricks and mortar of The Riverside Hotel, the attractive Long Bar with its cosy Chesterfield settees, belongs to the people of Monmouth. Any night of the week you can find the local postman and his son, the builder, fire chief, plasterers and painters and, of course, Dave. He sits on one of the custom-made bar stools at the end of the bar with his personalised beer glass, and if there is anything you need to know about Monmouth or the surrounding area, Dave can tell you.

The Riverside Hotel

The Riverside Restaurant is run by Richard Lammas. The atmosphere is created by brass coach lamps and flickering candlelight; the pink button-backed chairs ensure the diners comfort but it is the delicious cuisine that will keep you lingering at your table. Salmon from the neighbouring River Wye infused with fresh mint and served with a raspberry hollandaise is chef Richard's favourite recipe as the fish is top quality and so very fresh.

He asks his customers to be patient as he adds his own personal touches to each dish, but good food is always worth waiting for. Fresh apricots lightly poached and served with marsala sabayan sauce are a sweet finale to a different dining experience.

From commis cook at Gleneagles in Scotland to Executive Manager of 600-bedroom hotels in South East Asia, Rodney Dodd's experience alone makes him more than qualified to prove the standard of service required by today's traveller. Although his wife Judith has no formal training, her artistic flair and dedication to the public through her years as a professional dancer in the Royal Ballet Company stand her in good stead behind the bar. The Riverside Hotel has style and personality but most importantly, it is a friendly hotel.

The Riverside Hotel, Cinderhill Street, Monmouth, Gwent. Tel: 01600 715577 Fax: 01600 712668.

NEAR MONMOUTH

Further south down the beautiful Wye Valley and a short distance from Tintern Abbey is the village of **Whitebrook**. This particularly attractive area tempts many a traveller to break their journey and here you will find **The Crown at Whitebrook**. A first class restaurant and hotel remotely situated in the narrow and wooded Whitebrook Valley, just one mile from the River Wye and on the edge of the Tintern Forest. In this peaceful and tranquil setting, the proprietors, Sandra and Roger Bates, offer the very best in both cuisine and accommodation.

Specialising in enjoyable and delightful meals, with an authentic French flavour, dining in this intimate restaurant is a particular pleasure. The wide range of dishes, which combine the very best of Welsh ingredients with the long established traditions of true French cuisine, ensure that there is plenty to tempt even the most discerning palates.

House specialities include Guinea Fowl poached in wine with herbs and Fresh Wye Salmon with cream and brandy sauce.

The same exacting standards of the restaurant can be seen in the accommodation at The Crown. There are twelve modern bedrooms, all with bathrooms, that make staying in this hidden place a memorable holiday. The Crown Restaurant and Hotel is recommended by Egon Ronay, the AA (with three rosettes) and the RAC.

The Crown at Whitebrook, Whitebrook, Near Monmouth
Tel: 01600 860254 Fax: 01600 860607

Monmouth is to be our last port of call in the beautiful Welsh Borders country, for many it epitomises what they have come to feel about this special part of England. It's a gentle, peaceful place of great character and charm, which has largely been successful in keeping the more negative aspects of the 20th century at bay. Yet if you scratch the surface, you come across so much that intrigues within this rich tapestry of land, well worth the battles that have been fought over it through the centuries.

We do hope you have enjoyed reading our book and that it prompts you to discover some of the Hidden Places we have found, for yourself.

Safe journey.

Tourist
Information Centres

BEWDLEY
St. George's Hall, Load Street   Tel: 01299 404740

BRIDGNORTH
The Library, Listley Street   Tel: 01746 763358

BROADWAY
1 Costswold Court   Tel: 01386 852937

BROMSGROVE
Bromsgrove Museum,
26 Birmingham Road   Tel: 01527 831809

BROMYARD
1 Rowberry Street   Tel: 01885 482038

CHURCH STRETTON
Church street   Tel: 01694 723133

DROITWICH
St. Richards House, Victoria Square   Tel: 01905 774312

ELLESMERE
The Meres' Visitor Centre, The Mere   Tel: 01691 622981

EVESHAM
Almonry Museum, Abbey Gate   Tel: 01386 446944

HAY-ON-WYE
Oxford Road   Tel: 01497 820144

HEREFORD
1 King Street   Tel: 01432 268430

IRONBRIDGE
The Wharfage   Tel: 01952 432166

KIDDERMINSTER
Severn Valley Railway Station,
Comberton Hill   Tel: 01562 829400

LEDBURY
1 Church Lane   Tel: 01531 636147

LEOMINSTER
1 Corn Square   Tel: 01568 616460

LUDLOW
Castle Street   Tel: 01584 875053

MALVERN
Winter Gardens, Grange Road   Tel: 01684 892289

MARKET DRAYTON
51 Cheshire Street   Tel: 01630 652139

MUCH WENLOCK
The Museum, High Street   Tel: 01952 727679

OSWESTRY
the Heritage Centre, 2 Church Terrace   Tel: 01691 662753

OSWESTRY
Mile End Services   Tel: 01691 662488

PERSHORE
19 High Street   Tel: 01386 554262

REDDITCH
Civic Square, Alcaster Street   Tel: 01527 60806

ROSS-ON-WYE
Swan House, Edde Cross Street   Tel: 01989 562768

SHREWSBURY
The Music Hall, The Square   Tel: 01743 350761

TELFORD
The Telford Centre   Tel: 01952 291370

UPTON-UPON-SEVERN
Pepperpot, Church Street   Tel: 01684 594200

WHITCHURCH
The Civic Centre, High Street   Tel: 01948 664577

WORCESTER
The Guildhall, High Street   Tel: 01905 726311
                                                   &   01905 723471

INDEX

A

ABBEY DORE   276
ABBOTS MORTON   193
ACTON SCOTT   128
ALL STRETTON   133
ALMELEY   255
ALVERLEY   121
ASHPERTON   164
ASTERTON   137
ASTLEY ABBOTS   127
ASTON EYRE   127
ASTWOOD BANK   194
ATCHAM   73
AYMESTRY   244

B

BASCHURCH   24
BAYSTON HILL   95
BEWDLEY   223
BICTON   90, 277
BISHOP'S CASTLE   139
BISHOP'S FROME   227
BOSBURY   162
BRADNOR HILL   252
BRAMPTON BRYAN   249
BREDON   186
BREDWARDINE   281
BRETFORTON   183
BRIDGNORTH   122
BROADWAY   185
BROCKHAMPTON   299
BROMDON   112
BROMSGROVE   208
BROMYARD   234

BROSELEY   55
BROXWOOD   257

C

CASTLE FROME   163
CHADDESLEY
    CORBETT   216
CHELMARSH   117
CHIRBURY   92
CHURCH STRETTON   129
CLAVERLEY   121
CLEEDOWNTON   112
CLEOBURY MORTIMER   115
CLODOCK   274
CLUNGUNFORD   141
COALPORT   62
COLWALL   159
CONINGSBY   285
CRAVEN ARMS   109

D

DODDERHILL   202
DORSTONE   280
DROITWICH   199
DUDLESTON HEATH   39

E

EARDINGTON   116
EARDISLAND   239
EARDISLEY   256
EASTHOPE   128
EATON BISHOP   283
EDGEBOLTON   17
ELLESMERE   36
ELMLEY CASTLE   187

EVESHAM 177
EWYAS HAROLD 275

F

FECKENHAM 215
FLADBURY 191
FRANKWELL 87
FRODESLEY 135

G

GARWAY 302
GLEWSTONE 314
GOODRICH 306
GREAT BOLAS 16
GREAT MALVERN 156
GREAT WITLEY 225

H

HAMPTON LOADE 117
HANBURY 204
HARLEY 54
HARMER HILL 22
HARVINGTON 181
HAWFORD 204
HAY-ON-WYE 269
HEREFORD 283
HOARWITHY 301
HODNET 9
HOLDGATE 128
HOLME LACY 300
HOPE MANSELL 313
HOPE UNDER DINMORE 262
HOPTON WAFERS 116
HOW CAPLE 297
HUDDINGTON 204

I

INKBERROW 193
IRONBRIDGE 58

K

KENTCHURCH 302
KIDDERMINSTER 216
KILPECK 301
KINGTON 193, 249
KINNERSLEY 257

L

LEDBURY 165
LEEBOTWOOD 134
LEIGH 226
LEINTWARDINE 248
LEOMINSTER 231
LETTON 249
LICKLEY 212
LINGEN 249
LITTLE STRETTON 133
LLANSILIN 34
LONGTOWN 274
LOWER
    BROCKHAMPTON 234
LUDLOW 101
LYONSHALL 254

M

MADLEY 282
MAESBROOK 25
MAMBLE 223
MARCHAMLEY 10
MARDEN 230
MARKET DRAYTON 5
MELVERLEY 32
MICHAELCHURCH 274
MIDDLE LITTLETON 182
MIDDLEHOPE 128
MIDDLETON-IN-
    CHIRBURY 92
MINSTERLEY 92
MINTON 138

MOCCAS 282
MONMOUTH 316
MONTFORD 87
MORDIFORD 293
MORTIMER'S CROSS 243
MORVILLE 127
MUCH MARCLE 296
MUCH WENLOCK 51
MUXTON 69

N

NEEN SOLARS 114
NEWPORT 12
NOBOLD 89
NORTON 61

O

OAKENGATES 66
ODDINGLEY 204
OFFENHAM 183
OMBERSLEY 203
ORLETON 248
OSWESTRY 26

P

PEMBRIDGE 240
PERSHORE 187
PETERCHURCH 279
PINVIN 191
PONTESBURY 94
PRESTON WYNNE 229
PRESTON-ON-THE-
    WEALD 67

Q

QUATT 118

R

RATLINGHOPE 136

REDDITCH 213
ROSS-ON-WYE 307
ROWLSTONE 275
RUSHBURY 134

S

SALWARPE 204
SAMBROOK 15
SEDGEBERROW 178
SELATTYN 34
SHAWBURY 16
SHIFNAL 66
SHOBDON 243
SHREWSBURY 76
STAUNTON ON ARROW 241
STAUNTON ON WYE 262
STOKE LACY 228
STOKE POUND 206
STOKE PRIOR 206
STOKESAY 109
STOURPORT-ON-SEV-
    ERN 224
SUTTON ST. NICHOLAS 230
SYMONDS YAT 303

T

TARDEBIGGE 212
TELFORD 65
TENBURY WELLS 233
TEWKESBURY 168
THE FROMES 162
THE LENCHES 182
THE MARCHES 239
THORNBURY 233
TIBBERTON 204
TONG 69
TURNASTONE 279

U

ULLINGSWICK 229
UPPER ASTLEY 17
UPTON SNODSBURY 192
UPTON UPON SEVERN 170

V

VOWCHURCH 279

W

WALTERSTONE 274
WATERS UPTON 68
WELSHAMPTON 40
WELSHPOOL 93
WEM 18
WENTNOR 137
WEOBLEY 258
WEST FELTON 32
WESTBURY 91
WESTHORPE 128
WESTON-UNDER-
    PENYARD 312
WESTON-UNDER-
    REDCASTLE 11
 WHEATHILL 112
WHITCHURCH 40, 305
WHITEBROOK 317
WHITTINGTON 35
WIGMORE 248
WISTANWICK 12
WOOLASTON 90
WOOLHOPE 296
WOOTTON GREEN 120
WORCESTER 149
WORFIELD 127
WORTHEN 92
WROXETER 73
WYCHBOLD 205
WYRE PIDDLE 190

Y

YARPOLE 247
YEATON 24

THE HIDDEN PLACES SERIES

To order more copies of this title or any of the others in this series please complete the order form below and send to ;
M & M Publishing Ltd.
118 Ashley Rd. Hale, Altrincham, Cheshire. WA14 2UN.

TITLE		QUANTITY
Scotland	£8.99	....
Ireland	£8.99	....
Wales	£8.99	....
Lake District	£5.99	....
Northumberland & Durham	£5.99	....
Yorkshire	£5.99	....
Lancashire, Cheshire, & I.O.M	£5.99	....
Peak District & Potteries	£5.99	....
Welsh Borders (Shrops, Here, Worcs.)	£5.99	....
Heart of England (The Midlands)	£5.99	....
East Anglia (inc. Cambs & Essex)	£5.99	....
Cotswolds	£5.99	....
Wessex	£5.99	....
Devon & Cornwall	£5.99	....
Dorset, Hants, & I.O.W	£5.99	....
The South East	£5.99	....
Thames & Chilterns (Berks, Oxon, Bucks, Beds, Herts.)	£5.99	....

NB. FREE POSTAGE & PACKAGING
I enclose Cheque for £.................... made payable to:
M & M Publishing Ltd.
NAME...
ADDRESS..
....
POSTCODE..